Scripture in the Jewish and Christian Traditions

Stanley M. Wagner, General Editor

Scripture in the Jewish and Christian Traditions:

Authority, Interpretation, Relevance

Edited by
Frederick E. Greenspahn

Abingdon • Nashville

SCRIPTURE IN THE JEWISH AND CHRISTIAN TRADITIONS:
Authority, Interpretation, Relevance

Copyright © 1982 by University of Denver (Colorado Seminary)

Library of Congress Cataloging in Publication Data

Main entry under title:
SCRIPTURE IN THE JEWISH AND CHRISTIAN TRADITIONS.
  Includes index.
  Contents: "The authority of Scripture"/by Avery Dulles—
  "A Protestant view of biblical authority"/by John H. Gerstner—
  "Scripture and Mishnah"/by Jacob Neusner—[etc.]
  1. Bible—Evidences, authority, etc.—Addresses, essays, lectures.
  2. Bible—Hermeneutics—Addresses, essays, lectures.
  3. Bible—Criticism, interpretation, etc.—
  Addresses, essays, lectures. I. Greenspahn, Frederick E., 1946–
BS480.S349   220   82-4071   AACR2

ISBN 0-687-37065-5

MANUFACTURED BY THE PARTHENON PRESS AT
NASHVILLE, TENNESSEE, UNITED STATES OF AMERICA

CONTENTS

FOREWORD... 7

PART ONE—The Authority of Scripture

INTRODUCTION...9

1. The Authority of Scripture: A Catholic
   Perspective, AVERY DULLES, S.J.................13
2. A Protestant View of Biblical Authority,
   JOHN H. GERSTNER...............................41
3. Scripture and Mishnah: Authority and
   Selectivity, JACOB NEUSNER......................64

PART TWO—The Interpretation of Scripture

INTRODUCTION... 87

4. Jewish Biblical Exegesis: Presuppositions and
   Principles, MICHAEL FISHBANE.................. 91
5. The Bible in the Roman Catholic Church,
   BRUCE VAWTER, C.M........................... 111
6. Protestant Attitudes Regarding Methods of
   Biblical Interpretation, DAVID H. KELSEY... 133

PART THREE—The Relevance of Scripture

INTRODUCTION...163

7. The Hebrew Scriptures as a Source for Moral
   Guidance, SHELDON H. BLANK............... 168
8. Catholicism as an Integrationist Perspective,
   RICHARD P. McBRIEN........................... 183
9. Ancient Scripture in the Modern World,
   KRISTER STENDAHL............................. 201

NOTES.. 215

INDEX..229

FOREWORD

SINCE 1976, the Center for Judaic Studies of the University of Denver has served as a resource for the three major Christian theological seminaries in this region: The Iliff School of Theology, Conservative Baptist Theological Seminary, and St. Thomas Roman Catholic Theological Seminary. In a most unique academic arrangement, students from all the seminaries gather each semester at one seminary for a course in Judaic studies. Thus, for example, in one semester, we are almost certain to have the intriguing combination of a Jewish instructor and Conservative Baptist students (among others) at a Roman Catholic seminary. Other exciting combinations also are characteristic of these classes.

During these years, the Center has instructed more than five hundred seminarians in courses titled Archaeology and the Hebrew Bible, The Bible in Jewish Exegesis, The Development of Biblical Religion, Topics in Jewish Theology, The Land of Israel in History and Theology, Torah: Law and Salvation in Judaism, Judaism in the Time of Jesus, The Jewish Experience, Literature of the Rabbis, Jewish Philosophy, and Disputation and Dialogue: A History of the Jewish-Christian Encounter. The members of the Center faculty have regarded this teaching experience as among the most dynamic and rewarding in their academic life.

The context in which our instruction in Judaics takes place often requires, for clarification purposes, the presentation of

Jewish concepts, principles, themes, issues, and history side-by-side with corresponding elements in Protestantism and Roman Catholicism. We soon discovered, however, that seminarians, by and large, are woefully ignorant of religious traditions outside their own and that there exists a surprising paucity of suitable materials that could be utilized in the classroom.

As a result, the Center for Judaic Studies proposed a series of symposia in which leading exponents of Judaism, Protestantism, and Roman Catholicism would discuss fundamental theological issues within their respective religious traditions. We are most grateful to the Phillips Foundation of Minneapolis, through the good office of Dr. Paula Bernstein, for its vision and support in making those symposia possible. This volume contains the scholarly and lucid papers delivered at the first three symposia. The papers from the remaining programs are now being readied for publication.

We are especially thankful to Frederick E. Greenspahn, director of the Program of Ecumenic Studies at the Center for Judaic Studies, for his yeomen efforts both in organizing the symposia and in editing the papers included in this volume.

Our hope for this work is found in the Apocrypha:

> And I will light the lamp of understanding in thy
> heart, which shall not be extinguished.
> —*IV Ezra [II Esdras] 14:25 (APOT)*

Dr. Stanley M. Wagner
Director,
Center for Judaic Studies,
University of Denver

PART ONE
The Authority of Scripture

INTRODUCTION

THE BIBLE plays a central role in both Judaism and Christianity. It is read regularly in the course of communal worship, and it is cited to support any number of beliefs and practices. The centrality of a book, so characteristic of these religious traditions, was not, however, always a fact of life within the communities to which Jews and Christians trace their origins. In the earliest years of Christianity, the apostles were accorded authority on the basis of their direct contact with Jesus. Letters such as those by Paul do not appeal to the authority of a book, at least not one explicitly Christian, but rather to the authority of Christ himself, and secondarily to those who had learned from him.[1] As that generation passed, bishops then seem to have played a central role. Only slowly did holy books come to be accorded a major part in determining the nature of Christian practice and belief. Similarly, Israelite priests had been expected to deal with religious questions that were brought to them.[2] Their responses were called *torah*, instruction, and only in the course of time did this word come to refer to a book regarded as the basis of doctrine and practice.

The fact that there had not always been a Bible became a focal point for early Jewish-Christian polemics. To Paul, Abraham was an exemplar of faith, a man who had lived before the

Frederick Greenspahn has used his own interpretation of biblical passages.

promulgation of the law and yet was "reckoned as righteous" (Rom 4:3); Jewish tradition, perhaps responding to the Christian challenge, claimed that he had "kept the entire law, even though it had not yet been given."[3] Such statements reflect the fact that Abraham did not have a Bible, any more than Jesus or Paul had a New Testament. Scripture, which plays so central a role in Judaism and Christianity alike, simply did not then exist, much less enjoy a position of authority.

The importance of a written text might be traced back to the tablets Moses received at Mount Sinai; those, however, were not a book and could hardly have played as comprehensively authoritative a role as the Bible has since achieved. Although an apparently normative "book of the LORD'S law" is ascribed to the time of Jehoshaphat, who ruled over Judah in the ninth century (2 Chron 17:9), the authority of the written word emerges most clearly about two hundred years later with the discovery of a scroll during the reign of Judah's King Josiah.[4] The elevation of this text to a position of prominence signals the beginning of a shift from reliance on direct revelation, whether from priest or prophet, to reliance on the written word. This shift culminated in the later Jewish belief that revelation had ceased shortly after the Exile, although hope for its future restoration became a part of messianic aspirations.[5] With this shift toward emphasis on a written text as the source of divine guidance, it became unrealistic to expect a specific answer from God for every question; instead, one needed to search the pages of past revelation for guidance and direction, a situation that required suitable interpretive tools.

This belief that revelation had ceased, at least temporarily, carried with it the seeds of a further development. If biblical books were authoritative by virtue of having been revealed, only those books written before revelation ceased could be granted such status; therefore, *in principle,* there could be no new book containing divine revelation.[6] And so the same process that elevated Scripture to a level of primacy also effectively closed the canon.

The history of canonization, in the broadest sense—establishing official editions of holy books, collecting them, and ascribing authoritative status to them—is both complex and obscure.[7] Principles of selectivity clearly were involved at every step and, by implication, the recognition of authority. All that safely can be asserted is that by the end of the first Christian century, Jewish Scriptures seem to have taken on a normative form. A similar process is apparent also for the early church; although it is not entirely clear how early Christianity determined the content of its Old Testament canon, considerations and attitudes similar to those that determined the Jewish canon probably played a substantial part.[8] As for the New Testament, collections of Pauline writings were in evidence early in the second century, with authoritative Gospels appearing shortly thereafter.[9]

The emergence of a Bible was to have profound implications for both Judaism and Christianity. As long as direct revelation was believed available, revision was always a possibility: God's expectations for a particular situation might change in light of future developments. At the same time, one never could be entirely sure that a purported revelation was authentic. As the Bible itself amply demonstrates, people might present their own ideas as revelation, or indeed, God could even mislead people through inaccurate revelation.[10] However, once it had been decided that God's teachings were contained in a specific set of books and nowhere else, the relative value and the problematic of these characteristics were reversed. Determination of the accuracy of revelation ceased to be an issue; the location of God's teaching became an article of faith not subject to argument or in need of proof. In tandem with this newly gained certainty, however, change became a problem. God's teachings could not as easily be revised when circumstances changed.

Change is, of course, a constant reality. The religion of Abraham is not identical with either Christianity or Judaism as we know them today, although both have claimed him as an exemplar of their strikingly different religious ideals. This remarkable circumstance attests dramatically to the importance of Scripture, which has assumed a role not unlike that of the Constitution in American society—enduring as the fundamental document of the political system, even though successively diverse and occasionally conflicting explanations of its meaning can be authoritative. So it is that the rabbis, who are nowhere explicitly mentioned in the Jewish Bible, saw themselves as intended by the commandment: "If a legal issue be too difficult for you . . . then you shall get up and go to the place which the LORD, your God, will choose for you and go to the priests, the Levites, and the judge who will be at that time and inquire so that they can inform you of the legal obligations" (Deut 17:8-9).[11] Similarly, Jesus, also never mentioned in the Hebrew Scriptures, was viewed by the Christian church as the fulfillment of promises found on almost every page.[12] So, too, the Reformers could claim to rely on Scripture alone, while Roman Catholicism saw in the same Scripture a mandate for those institutions the Reformers rejected.

Despite certain obvious differences in that which is regarded as scriptural by the various traditions, there is a great deal that is common and authoritative to all.[13] Yet, as will become clear, the *kind* of authority ascribed to Scripture varies among, and even within the different groups. Traditional Judaism looks to the Bible as a source of law. Consequently, more authority is attributed to the Pentateuch (Torah) than to later sections (Prophets and Writings); for similar reasons, the narratives within the Pentateuch itself often are regarded as of less importance than the legal material that makes up its bulk.[14] Alongside this nomistic perspective, one can trace to the biblical period a quite different tendency, which elevates Torah to metaphysical status, ultimately regarding the holy book as an earthly manifestation of the divine wisdom that governs all aspects of the universe.[15] For Christianity, the Old Testament is most often perceived as a theological promise, fulfilled in the coming of Christ. Thus there has been a tendency for normative Judaism to focus upon Scripture's concrete meaning, whereas its spiritual role has been emphasized more often in Christian tradition. As a result, both Judaism and Christianity can enshrine the same body of Scripture and accord it central authority while interpreting it in quite dissimilar ways. By focusing on different sections of Scripture and differing dimensions of scriptural truth, they are able to make this one book more than one.[16]

ALTHOUGH IT IS OBVIOUS that the Bible plays a central role in Jewish and Christian traditions, the nature of that role is not always carefully defined. Who decides which writings constitute "Bible," and how is that decision made? What kinds of authority are to be ascribed to these writings? How is the biblical teaching on a given subject determined? What, if any, other sources of guidance are to be consulted; and how can this procedure be justified? Although the Roman Catholic tradition possesses the means for responding to such questions in a clear and official way, its positions have been neither static nor monolithic. Thus together, the questions with which it has grappled and the ways it has sought to deal with them can serve as a paradigm, exemplifying many of the issues and approaches used by other traditions as well. —F.E.G.

The Authority of Scripture: A Catholic Perspective

AVERY DULLES, S.J.
CATHOLIC UNIVERSITY OF AMERICA

FOR MANY OF OUR CONTEMPORARIES, the term *authority* is a pejorative one, evoking suspicion and hostility. It suggests a blank check, a dehumanizing alienation, an irresponsible abdication of one's own reason and critical powers. Only when we reflect more carefully do we see how authority can be consonant with reason and helpful to human progress. All the sciences advance through trusting acceptance of their own approved methods, through reliance on the scientific community and its acknowledged leaders, and through appropriation of hitherto assured results. The historical sciences, in particular, depend on authority, for in most cases the facts are not recoverable except through the reports of reliable witnesses. Historical reason critically evaluates the reports, and it accepts—not blindly, but with open eyes—those it finds reason to trust. And this procedure suggests my own understanding of *authority: that which* (or *those whom*) *one has reason to trust.*

If we are better off religiously than were primitive pagans, it is because we benefit from a religious heritage that has been built up over many centuries. The writings of the great masters of religious thought are classics, analogous to the works of Plato, Homer, and Sophocles. Such writings never grow old.

Avery Dulles, S.J., has used the Revised Standard Version of the Bible for his Scripture references.

They are studied anew in every generation and give rise to a tradition of interpretation. For Jews and Christians, the Bible is the fundamental religious classic. It differs from the classics of philosophy and literature because the biblical writers, according to their own claim and the belief of the community of faith, were not simply expressing their own personal insights. They were witnessing to a divine revelation which they had received as a pure gift in trust for others, including their posterity. To anyone who accepts this claim and belief, the testimony of the biblical witnesses shares, in some sense, in the authority of God himself. My objective here is to clarify the extent and significance of this sharing as understood in contemporary Roman Catholicism. After a preliminary word concerning the sources in which the official Catholic teaching on this subject may be found, I shall treat in succession the following questions: the canon, texts and versions, inspiration, inerrancy, interpretation, the sufficiency of Scripture, and the uses of Scripture.

Sources of Catholic Teaching

The official positions of the Roman Catholic Church regarding the Bible are found principally in papal and conciliar documents.[1] Most important, these documents include the decisions concerning the canon issued by local councils and popes in the fourth and fifth centuries; the statement of the Council of Florence (1442) regarding the canon; the decrees of the Council of Trent (1546) on the canon, on Scripture and tradition, on the authority of the Vulgate, and on the interpretation of Scripture; and the decrees of Vatican Council I (1870) on the inspiration and interpretation of Scripture. More recently, three popes issued important biblical encyclicals: *Providentissimus Deus,* Leo XIII, 1893; *Spiritus Paraclitus,* Benedict XV, 1920; and *Divino afflante Spiritu,* Pius XII, 1943. Still more recently, in 1965 Vatican Council II issued its *Dogmatic Constitution on Divine Revelation (Dei Verbum).* These major sources are supplemented by various responses and instructions issued since 1905 by the Pontifical Biblical Commission and, at various times, by the Holy Office.

These various official documents obviously are not all of the same weight. From the standpoint of authority, the decrees of the last three ecumenical councils (Trent, Vatican I, and Vatican II) are of the highest dignity. Several canons of Trent and Vatican I, set forth under pain of anathema, have greater juridical force than any other conciliar statements. Vatican II made no new dogmatic definitions and imposed no canonical sanctions for violations of its teaching.

On the other hand, it must be recognized that more recent teaching possesses a certain primacy of authority, inasmuch as it speaks more directly to contemporary questions in light of all the knowledge modern scholarship has made available. In reading older documents, one must bear in mind that they often address issues and problems not our own and that they do so on the basis of limited information and with the vocabulary and thought-categories of an earlier period.[2] Generally speaking, documents written more than a generation ago must be used with caution as representing the positions of contemporary Roman Catholicism; they often need to be reinterpreted or updated to be properly understood and applied today. To some extent, Vatican II has provided an official modern interpretation of the total Catholic heritage, including understanding of the Bible. The council reaffirmed the essentials of the Catholic tradition, but it did so in a fresh context. Thus we may rely principally on the documents of Vatican II as an introduction to present-day Catholic doctrine concerning the Bible and its use.

Except for several brief but important statements issued by Trent and Vatican I, the Roman Catholic Church has not issued any infallible or irreformable pronouncements in regard to the Bible. With these exceptions, official Catholic teachings on Scripture may be regarded as fallible and therefore subject to challenge. A Catholic scholar who is convinced, for reasons that seem solid, that the official teachers have erred may, with due modesty, propose a contrary view. Some older magisterial statements about the Bible have for all practical purposes been reversed. In principle, it must be allowed that certain currently official positions may also be reversed at some future time.

It would be a mistake to imagine that the Catholic understanding of Scripture is totally contained in official documents. In most cases the ecclesiastical magisterium—that body which formulates official doctrine—contents itself with a supervisory, judicial role. It allows the burden of day-to-day teaching to be borne by individual Catholics. Only when some serious crisis, error, or controversy arises does the magisterium intervene with an authoritative statement. When it does intervene, it usually says only as much as is necessary to preclude a serious error. Popes and councils have not attempted to set forth a complete and coherent doctrine regarding Scripture. To achieve systematic completeness is rather the task of private theologians. Provided that theologians do not offend against the settled doctrine of the church, they are free to synthesize the data as they think best. The force of official teaching is therefore predominantly negative. Taken in itself, it does not provide or attempt to provide the kind of positive intelligibility for which one looks in theological treatises.

In a sense, therefore, one cannot fairly set forth *the* Catholic teaching concerning Scripture. The church leaves its members free to follow any theological theories within the bounds of orthodoxy. Orthodoxy itself provides not so much a doctrine as a set of negative norms which serve as guidelines for theological speculation.

The generalizations made in the last two paragraphs admit of some exceptions. The biblical encyclical of Pius XII, *Divino afflante Spiritu,* was intended to encourage biblical scholarship, rather than to prevent errors. For this reason it is more positive in tone than many previous papal pronouncements. Vatican II's teaching also attempted to provide positive encouragement and to overcome an excessively timid or restrictive interpretation of previous church teaching. Nevertheless, even Pius XII and the Second Vatican Council were content to set forth general norms and sought to avoid seeming to impose positions that should be left open to theological speculation and debate. On many points, therefore, the official documents are deliberately ambiguous.

In concentrating on the official teaching of the church, I shall abstain from setting forth the positions of individual theologians, although such positions often give deeper insight into what Catholics believe and think about the Bible.

The Canon

In accepting a canon of biblical writings, the Catholic Church implicitly declares that these writings have special authority for and in the church. In Greek, the word *canon* means a *rule* or *standard* and, in that sense, an *authority*. In any treatment of the authority of the Bible, therefore, some attention must be given to the problem of the canon.[3]

Although debates concerning the books to be read as Scripture are almost as old as the church itself, it was chiefly in the fourth century that agreed-upon lists of biblical books were drawn up. The process required considerable discussion and involved pastors and theologians representing different churches in the East and West. As far as the Catholic Church is concerned, the authoritative decisions were those adopted in several North African local councils toward the end of the fourth century and reaffirmed by several popes in the fifth century. This canon was reasserted in the fifteenth century by the Council of Florence, in its Decree of Union with the Jacobites. In the face of certain doubts raised by humanistic scholars and by the Protestant Reformers, the Council of Trent, appealing to the settled tradition of the church, imposed the canon of Florence under anathema. The First Vatican Council in 1870 declared that all the books listed by Trent were "sacred and canonical" (DS 3006, 3029).

The precise import of the decisions concerning the canon is open to discussion. It often has been alleged that in drawing up the canon, the church vouches for the fact that these books *and no others* are sacred, inspired, and divinely authoritative. But canonization also can be interpreted to mean that these books, *and perhaps others,* are sacred, inspired, and divinely authoritative. In the latter case, the church would leave open the possibility of adding to its canon.

In some respects, the decision concerning the canon is a

practical one. It asserts that certain books are edifying and recommends them for use in piety, liturgy, and teaching. Understood in this way, the canon need not be taken as having been revealed by God and imposed on the church. It is quite possible to say that the church selected certain books in which it perceived a reliable and edifying expression of God's revelation in the constitutive period. In recent theological discussion, there is a general tendency to admit that the exact limits of the canon rest upon the discretionary decision of the church. There is no proof that the church could not have drawn the limits of the canon either a little more broadly or a little more narrowly. If the church had accepted a work such as Third or Fourth Esdras into its Old Testament, or First Clement into its New Testament, it would presumably have been able to live with that decision.

Inasmuch as the same list of canonical books has been recognized in Roman Catholicism since the fourth century, it seems very unlikely that the list will be changed in the future. In view of past definitions, it is hard to see how the church could ever declare that any book now in its canon is no longer to be considered sacred or inspired. Although it could cease to use a given book in its liturgy, it always will look to all the canonical books for the full content and context of its faith.

Could the church add any books to its present canon? To the best of my knowledge, the canon never has been defined in an exclusive sense. Thus it seems possible, at least in theory, that a new book could be added. Conceivably, therefore, the Catholic Church, in the course of union negotiations with a Coptic or an Armenian church, might be able to admit the canonicity of a work such as Third Maccabees or Fourth Esdras. Or again, if a new Pauline letter of uncontestable authenticity were unearthed in some cave in the Judaean desert, there could be discussion as to whether it too could be added to the Catholic canon. The absence of any tradition in favor of such a book would make its reception into the canon very unlikely, but the case for inclusion could at least be argued.

Protestants and Catholics use the same New Testament, but differ slightly in regard to the Old Testament. For the most part, Protestants follow the Hebrew Bible, which omits seven books (and fragments of two others) of the forty-six included in the Catholic Old Testament. Scholarly opinion has not yet reached a consensus as to which books Jesus and the apostles would have recognized as Scripture. Most Catholics and some Protestants maintain that the wider (Catholic) canon more closely corresponds with the books used as Scripture in the time of Jesus and that the narrower canon of the present Hebrew Bible is the result of a decision reached by the Palestinian rabbis about the end of the first century after Christ. Since the time of Jerome, however, some Christians have preferred the narrower Old Testament canon, and some respected Catholic theologians favored that position during the Middle Ages and the Renaissance. The seven disputed books (sometimes called deuterocanonical) scarcely can be regarded as central to the Bible. Yet they are valuable in their own way. Even if they were not in the canon, these books would need to be consulted for a better understanding of the faith of the Jews in the century before Christ. In practice, Protestants as well as Catholics make use of these books, and also of other intertestamental works which are regarded by Catholics, too, as apocryphal.

In this connection, it is worth noting that not all books of the Bible are on the same level of religious importance. In general, one may say that in the Old Testament, Christians make the most extensive use of Genesis, Exodus, the Psalms, and the major prophets—especially Isaiah. In the New Testament, the four Gospels and the great Pauline letters hold places of special importance. Some theologians, chiefly from the Lutheran tradition, have proposed that there be a "canon within the canon," but this idea has not appealed to Catholics or, in fact, to most Protestants, since it seems to authorize theologians to impose their own preferences, closing their eyes to biblical writings that do not appeal to them. Often, we most need to hear the testimony of the biblical witnesses whose messages seem to us strange and difficult to accept.

The Catholic Church, like other Christian bodies, generally has tended to regard the Old Testament as subordinate to the New. The Council of Trent, for example, declared that the church is bound to the Gospel, which was promised beforehand through the prophets of the Old Testament but first promulgated through Christ and the Holy Spirit (DS 1501). Vatican II, in its *Constitution on Revelation,* repeated St. Augustine's idea that by God's wise disposition, the New Testament lay hidden in the Old, whereas the Old is made manifest in the New (*DV* 16). Thus the relationship between the Old and New Testaments is predominantly understood in terms of a dialectic of promise and fulfillment. Some have suggested, however, that this schematization is not adequate. It is not true that everything in the Old Testament is better or more clearly stated in the New. In many respects the Old Testament remains unsurpassed, even unequalled. Thus it retains its value, not simply as promise but also as revelation.

Texts and Versions

The canon as discussed up to this point is simply a list of titles. The list is of little help until we knew what is printed under the titles. The councils of Trent and Vatican I had something to say on this question, too. They taught that the approved books "as a whole, with all their parts, as they have been accustomed to be read in the universal Church [*in Ecclesia catholica*] and as they are given in the old Latin Vulgate edition," are to be received as "sacred and canonical" (DS 1504; cf. 3006). Presumably both criteria alluded to here must be verified to establish beyond doubt that a given passage belongs in the Bible.[4] Insertion into the Vulgate is regarded as the clearest sign that the passage in question has been continually used as Scripture in the Latin church, but one must inquire further as to whether the Eastern churches, too, always have read it as Scripture. The councils have not determined in detail which disputed passages meet the criteria just given. Most Catholic scholars would readily agree that the story of the adulterous woman (John 7:53–8:11) and the longer ending of Mark (16:9-10) are canonical, but neither of these cases has been settled by an authoritative statement of the magisterium.[5]

The Vulgate never has been accepted as an inspired text, but only as a substantially reliable translation, free from

doctrinal error. In this sense it was approved by Trent, which
also called for a critical edition of that text (DS 1506-8). Pius
XII, in *Divino afflante Spiritu,* held that the books are inspired
in the "original languages" but did not specify those original
languages. In general the church has been inclined to follow
Jerome, who looked to the Hebrew for the originals of the
protocanonical books, to the ancient Greek Bible for most of
the deuterocanonicals, and there also for the sections of
Daniel and Esther not found in the Hebrew. For Tobit and
Judith, Jerome relied on Aramaic recensions no longer
extant. Modern Catholic editions of the Old Testament rely
predominantly on the Jewish Masoretic tradition for their
versions of the protocanonical books.

There has been periodic discussion of the authority of the
Greek Septuagint edition of the Hebrew Bible. Many of the
Church Fathers—from Irenaeus and Clement of Alexandria
to Augustine and Isidore—believed that the Septuagint was
inspired. Even Jerome, notwithstanding his preference for the
Hebrew, did not reject the inspiration of the Septuagint.
Under the influence of Jerome, however, Christian scholars
came increasingly to look upon the Septuagint as a mere
translation, to be judged in the light of the Hebrew original.
This opinion was all but universally accepted in modern times
until about 1950, when several Catholic scholars rather
tentatively proposed that it might be possible to go back to the
patristic opinion that the Septuagint was inspired, even—or
especially—where it departs from the Hebrew.[6] If this view is
correct, Alexandrian Judaism played a more significant role in
the history of revelation than has been usually recognized.

For much of the Old Testament, the choice is not simply
between the Hebrew and the Greek. In addition to the
Septuagint, there were several other ancient Greek versions,
known to us only through fragments. As for the Hebrew, the
Masoretic text, excellent though it is, was drawn up many
centuries after Christ. Thanks especially to the Qumran
discoveries, we now have, for certain books, rather complete
Hebrew versions which differ notably from the Masoretic. In
some cases these non-Masoretic recensions closely resemble
the Septuagint. For certain portions of the Old Testament,

therefore, the question as to which version is the "inspired text" remains undecided. Some theologians prefer to speak of inspired *traditions* rather than simply of inspired books. Thus the question of the canon leads directly to that of inspiration.

Inspiration

Since patristic times Catholic theologians have asserted, with something like unanimity, that the whole Bible is inspired. Against certain minimizing views, this belief was solemnly defined by Vatican I (DS 3006, 3029), which evidently understood the term *inspiration* to mean a positive antecedent influence upon the sacred writer sufficient to render God the author of the books and all their parts. In another context, Vatican I referred to the Bible as the "written word of God" (DS 3011). After repeating the substance of Vatican I's teaching on inspiration, Vatican II added: "To compose the sacred books, God chose certain men who, all the while he employed them in this task, made full use of their powers and faculties so that, though he acts in them and by them, it was as true authors that they consigned to writing whatever he wanted written, and no more" (*DV* 11, Flannery).

Vatican II's statement is noteworthy for its affirmation that the human writers were not mere secretaries but true authors, thus by implication repudiating certain "dictation" theories. Generally speaking, contemporary Catholic theologians reject the idea that by inspiration, God directly infused words or ideas into the minds of the biblical writers. Inspiration does not relieve its recipients of the necessity of applying their own powers to the research and composition from which books result. It assures only that those powers are so effectively assisted that the resulting books will serve as God intends for the guidance of the church.

Understood in this way, the doctrine of inspiration is closely linked to that of canonicity. In giving a historical revelation, God implicitly signifies that it be transmitted in reliable form to later generations. For this to occur, the recipients of the revelation must express their faith so as to make that faith accessible to posterity. The production of the canonical Scriptures is one of the principal ways in which the revelation given to Israel and to the apostolic church is preserved from corruption or oblivion.

Perhaps a word should be added at this point about divine authorship of the Bible. The idea that God is author of both the Old and New Testaments (or covenants) has appeared in many church documents since patristic times, and in the modern councils (Florence, Trent, Vatican I, and Vatican II) it is applied to the Scriptures. But the meaning of *authorship* in this connection is far from clear. Many theologians have held that God is literary author, in the sense that he conceives and communicates not only the ideas, but even the literary expression. However, in that case it would be difficult to consider the human writers as more than secretaries.

In view of the insistence of Vatican II that the human writers are true authors, perhaps we are invited to rethink the sense in which God is author. The term *auctor* in Latin (or *archēgos* in Greek) does not necessarily mean *literary author,* but rather *originator.*[7] Thus it is possible to say that God is author of the Bible in the sense that God initiates and controls the process whereby it is written, even though he does not dictate or miraculously infuse the ideas and words. In this view God would be, in the first instance, the author of the people of Israel and of their faith, and of the development of that faith through Jesus Christ. Inasmuch as God personally involves himself in salvation history, God could be called the author, indirectly, of the documents whereby the people of God express their faith in a divinely guided and reliable fashion.

Thus conceived, biblical inspiration results in a body of traditional literature which represents the faith of the people of God at various stages of development. In a special way, it expresses the faith of the prophetic and apostolic leaders who helped to shape the faith of Israel and of the church. A sufficient deposit of that inspired literature has survived to allow the church of subsequent centuries to constantly test its own teaching and piety against that of the recipients of the Jewish and Christian revelation.

Sometimes it is asked whether the Bible is the only inspired body of literature. The Catholic Church has never taught that it is. Modern scholarship has abundantly shown that the patristic and medieval writers spoke freely of the inspiration of Church Fathers and of councils.[8] In more recent times Christians have begun to ask whether the Koran and the sacred books of Hinduism and Buddhism also might not be, in some sense, inspired. There are no grounds for antecedently denying that this is possible, in the sense that the grace of the Holy Spirit may have assisted non-Christians in their religious searchings and discoveries. But if we define inspiration in terms of the goal of providing the church with an authentic record of its original patrimony, inspiration is proper to the Bible. Biblical inspiration, by definition, is that which results in a book that Christians can accept as a canonical expression of their own faith, as given in the constitutive period of revelation. Although other writings may be, in some sense, inspired—inasmuch as their authors were working with the grace of the Holy Spirit—they are not inspired Christian Scripture.

Inerrancy

The doctrine of inerrancy often has been seen as a corollary of inspiration, or of divine authorship. If God is author by way of inspiration, it seems to follow that whatever the human writers said, God said. Since God can neither deceive nor be deceived, the Bible itself must necessarily be free from error. Thus every declarative sentence in the Bible, no matter what its content, could be seen as peremptory authority. Many classical theologians adopted approximately this line of argument, and it may be found in rather similar terms in the encyclical of Leo XIII, *Providentissimus Deus*.

Although inerrancy of Scripture has been rather unanimously upheld since patristic times, careful students of the Bible always have been aware of serious objections to the doctrine. For example, there are internal contradictions in the Bible itself, with regard to not only historical and scientific matters, but even religious and ethical teaching. Furthermore, the accounts of the creation in Genesis, if accepted literally, do not agree with modern scientific theories about the origins and structure of the universe. Modern history and archaeology also have raised grave difficulties with the historicity of many factual statements in the Bible. When critical scholarship began to be applied to the Bible as it is to other historical sources, the doctrine of inerrancy was fiercely attacked, and conservative theologians, both Protestant and Catholic, then reacted defensively.

It is of interest to note that no ecumenical council ever has taught the inerrancy of Scripture. In the early drafts of Vatican II's *Constitution on Revelation,* the term *inerrancy* appeared in a chapter heading, and the provisional text asserted, along the same lines as *Providentissimus Deus:* "It is utterly unlawful to admit that the sacred writer has erred, since divine inspiration of its nature excludes and rejects all error in any matter, religious or profane, with the same necessity that God, the Supreme Truth, can be the source of no error whatsoever." This text, however, met with sharp opposition on the council floor. As a result, it was radically revised, and *inerrancy* was dropped from the heading. The final version states: "Since, therefore, all that the inspired authors, or sacred writers, affirm should be regarded as affirmed by the Holy Spirit, we must acknowledge that the books of Scripture, firmly, faithfully, and without error, teach that truth which God, for the sake of our salvation, wished to see confided to the sacred Scriptures" (*DV* 11, Flannery).

Comparing the two texts, one might say that the council backed away from absolute inerrancy. But because *inerrancy* itself suggests *total* freedom from error, the council preferred not to use the term at all; not rejecting total propositional inerrancy, Vatican II stopped short of positively teaching it. The final statement can be interpreted as accepting qualified, or limited, inerrancy—that is, inerrancy with regard to that truth which God wished committed to the Scriptures for the sake of our salvation.

The final text of Vatican II's statement could be misunderstood as indicating that the Bible is a patchwork of errant and inerrant passages. Reading the sentence as a whole, however, one can see that the council looked upon the divinely intended truth as a predicate of the Bible in its entirety, not just of certain parts—for everything written in the Scripture was inspired by the Holy Spirit. Thus the Bible as a whole inculcates the salutary truth for which God inspired it. Particular mistakes on the part of individual authors need not interfere with this value of the Bible as a totality, for even a passage that contains a materially false statement may be expressive of the community's valid perception of its own relationship to God. Many of the biblical writers' misunderstandings are corrected elsewhere in Scripture, and the very record of those misunderstandings helps us to appreciate how gradually God's revelation penetrates human minds and hearts.

Understood in this global theological perspective, the integral truth of the Bible is a mere aspect of its canonicity. In accepting a book as canonical, the church authenticates it as a normative guide for belief and worship. Since the church could not bind itself to anything that might be error, the adoption of the canon is an implicit affirmation of trustworthiness. The Bible is accepted as giving a true account of the faith of the people of God in its formative period—a faith that Christians regard as reaching its unsurpassable fulfillment in Jesus Christ as the self-revelation of God.

The less rigid stance of the contemporary Catholic Church toward inerrancy makes room for a more critical approach to the Bible than was considered permissible in recent centuries. Many older official Catholic documents were defensively drawn up against the assaults of "higher criticism." But since not every sentence of the Bible is guaranteed against every kind of error, it is possible and useful to try to dig behind the biblical texts to see how they are related to the actual events of the history on which they are based. *Divino afflante Spiritu,* with its recognition of form criticism, stopped short of encouraging a critical stance toward any intention of the biblical writers. Even the Instruction of the Biblical Commission on "The Historical Truth of the Gospels," issued in 1964, contents itself with recognizing the various forms of historicity that might be attributed to various passages. Vatican II, however, seems to open the way for Catholic critics to affirm that the biblical writers, even though they intended to vouch

for something as being scientifically, historically, or religiously correct, may have been mistaken. Only under the
formality of its "salutary truth" is the whole Bible protected
against error. Stimulated by this more open attitude, Catholic
biblical scholars have joined their Protestant colleagues in
seeking to probe beyond the biblical texts and to recapture the
privileged experiences on which the faith of the biblical people
was founded. These experiences are viewed as having
constitutive authority, even for the Bible itself.

Interpretation

The problem of interpretation will be touched upon rather
briefly. It cannot be entirely omitted, for Scripture has
authority for the church and for its members only to the extent
that the divinely intended meaning of the Scripture can be
ascertained. Church authority, as we shall see, plays an
important role in the interpretation of Scripture.

Since early patristic times, Christian authors—following
Jews such as Philo—have recognized various levels of
meaning in the Bible. Sometimes the plurality of meanings
was presented in superstitious or fanciful ways, to the
detriment of sober piety and common sense. The more
judicious medieval theologians, including Thomas Aquinas,
affirmed the primacy of the literal meaning as the one on
which all spiritual meanings must be founded. Reacting
against certain excesses of allegorization, theologians of the
sixteenth century, both Protestant and Catholic, tended to
concentrate on the literal sense. In the biblical encyclicals,
especially *Divino afflante Spiritu,* Catholic exegetes were
urged to seek out first the literal meaning and to affirm
spiritual meanings only where these were clearly and
demonstrably intended by God. Pius XII sought to establish
some criteria for ascertaining the existence of an authentic
spiritual sense in certain passages.[9]

In recent decades the new literary criticism, reinforced
by modern tendencies in philosophical hermeneutics, has
somewhat clouded the distinction between the literal sense
(understood in *Divino afflante Spiritu* as the sense of the words

themselves intended by the sacred author) and the spiritual sense (allegorical, typical, or whatever). There is widespread opinion that words generally carry meanings beyond the intentions and perceptions of those who speak and write them and that classical texts, as the subject of prolonged reflection by a historical community, generate a tradition of meanings related to but not identical with those originally intended. Further, it is pointed out that the Bible, as an inspired document, expresses a progressively deeper understanding of the faith entrusted to God's people. Impelled by the divine Spirit, the authors of Scripture spoke better than they knew; their words conveyed implications that could be unfolded only in the light of subsequent revelation.

Finally, it is contended by many theologians that the canon binds the biblical books into a single collection, in which any one book may be legitimately interpreted in light of the others.[10] To some extent, the editors of the canon intended that the various traditions should be read with reference to one another. The meaning of Scripture, then, would not necessarily be the meaning of a given text taken in isolation, but rather the resultant meaning of all the texts, just as the meaning of a documentary film would not be the meaning of particular statements made by one character or another. Vatican II could therefore assert: "Since holy Scripture must be read and interpreted according to the same Spirit by whom it was written, no less serious attention must be given to the content and unity of the whole of Scripture, if the meaning of the sacred texts is to be correctly brought to light" (*DV* 12). A little farther on we read: "The books of the Old Testament with all their parts, caught up into the proclamation of the gospel, acquire and show forth their full meaning [*plenam significationem*] in the New Testament . . . and in turn shed light on it and explain it" (*DV* 16, Scripture refs. omitted).

On the basis of passages such as these, it seems defensible to speak of something like a deeper literal meaning which lies beyond the horizons of the individual human author and yet is truly present in the Bible taken as a whole. This meaning corresponds approximately to certain modern exegetes' "fuller meaning" *(sensus plenior)*, but the terminology is far from settled. Whatever terms are used, it seems correct to say that the church is concerned not so much with what the inspired writers consciously intended by their words, but with what can be found in their words by one who reads them in an informed way, in light of the whole Bible and the whole tradition of the church.

Who can rightly interpret the Scriptures? It is an axiom of Catholic exegesis, repeated, as we have just seen, by Vatican II, that the Bible must be read "according to the same Spirit by whom it was written." For anyone who looks on the Bible as inspired, this evidently means that the reader must be open to the present activity of the Holy Spirit. Although a purely profane exegesis, according to historical/critical principles, can say many true things, it will not penetrate to the heart of the divinely intended meaning. Scripture is written to direct believers in their faith and worship, and unless we are disposed toward such religious activities, we shall inevitably remain at the surface.

After considering these general assertions, one can better understand certain official church rulings regarding interpretation. The Council of Trent, seconded by Vatican I, forbade interpretation of the Scriptures in a way contrary to the unanimous teaching of the Fathers (DS 1507, 3007). The assumption was that the Fathers, having enjoyed the guidance of the Spirit of Christ, could not have been universally misled about what God intended to communicate as a matter of faith through the Bible. While it may be difficult to specify any given text that has been infallibly interpreted through a consensus of the Fathers, the fact remains that Catholic exegetes look to the Fathers as highly adept at penetrating the spiritual and theological significance of God's Word in the Bible.[11]

Regarding the Bible as the "Book of the Church" par excellence, the councils have repeatedly insisted that it is the right and duty of the church, through its official teaching body, or magisterium, to give judgments concerning the true meaning of Scripture (DS 1507, 3007). Vatican II, taking up this theme, asserted: "The task of authentically interpreting the word of God, whether written or handed on [in the form of

tradition], has been entrusted exclusively to the living
[magisterium] of the Church, whose authority is exercised in
the name of Jesus Christ" (*DV* 10). A few paragraphs farther,
the constitution added that the interpretation of Scripture "is
subject finally to the judgment of the Church, which carries
out the divine commission and ministry of guarding and
interpreting the word of God" (*DV* 12).

At this point one encounters the rather complex question,
How is the "authentic" interpretation of the magisterium to
be seen in relation to the exegetical labors of scholars of
Scripture? It is important to note that the magisterium is not
entitled to interpret the Bible in an arbitrary or whimsical
manner. According to Vatican II, "this teaching office is not
above the word of God, but serves it" (*DV* 10). In seeking out
the true meaning, the magisterium is dependent in some
measure upon biblical scholars, whose preparatory study, in
the words of *Dei Verbum,* is valuable so that "the judgment of
the Church may mature" (*DV* 12). Thus the exegetes are not
unilaterally subject to the magisterium; there is a kind of
mutual dependence, as each group carries out its own proper
function within the Body of Christ.

Some have imagined that Catholic exegetes are not free to
pursue honest scholarship, inasmuch as they are antecedently
bound to interpret the Scriptures as the magisterium has
interpreted them. This conclusion would be, for several
reasons, unwarranted. First, it must be noted that while the
church, in a general way, bases its teaching on Scripture, it
rarely points to texts as having certain specific meanings. Even
when particular texts are cited, the citation is generally
intended to show that the texts in some way support the
teaching of the church, without affirming that they mean
exactly what the church is teaching. Second, when the
magisterium does affirm that a given text has a particular
meaning, it rarely if ever uses the full weight of its infallible
teaching authority to define irrevocably that such is the
meaning of the text. As Pius XII put it, "There are but few
texts whose sense has been defined by the authority of the
Church," and thus "the skill and genius of Catholic
commentators may and ought to be freely exercised, so that

each may contribute his part to the advantage of all."[12] Third, even though the meaning of several biblical texts has been infallibly defined, there is no assertion that the definitions in question express the full and only meaning of the texts. In fact, it may in some cases be doubted whether the magisterium refers to the literal meaning of the text in its original historical setting, or in the minds of the inspired authors.

To make this last point concrete, one may question the binding force of the canons of Trent, to the effect that the expression "unless one is born of water and the Holy Spirit" (John 3:5) refers to the water of baptism (DS 1615), and the statement "Whose sins you shall forgive, they are forgiven" (John 20:23) has reference to the sacrament of penance (DS 1703, 1710). These canons do not oblige the exegete to hold that the biblical passages refer only to the sacraments of baptism and penance. Without directly contradicting the canons, one might hold that the Evangelist, or Jesus himself, might have had other meanings in mind, or that the contemporary believer, while not excluding the meaning affirmed by Trent, could find a wider intelligibility in these texts.

In short, the ecclesiastical magisterium does not seek either to reduplicate the task of the scholarly exegete, whose primary role is to seek out the literal sense as it would have been understood in its earliest setting; or to preempt the insights of the speculative theologian, who seeks systematic understanding; or to disagree with the devout reader, who may find particular meanings especially relevant to his or her present situation. The magisterium is concerned rather with setting limits as to what may be taught without contradicting the general doctrine of the church. The dogmatic judgments proclaimed by the magisterium, while they bear a certain relationship to the scholarly and spiritual interpretations, need not perfectly coincide with either. The distinction of functions between the scholar, the prayerful reader, and the pastoral magisterium assures, in principle, that none of the three will usurp the prerogatives of the others. Where usurpation of functions does occur, it is an abuse that can and must be corrected.

The Sufficiency of Scripture

Since the sixteenth century there has been a prolonged debate between Protestants and Catholics as to whether the Bible alone is a sufficient standard of doctrine. At Worms, Luther set the precedent of appealing to the Bible rather than to popes and councils: "Unless I am convinced by the testimony of the Scriptures or by clear reason (for I do not trust either in the pope or in the councils alone, since it is well known that they have often erred and contradicted themselves), I am bound by the Scriptures I have quoted and my conscience is captive to the Word of God."[13] The Council of Trent gave an initial Catholic response—namely, that the truth of the gospel and the norms of Christian conduct are "contained in written books and unwritten traditions" that have come down to us from the apostles, and therefore equal piety and reverence should be paid to the traditions and to the books of sacred Scripture.

Although Trent did not explicitly teach that there is any revealed truth not contained in Scripture, post-Tridentine Catholic theology took the position that some revealed truths are conveyed to us by tradition alone. The schema for the Sources of Revelation drawn up by the Preparatory Commission for Vatican Council II reflected this view in its statement: "Holy Mother Church has always believed and believes that the full revelation is contained not in Scripture alone but in Scripture and Tradition, as in two sources, though in different ways."[14]

In the past few decades many Protestants have distanced themselves from the "Bible alone" formula, and conversely, many Catholics have abandoned the idea that certain revealed truths are given in "tradition alone." Protestant theologians have frequently pointed out that the Bible alone is not an adequate source, since the Bible is never alone. It is always read within an ecclesiastical tradition—if only the tradition of "Bible alone." The only real alternative to good tradition is bad tradition. These and other similar points were made at the Montreal meeting of the Faith and Order Commission of the World Council of Churches (1963).[15]

Meanwhile, in the autumn of 1962, the fathers at Vatican II
rejected the schema on the Sources of Revelation that had
been prepared for them. They particularly objected to the
two-source theory in the passage just quoted. The new draft,
which was prepared in 1963 and became, with some revisions,
the *Dogmatic Constitution on Divine Revelation,* was deliberately worded in such a way as to avoid the implication that
tradition contains any revealed truth that is not also in
Scripture. It implies rather that Scripture and tradition
together constitute a single source. "There exist a close
connection and communication between sacred tradition and
sacred Scripture. For both of them, flowing from the same
divine wellspring, in a certain way merge into a unity and tend
toward the same end" (*DV* 9).

Not only did Vatican II intimately conjoin Scripture and
tradition; it gave a certain priority to Scripture. Sacred
Scripture is unequivocally called the Word of God, both in
Article 9 and in Article 24 of *Dei Verbum.* The latter states:
"The sacred Scriptures contain the word of God and, since
they are inspired, really are the word of God." The council
never states that tradition is the Word of God, but only that it
"hands on" that Word and makes it active in the church, so
that "God, who spoke of old, uninterruptedly converses with
the Bride of His beloved Son" (*DV* 8).

Thus one perhaps may find between the lines of *Dei Verbum*
a certain qualified *sola Scriptura.* Scripture alone, the
constitution seems to say, is the Word of God. Does this mean
that Scripture is all we need and that tradition is superfluous?
According to the council, tradition is necessary in order for
the Bible to be interpreted with assurance and accuracy. As
the council puts it: "It is not from sacred Scripture alone that
the Church draws her certainty about everything which has
been revealed. Therefore both sacred tradition and sacred
Scripture are to be accepted and venerated with the same
sense of devotion and reverence" (*DV* 9). As a particular
instance of the necessity of tradition, the council states that it
is through tradition that the church's "full canon of the sacred
books becomes known" (*DV* 8).

Does this mean that the canon is known by tradition only,

with no consideration of the biblical books themselves? Some Catholics seem to speak as if this were the case, but there is little plausibility in the concept that the tradition could have grown up without some appraisal of the books. If the apostles ever certified a list of biblical books (a most unlikely hypothesis), their testimony was not appealed to or apparently not remembered during disputes about the canon in subsequent centuries. The tradition that validated the Scriptures appears rather to have arisen in the churches. As they used the books in preaching, teaching, and worship, they experienced the spiritual benefits that flowed from the Scriptures. The convergent traditions of many churches were taken as evidence of the inspired and normative character of the books themselves. Thus the formation of the canon admirably illustrates the mutual coinherence of Scripture and tradition.

With regard to the sufficiency of Scripture, it still must be asked whether the Protestant and Catholic positions as here presented do justice to contemporary religious experience as a theological locus. Tradition, as usually understood, refers to a patrimony handed down from the past. But a number of modern authors tend to understand it as the living consciousness of the church, so that the contemporary experience of believers may be included in an expanded notion of tradition. In line with this school of thought, Vatican II speaks of tradition continually developing in the church as believers meditate on the patrimony of faith in light of their spiritual experience (*DV* 8).

Within the limits of this essay, it is impossible to discuss the development of the notion of tradition itself over the centuries. It should, however, be observed that when Vatican II spoke of *tradition,* it was using a concept rather different from that of Trent, which spoke of *traditions* (in the plural). By the time of Vatican II, there was a ready acceptance of change and development in the understanding of faith, and hence of a fluid and dynamic concept of tradition. Only in the light of this shift can one adequately understand the modern Catholic view of the development of dogma—another theme which limitations of space prevent us from pursuing.

The mandate here, however, does call for some treatment of the extent to which church structures are under the authority of Scripture. Sixteenth-century Catholics, like their Protestant counterparts, sought to ground the principal structures of the church, including the sacraments and the ecclesiastical ministry, in the apostolic revelation as attested by the New Testament. Today the tendency is to recognize that the forms of sacramental worship and church polity have developed from rather rudimentary seeds given in apostolic times. A careful comparison of the statements of Trent and Vatican II would substantiate this shift of consciousness.

Apart from the essential structures of sacrament and ministry, there exists in Roman Catholicism a vast array of secondary structures relating to worship and government. Historical accretions such as archbishops, patriarchs, dioceses, deaneries, and parishes, the college of cardinals, the rubrics of sacramental and nonsacramental worship, the discipline of the clergy, and all such matters are subject to the governing power of the church, which may modify, abrogate, and innovate as circumstances seem to require. Rules concerning holy days and fasts, the style of life of priests and other religious, and numerous matters of this kind are regulated by the canonical powers vested in the hierarchy— powers analogous to the government of a secular state. Just as legislative and executive decisions need not be specifically authorized by the constitution of a secular state, so the canonical regulations of the church need not be specifically authorized by Scripture or by apostolic tradition. It is sufficient that they not violate the letter or the spirit of the revelation originally given in Christ.

The Uses of Scripture

Thus far we have concerned ourselves primarily with Scripture insofar as it is an authoritative source of doctrine. This is the aspect under which the magisterium has principally discussed the Bible, but the Bible has many other uses. The varied purposes of Scripture are suggested in this familiar text: "All Scripture is inspired by God and profitable for teaching, for reproof, for correction, and for training in righteousness, that the man of God may be complete, equipped for every good work" (2 Tim 3:16).

The Council of Trent, in its reform decrees, sought to reactivate these multiple uses of Scripture. Solicitous "that the heavenly treasure of the sacred books which the Holy Ghost has with the greatest liberality delivered to men may not lie neglected," the council ordained and decreed that bishops and ecclesiastical superiors should provide for regular biblical study and preaching.[16] The papal encyclicals of Leo XIII, Benedict XV, and Pius XII did not fail to mention the value of the Bible for personal prayer, liturgy, preaching, and theological reflection. These themes were taken up with added emphasis by Vatican II.

The *Constitution on the Sacred Liturgy* points out that the "real presence" of Christ should not be restricted to the Eucharist or to the Sacraments. Christ also is present in the community that gathers to pray and in the Word of Scripture that is read in the assembly (*SC* 7). Farther on in the same constitution, we read:

> Sacred Scripture is of paramount importance in the celebration of the liturgy. For it is from Scripture that lessons are read and explained in the homily, and psalms are sung; the prayers, collects, and liturgical songs are scriptural in their inspiration, and it is from Scripture that actions and signs derive their meaning. Thus if the restoration, progress, and adaptation of the sacred liturgy are to be achieved, it is necessary to promote that warm and living love for Scripture to which the venerable tradition of both Eastern and Western rites gives testimony. (*SC* 24)

The liturgical reforms initiated by Vatican II are essentially linked with the more abundant use of Scripture. For example, the *Constitution on the Sacred Liturgy* declares: "In sacred celebrations there is to be more reading from holy Scripture, and it is to be more varied and suitable" (*SC* 35). In the same article, Bible services are given special encouragement.

The most extensive treatment of the uses of Scripture is to be found in the sixth chapter of the *Dogmatic Constitution on*

Divine Revelation, which deals with "Sacred Scripture in the Life of the Church." This chapter begins with a bold comparison of the Bible with the Eucharist. The faithful, it declares, are to be nourished "from the table of both the word of God and of the body of Christ" (*DV* 21). Here the Word of God means especially the Bible, for it alone, according to the constitution, offers that Word immutably in the words of the prophets and the apostles. All preaching in the church is to be ruled by the Bible, "for in the sacred books, the Father who is in heaven meets His children with great love and speaks with them; and the force and power in the word of God is so great that it remains the support and energy of the Church, the strength of faith for her sons, the food of the soul, the pure and perennial source of spiritual life" (*DV* 21).

Throughout this chapter, the council repeatedly makes mention of the inner power of the Word of God, which exerts a transforming influence on those whom it encounters. It is not sufficient for the faithful to be told about the Scriptures. It is also important that all have ready access to the Bible itself, so as to gain from their frequent reading "excelling knowledge of Jesus Christ" (Phil 3:8, quoted in *DV* 25). If in the past there had been a certain fear that the faithful might be led astray in their attempts to find God in the Scriptures, that fear seems to have been allayed. Vatican II sets forth the principle: "Easy access to sacred Scripture should be provided for all the Christian faithful," and to this end it recommends modern translations into various languages (*DV* 22).[17] Particular attention is given to the importance of praying as one reads the Scriptures, "so that God and man may talk together" (*DV* 25).

The constitutions on the liturgy and on revelation are at one in insisting on Bible study for the preparation of preachers and others engaged in the ministry of the Word. Homilies and catechesis are to be given a solid biblical base (*DV* 24). So, similarly, theology is to be taught in such a way that its "soul" will be sacred Scripture—a principle which Vatican II, in its *Constitution on Revelation* (*DV* 24) and in its *Decree on Priestly Formation* (*OT* 16), takes over from Leo XIII.

Finally, it deserves to be mentioned that Vatican II relates the value of Scripture to the ecumenical movement. The *Decree on Ecumenism* praises Protestants for seeking God in the Bible "as He speaks to them in Christ" (*UR* 21). As if to answer the anticipated objection that seeking is not the same as finding, in the following article the decree goes on to point out that the faith of Protestant Christians is strengthened by their reverence for God's Word and by their meditation on the Bible. Thus it is easy to understand how the council can proclaim that in dialogue with Protestants "the sacred utterances are precious instruments in the mighty hand of God for attaining that unity which the Savior holds out to all men" (*UR* 21).

Although the biblical revival since Vatican II may not have been as deep and far-reaching as some of the council fathers had hoped, there can be no doubt that renewed attention to the Scriptures has been one of the most efficacious sources of religious regeneration in the past twenty years. Encouraged by the council, Bible study groups and prayer groups have flourished in many parts of the world. These groups are frequently ecumenical in character, and sometimes they are linked with the charismatic movement. Generally speaking, the Bible holds a more central place in the prayer of individual Catholics and in the public worship of that church than it has for many centuries.

To the extent that the Bible is restored to its centrality in the life of the church, the church is internally strengthened as a community of faith. But the efficacy of God's Word in Scripture, as understood by the Catholic Church, far exceeds its power to effect an inner reform of the church itself. The Scriptures are revered by all Christians and, in great part, by Jews and Muslims. God's Word in the Bible is directed ultimately to humanity as a whole, "for not only the Church, but every man lives in his ultimate depths more from the word of God than from the bread that is granted him by his mortality on earth."[18]

Precious though the fruits of the biblical revival have been, biblical theology has its limits, and these have been acutely experienced in the decade since Vatican II. One of the aims of the council itself, as conceived by Pope John XXIII, was to bring the church into a more vital relationship to the modern world. But the modern world no longer thinks in biblical categories, and its concerns are quite different from those of the Jews of old. The Catholic Church, therefore, cannot settle for a biblical theology that simply repristinates the mentality of the biblical writers. The Bible can speak with full power only when its message is brought into correlation with present-day questions. Nor can its value be fully appreciated if it is used uncritically, in an authoritarian manner. Since 1965, many Catholic theologians have sought to press beyond the kind of biblical theology enshrined in Vatican II's constitutions on the liturgy and revelation, and in its *Decree on Ecumenism.* Attempts are being made to recapture the religious experience which underlies the biblical accounts and to relate this in some way to contemporary religious experience. A critical discussion of these efforts, however, would take us far beyond the scope of this essay.

THE NATURE and extent of biblical authority has become, over the past two centuries, the focal point of a major debate within Protestantism. Some look to the Bible for guidance only in spiritual matters; others argue that since the entire Bible comes from God, its authority in all matters is beyond question. Those who hold the latter position, recognizing the presence of metaphor, do not always read the Bible literally; still, the result of their perspective is to extend the reliability and hence the authority of Scripture beyond the realm of theology. So viewed, every biblical statement—historical as well as ritual, scientific as well as ethical—becomes divinely based.

According to this position, one proof of the Bible's divine origin is derived from Jesus' acceptance of its authority, from which it is inferred that he certified its reliability in any and all matters. Such a theory clearly cannot apply to the New Testament, for which alternative arguments must be marshaled. Two other claims are equally characteristic of this perspective. First, inerrancy is ascribed only to the original copies (autographs) of scriptural works; errors in our editions of the Bible are to be understood as the result of faulty transmission. Second, proponents of this position argue that theirs is the classical Protestant, and even the classical Christian position.

—F.E.G.

A Protestant View of Biblical Authority

JOHN H. GERSTNER
PITTSBURGH THEOLOGICAL SEMINARY

THIS ESSAY will present the fundamental view of biblical authority as observed by orthodox Protestantism through the ages. There being considerable deviation from this view among contemporary Protestants, this too will be noted, without losing a focus on the persistent classical stance. The reason for the Protestant position will be explained—that the Son of God certified the Bible as the Word of God—and three current efforts to avoid Christ's authoritative verdict will be critiqued. In conclusion, the Bible as the Word of God applied to society—specifically, the home, the state, and the church—will be considered briefly.

The Classic Protestant Doctrine: The Bible Is the Word of God

The precise authority of the Scripture, according to traditional and orthodox Protestantism, is the authority of God. Throughout the ages, the byword of the church has been, "What the Bible says, God says." That is our view of the Bible. Roman Catholics sometimes have teased us, saying that we believe in a paper pope. They could go a step farther and say that we believe in a paper God, for though we do not believe that God has become incarnate in printer's ink, we do

---

John Gerstner has quoted passages from the New American Standard Bible, the Revised Standard Version, and the King James Version.

believe that what he has inspired in the sacred text is nothing less than his very Word, to be believed and obeyed as if he were appearing before us and speaking to us. Indeed, the Westminster Confession of Faith, one of the creeds of Protestantism, refers to "the Holy Spirit speaking in the Scripture."

To this day, the United Presbyterian Church in the U.S.A. requires its officers to affirm this vow: "Do you accept the Scriptures of the Old and New Testaments to be, by the Holy Spirit, the unique and authoritative witness to Jesus Christ in the Church universal, and God's word to you?"[1] One can sense the dynamism of that statement. It is by the active working of the Holy Spirit, the third person in the Godhead, that the Scriptures are "God's word to you," the individual believer. We do not consider the Book itself sacred (as the Sikhs seem to worship their holy book, calling it Mr. Granth and genuflecting), but what the Scriptures teach we regard as sacred. That teaching we do hear and obey, because and only because it is God's Word. Thereby we worship its Author, since he says in the Scripture, "To obey is better than sacrifice" (1 Sam 15:22 RSV).

This sentiment is by no means limited to the Presbyterian Westminster standards, but is a heritage common to Protestantism. The Lutheran Formula of Concord states:

> We believe, confess, and teach that the only rule and norm, according to which all dogmas and all doctors ought to be esteemed and judged, is no other whatsoever than the prophetic and apostolic writings both of the Old and of the New Testament. . . . But other writings, whether of the fathers or of the moderns, with whatever name they come, are in nowise to be equalled to the Holy Scriptures, but are all to be esteemed inferior to them, so that they be not otherwise received than in the rank of witnesses.[2]

In the French Confession of Faith, we read that "inasmuch as [the Bible] is the rule of all truth, containing all that is necessary for the service of God and for our salvation, it is not lawful for men, nor even for angels, to add to it, to take away from it, or to change it."[3] The American revision of The

Thirty-nine Articles of the Church of England reads: "Holy Scripture containeth all things necessary to salvation: so that whatsoever is not read therein, nor may be proved thereby, is not to be required of any man, that it should be believed as an article of the Faith, or to be thought requisite or necessary to salvation."[4] To this same principle witnessed all Protestant creeds.[5]

It follows that if the Bible is the very Word of God, the precise character of the authority of the Bible in the classic Protestant tradition can be stated in the one word—*inerrant*. The inerrancy, or infallibility, of the Bible is the usual modern, or at least American way to express the traditional position. *Inerrant* expresses the belief that Scripture in its original manuscripts is without any error whatsoever, in anything that, fairly interpreted, it teaches. This is sometimes called the inerrancy of the autographs. The reference to the autographs does not mean, of course, that the orthodox demand that the original handwriting of the scribes of Scripture be produced. As close an approach as possible (by the science of textual criticism) must be attempted. No doctrine can be based on a demonstrably nongenuine text, and no errors based on errant texts can be considered errors in the Bible. On the other hand, if the text is shown to be genuine—that is, derived from the original manuscripts—any single text soundly construed inerrantly demonstrates whatever it deliberately asserts. In the famous words of the great proof texter Martin Luther, "One little word shall slay him [the Devil]."[6]

These two words—*God* and *inerrancy*—are, in the orthodox mind, utterly inseparable. God, by definition, is incapable of error or deceit. His omniscience means that he cannot be ignorant and his veracity means that he cannot lie. Consequently, in general, theism would say that God cannot, in any sense, err. If, therefore, the Bible is inspired by him in such a way as to be his Word, the Bible cannot err. To say that the Bible can be God's Word and still can err is to blaspheme. We believe that when anyone, anywhere, contends that the Bible is in error, in that very statement that person shows that he does not believe the Bible to be the Word of God. We readily admit that if the Bible is not the Word of God, it can err; but we believe that anyone will grant us that if the Bible is (and does not merely contain or point to) the Word of God, it cannot err.[7]

Contemporary Protestant Deviations

We are laboring this point because there are Protestants today who are saying that the Bible *is* the Word of God, but that it can err.[8] This, we insist, is not only nonsense, but blasphemy, and although it departs from the traditional Protestant position of inerrancy, does not admit doing so. It therefore is departing from biblical authority, for the Bible has authority insofar, and only insofar as it is the Word of God. I repeat that no one will ever say that God can err. If therefore some teach that the Bible can err, they must admit that they no longer believe that the Bible is completely the Word of God.

It must be granted that much of modern Protestantism is no longer traditionally Protestant. Nowhere is this more evident than in its view of the Bible. Many neo-Protestants themselves admit this. Karl Barth, for example, says:

The Reformers took over unquestioningly and unreservedly the statement on the inspiration, and indeed the verbal inspiration, of the Bible, as it is explicitly and implicitly contained in those Pauline passages which we have taken as our basis, even including the formula that God is the author of the Bible, and occasionally making use of the idea of a dictation through the Biblical writers. How could it be otherwise? Not with less but with greater and more radical seriousness they wanted to proclaim the subjection of the church to the Bible as the Word of God and its authority as such. . . . Luther is not inconsistent when we hear him thundering polemically at the end of his life: "Therefore, we either believe roundly and wholly and utterly, or we believe nothing: the Holy Ghost doth not let Himself be severed or parted, that He should let one part be taught or believed truly and the other part falsely. . . . For it is the fashion of all heretics that they begin first with a single article, but they must then all be denied and altogether, like a ring which is of no further value when it has a break or cut, or a bell which when it is cracked in one place will not ring any more and is quite useless" *(Kurzes Bekenntnis vom heiligen Sakrament* 1544 W. A. 54, 158, 28). Therefore Calvin is not guilty of any disloyalty to the Reformation tendency when he says of Holy Scripture that its authority is recognised only when it . . . is realised that *autorem eius esse Deum.* In Calvin's sermon on 2 Tim. 3:16f. (C.R. 54:238f.) God is constantly described as the *autheur* of Holy Scripture and in his commentary on the same passage we seem to hear a perfect echo of the voice of the Early Church.[9]

John E. Smith, general editor of Yale University Press' *Works of Jonathan Edwards,* writes of America's greatest theologian that "Edwards accepted totally the tradition established by the Reformers with respect to the absolute primacy and authority of the Bible, and he could approach the biblical writings with that conviction of their inerrancy and literal truth."[10]

Probably the best-known liberal acknowledgment of this historic shift is that of Chicago's Kirsop Lake, the New Testament scholar:

> It is a mistake often made by educated persons who happen to have but little knowedge of historical theology to suppose that fundamentalism is a new and strange form of thought. It is nothing of the kind. . . . No, the fundamentalist may be wrong; I think he is. But it is we who have departed from tradition, not he, and I am sorry for the fate of anyone who tries to argue with the fundamentalist on the basis of authority. The Bible and the *corpus theologicum* of the Church is on the fundamentalist side.[11]

Not all Protestants are so candid. Not liking to be out of line with history, they attempt to bring history into line with themselves. If one were not knowledgeable, one could well imagine that inerrancy was unheard of until it was bruited abroad in the backwoods of America a century or so ago.[12]

In any case, I will present the classic view, which is still held by millions of Protestants. It was a Roman Catholic, G. K. Chesterton, who once observed that most church people do not know what Christianity is, and if they ever learn, they will realize they don't like it. Be that as it may, let us consider now the traditional case for biblical authority that many in the

Protestant churches still confidently advance and which, though often ignored, remains unrefuted.

The fundamental case for the Bible, as we see it, is this: The Bible is the Word of God because the Son of God says so.

It has often been demonstrated that Jesus Christ identifies the Bible as the Word of God. This data has been well summarized by John W. Wenham in a recent essay on that subject.[13] I will simply use his own brief summary of his work so that I may get on with my pleasant task, which is to show the significance of this stupendous fact—that Christ approves (and thereby proves) the Bible's inspiration—and especially to meet the inevitable attacks that follow that assertion.

But first, Christ on Scripture, from the pen of Wenham:

First, Jesus taught the truth of Old Testament *history,* treating the historical narratives as straight-forward records of fact. He refers to: Abel (Luke 11:51), Noah (Matt. 24:37-39; Luke 17:26, 27), Abraham (John 8:56), the institution of circumcision (John 7:22), Sodom and Gomorrah (Matt. 10:15; 11:23, 24; Luke 10:12), Lot (Luke 17:28-32), Isaac and Jacob (Matt. 8:11; Luke 13:28), the manna (John 6:31, 49, 58), the wilderness serpent (John 3:14), David eating the shewbread (Matt. 12:3, 4; Mark 2:25, 26; Luke 6:3, 4), David as psalm-writer (Matt. 22:43; Mark 12:36; Luke 20:42), Solomon (Matt. 6:29; 12:42; Luke 11:31, 12:27), Elijah (Luke 4:25, 26), [and many more].

Although truth may be conveyed by parable or allegory or even historical fiction, there is no evidence that Jesus thought of the Old Testament historical narratives in these terms. Indeed, he puts the visit of the Queen of the South, recorded in the book of Kings, side by side with the story of Jonah (Matt. 12:41, 42).

Second, Jesus endorsed the Old Testament's *teaching.* It was the court of appeal in controversy with the Pharisees (Matt. 15:1-9; Mark 7:1-13) and the Sadducees (Matt. 22:29; Mark 12:24): "You are in error, because you do not know the Scriptures or the power of God." It is the guide to ethics: "All the Law and the Prophets hang on these two commandments" (Matt. 22:40).

That this is Jesus' own standpoint and not just a position adopted to accommodate himself to the beliefs of his hearers is shown in the temptation narratives. Here he answers the keenest thrusts at his inmost soul by a threefold quotation of Scripture, which he prefaces by the words "It is written." (Matt. 4:4, 6, 7; Luke 4:4, 8).

That it is not due to his human limitations is shown by his teaching after he was raised from the dead. For "beginning with Moses and all the Prophets, he explained to them what was said in all the Scriptures concerning himself" (Luke 24:27).

Third, Jesus affirmed the inspiration of the Old Testament *writings.* He is well aware of the sins of the Old Testament saints and does not espouse the modern notion that the *men* were inspired rather than their writings. Though he mentions the human authors as real authors—Moses, Isaiah, David, Daniel (Mark 7:10; 7:6; 12:36; Matt. 24:15)—he nevertheless indicates that their authority derives from the fact that their teachings were given by God. . . .

Jesus often speaks simply of "Scripture," God being the implied author ("The scriptures . . . bear witness to me," John 5:39). "Have you not read" is equivalent to "Do you not know that God has said?" (Matt. 12:3; 19:4; 21:16; 22:31; Mark 2:25; 12:10; Luke 6:3). "It stands written" is used in many contexts (Matt. 11:10; 21:13; 26:24). The Old Testament is Scripture to Christ because it has God as its primary author (which other writing does not).

We conclude that for Jesus the Old Testament was true, authoritative and inspired. To him the God of the Old Testament was the living God and the teaching of the Old Testament was the teaching of the living God. What Scripture said, God said.[14]

We need not say anything about Christ's approval of the then future New Testament, because his certification of the apostles as those whom the Spirit would lead into "all truth" is evidence enough for the completion of the canon, all of which Christ indicates to be the Word of God and therefore inerrant.

Contemporary Objections

We turn now to efforts to undermine the testimony of Christ. I say *undermine* because no Christian, at least, will seem to disagree with Christ. If he does disagree, he must somehow try to show that it is not Christ with whom he is disagreeing; in this way he undermines without seeming to disagree.

Kenosis Doctrine. The first "explanation" of Christ's high view of Scripture results in an exceedingly low view of Christ's nature. I am afraid it amounts to nothing less than blasphemy, if Christ was the Son of God. Not that those who offer this explanation necessarily intend or realize blasphemy, but it amounts to that by implication, nonetheless. I refer to various kenosis doctrines, which hold that Christ emptied himself of deity during his Incarnation.

Let us look at the situation that created kenotic doctrine. It was acknowledged, to begin with, that Christ did indeed teach the inspiration of the Bible as the inerrant Word of God. As Jülicher and many other radical—as far as the Bible is concerned—scholars have admitted, "Jesus war ein Fundamentalist." But it was assumed by liberal minds that the Bible is not the inerrant Word of God. So they had a problem. The Son of God could not possibly, they reasoned, be ignorant of the fact (of which they themselves were well aware) that the Bible is not the Word of God. This then was their dilemma: The Son of God taught that the Bible is the Word of God; but the Son of God would have known that the Bible is not the Word of God. So if they could not deny that Christ did teach that the Bible is the Word of God, and they themselves could not admit that the Bible is the Word of God, something had to give. And that something could be only the conviction that Christ was the Son of God.

Yet to deny that Christ was the Son of God is not easy either, for Christians. The problem then becomes: How can one consider Christ to be the Son of God and, at the same time, not the Son of God? How can one deny the deity of Christ but not deny the deity of Christ? That is a christological problem of no mean difficulty, but the nineteenth century hit on the solution—a truly brilliant one! It was the kenosis doctrine. This was the theory that made it possible for Christ to be both the Son of God and not the Son of God. He supposedly emptied himself of his deity (or some attributes of that deity) for the duration of his Incarnation. Thus he remained the Son of God, and yet was not the Son of God (or fully the Son of God) during his Incarnation. This hopelessly confusing theory probably never would have occurred to anyone, or been seriously maintained, if it had not been for the relentless pressure against inerrancy. "This is the curse of evil deed that of new evil it becomes the seed." But it did seem so effectively to solve the problem—that the Son of God "wrongly" taught that the Bible is the Word of God—that some Christians were willing to overlook the problems in the theory itself.

It was one of those cases of curing a headache by decapitation. It was so good to be free of the headache that, for awhile, one hardly noticed the decapitation. This is somewhat like the soldier whose enemy slashed at him with a sword but, the soldier thought, missed. Greatly relieved, the soldier taunted, "You missed," only to hear the enemy reply, "Wait till you shake your head." Kenosis did indeed solve the problem of the Son of God "errantly" supposing the Bible to be the inerrant Word of God. He was not at that time the inerrant Son of God, and that is why he errantly thought that the Bible was inerrant. The liberal had accomplished his great goal—he had removed the greatest of all arguments for the inerrancy of the Bible but did not, he thought, sacrifice the divinity of Jesus Christ. A masterful theological performance it surely seemed. There is little doubt that many who defended this way out of their inspiration problems thought that it was a valid way, which both acknowledged error in Christ and affirmed his deity—but that was before they shook their heads.

Kenosis did seem, on the surface, to have valid biblical authority. Thus the refutation of the inerrant Bible could come from the Bible itself. It was from Philippians, chapter 2, that we learned implicitly of the possible errancy of all the rest of the Bible. For if the Son of God could err with respect to the Bible, a fact which that chapter was supposed to imply, how could the Bible itself be inerrant?

How is Philippians 2 supposed to teach the theory that was such a "godsend" to disbelievers in the inerrancy of Scripture? Incidentally (we may note in passing) it never seemed to be noticed that if Philippians 2 taught that the Son of God, by his kenosis, could err about the Scripture and that therefore all Scripture could be in error, then this indictment should apply to that chapter as well. Rather, the liberal mind tacitly accepted the inerrancy of Philippians in order to provide a basis for the errancy of all the rest of Scripture.

Our passage, speaking of Christ, reads: "Although He

existed in the form of God [he] did not regard equality with God a thing to be grasped, but emptied Himself, taking the form of a bond-servant, and being made in the likeness of men. And being found in appearance as a man, He humbled Himself by becoming obedient to the point of death, even death on a cross" (vss 6-8 NAS). One admits that at first glance, the text seems to suggest that the Son of God emptied himself of deity when he took the form of a man. A more careful examination will show that Philippians merely says that Christ emptied himself—not of *what* he emptied himself. The text itself does not answer that question. But a moment's reflection will suggest that of which he did *not* empty himself. The Son of God certainly could not empty himself of the "form of God" *(morphe tou theou)* in which he timelessly existed *(huparchon),* for one very good reason. He could not empty himself of deity, because deity cannot be emptied. That which is unchangeable, infinite, eternal cannot cease to be unchangeable, infinite, and eternal, for then it would not be or ever have been infinite, unchangeable, and eternal. God could not be life eternal if he ceased to be life for even thirty seconds, much less thirty years. God could not be the creator and sustainer of all everlastingly, if for one moment he ceased to be—not to mention the fact that in that one moment, all things everlastingly dependent on him would cease to be. The all-wise God would not be the all-wise God if for a split second his knowledge were confined to the limitations of a human intellect. Kenoticists have affirmed that one or more of these attributes, or all of them, were emptied out for the period (or a part) of the Incarnation; but the emptying of any one of these attributes is fatal, because the glory of God lies in the possession of all his attributes (which are really one). If even one of them were missing, the glory of God would cease, and God himself would cease to be God. And since the essence of God is one, any deficiency in any one of the three Persons in the blessed Trinity is a fatal deficiency in the one and only divine essence.

So Paul assumes that we know this much: Whatever the emptying does refer to, it could not extend to the "form of God." It must pertain to the "form of man." That is the way the text itself reads: "emptied Himself, taking the form of a bond-servant." For God to take the form of a bond-servant (man) was emptying indeed. Of course, he remained ever God, as God ever does, or he is not ever God; but for such a divine person to take the form of man was a stoop so great that "emptying" is an understatement. So Christ emptied Himself by adding to himself a nature infinitely below Himself (John 16:13). Therefore to suppose that the Son of God actually emptied himself of his eternal Self would be nothing less than blasphemy, for it would be a denial of God, a temporary deity being no deity at all. So the kenosis of Philippians, chapter 2, far from teaching that deity emptied itself of deity, taught that deity *added* to itself *humanity*.

Consequently, returning to our main theme, when Christ taught that the Bible is the Word of God, it was the Son of God Incarnate who taught that doctrine. No one—but *no* one—will say that the Son of God could err about the Word of God. He knew everything and he certainly knew his own Word.

Suborthodox Christology of Some Traditionalists. I say that no consistent person will say that the Son of God could err. Therefore, if Christ said that the Bible is the Word of God, the Bible *is* the Word of God. But this error of biblical errancy (or limited inerrancy, which is the same thing) dies hard. Errantists still will say: Granted that the Son of God could not err; but could not the Son of man err, being man, truly man? After all, they argue, even this kenosis passage surely says that the Son of God did empty himself by taking on humanness. Did that not lay him open to error? Is it not human to err?[15] Is it not human even for the Son of God Incarnate to err? And, they continue, since you admit that Christ was truly human, must you not also admit that, after all, he could have erred? Unless, that is, you become heretical yourself by denying his genuine humanity (so that we, the liberal Protestants, must avoid denying Christ's deity, while you, the orthodox Protestants, must be careful to avoid denying his humanity). Could we not all, they ask, agree on this statement: "The Son of God in his humanity may have erred in not recognizing that the Bible itself was also the word of men and therefore liable to error," without our impugning in the least the deity of the Son of God?

And here liberal Protestants seem able to embarrass evangelicals, for many evangelicals are vulnerable at this point. The liberals correctly observe that some conservatives speak as if Christ could have succumbed to temptation (though he did not). Conservatives often say that Christ might have yielded to temptation—otherwise, it would not have been a real temptation. So liberals will press their advantage here: If Christ might have sinned in yielding to temptation (though he did not) must you inerrantists not admit that he might have erred in his estimate of the Bible? If you, they say, admit that Christ might have erred in thinking the Bible was without error, we, the liberals, will prove to you that he did actually err. You must admit that we may be right, must you not?

I must, in all fairness, say that some of my brother evangelicals cannot deny this line of reasoning and must rethink their belief that Christ might have succumbed to temptation because he was truly human. Otherwise, they would be forced to admit that Christ the Lord may have erred in his estimate of Scripture. Then it would need to be proved that he did not err. In that case, evangelicals no longer could use the testimony of Christ regarding Scripture to settle the matter of its inerrancy. They must, then, first prove that Christ, being fallibly human, nevertheless did not make an errant judgment. It goes without saying that followers of Christ always must argue consistently. So I repeat, if we once admit that Christ might have sinned, it follows that any statement of his may be an instance in which he actually may have erred, and we must then withdraw the very strongest of all our arguments in support of the inerrancy of Holy Scripture—that Jesus Christ endorsed it as such.

I do not, and I trust that traditional Protestants will not withdraw this strongest of all arguments, for we need not grant—indeed, cannot grant—for one moment that Jesus Christ ever could have sinned or ever could have erred. Why? Not because he was not human, but because his humanity was upheld in its integrity by his deity, which never could permit sin or error in anything. If some liberal Christians learn something about the Word of God from this controversy, some traditional Christians may well learn something about the Son of God. Let me explain.

Let us for a moment compare the first and second Adams. Augustine has said that the first Adam was capable of sinning or of not sinning *(posse peccare; posse non peccare)*.[16] This could truly be said of a mere man, which the first Adam was. But how could that ever be said of a man who was in indissoluble union with God (the orthodox doctrine of the Incarnation)?[17] If we were to suppose for a moment (may God forgive us) that human nature in personal union with God could sin, would this not be blasphemy? No, you say, because we are speaking about a man who sins, and that is not blasphemy. But we are not now speaking of a mere man. We are speaking of sin of human nature in personal union with God, and that is blasphemy. Why, you ask, since Christ would not be sinning as God but as man? You will admit that to say that God can sin is blasphemy. But you are not, you insist, saying that God can sin, but that man can sin. Oh, yes, we reply, you are saying that man-in-personal-union-with-God can sin, and that is blasphemy, because though God would not be conceived of as committing the sin, he nevertheless would be involved in the sin by virtue of his union with the sinning man.

Jesus Christ was not a human person, but divine, and everything he did in his human nature is always attributable to his divine person, which was his only person. He was not a human person such as Adam, who could sin and to whom sin could be attributed without blasphemy. He was a divine person, to whom sin cannot be attributed without blasphemy. God's eyes are too pure to behold iniquity, not to mention admitting it into his very bosom, so to speak. No, corruptible human nature is made incorruptible by being united with the incorruptible divine nature. If a human nature could remain corruptible while in union with the incorruptible divine nature, even the divine nature would no longer be free from possible corruption. This is horrible to contemplate, for mere possible corruption is corruption in a God who is incapable of corruption—a God who does not merely *not* lie or do wrong, but who *cannot* lie or do wrong. The "Prince of this World" could have come and found something sinful in Christ, as it were. He could have found him as corruptible as the first Adam. And incidentally, there is no reason to deny that the second Adam, under the circumstances he encountered, would be far more vulnerable to corruption that the first Adam, who was created in ideal surroundings without a history of human sin, corruption, or evil example. Remember, we are now speaking of the second Adam (Christ) as if he were not a divine person. In this supposition, the divine person could not prevent him from sinning and thus would allow corruption to come into intimate association with the very essence of deity.

Here arises another intramural problem, which can be seen to lie close to the heart of the most important argument for errancy, and that is possible error in the Son of God himself. Obviously, if the Son of God could err, it would be impossible to prove that the Word of God cannot err. And if the Son of God could err, who would care whether the Word of God can or cannot? The Word of God has no real significance, apart from the Son of God. The Word of God would be worthless if it inerrantly bore witness to a Son of God who was capable of error—who was not the holy and undefiled Lamb of God without blemish and without the possibility of ever being with blemish.

But to come to the intramural question some evangelicals ask: How could the temptation of Christ be genuine if he were incapable of succumbing to it? Let me restate that question and see whether you do not notice its absurdity. How could the temptation of Christ be genuine if he could not succumb to it? What does the possibility of succumbing have to do with whether temptation exists? Succumbing has to do with the *outcome* of temptation, not its nature. Obviously, temptation could exist even if the person tempted were infinitely above succumbing to it (just as, at the opposite end of the scale, Satan is constantly "tempted" to do more evil, even though he cannot possibly resist). Even humans can be euphemistically called untouchables, although they nevertheless are constantly tempted, and tempted all the more because they have a reputation for being untouchable. Temptation is one thing; resisting it or succumbing to it is another. One can neither resist nor succumb to temptation unless one is tempted in the first place. The words *resist* and *succumb* are meaningless apart from temptation, but temptation itself does not necessarily imply one or the other. In the case of the first Adam, either could have followed; in the case of the fallen sons of Adam, succumbing always follows; in the case of the second Adam, succumbing never follows and never could follow. One thing is clear—temptation is one thing, and the response to it is another. So we should never say that Christ was not tempted simply because he could not succumb to it.

Christ was truly tempted in all points, just as we are, but without sin or the possibility of sinning (Heb 4:15). Sin was impossible for Christ, as the devil knew (but was always forgetting), and as we should know and never forget. Because it was impossible for Christ to sin, it did not follow that he did not sweat drops of blood in resisting and overcoming temptation. Precisely because Christ was human, the resistance was difficult. God would never have let him succumb, but he would and did let him enter into temptation (he even led him into it [Matt 4:1]) and emerge from it victorious through great agony of soul and body. His humanity was genuine, the fact that it was upheld by his divine person notwithstanding.

So in conclusion, we return to orthodoxy's most fundamental argument for the inerrancy of the Word of God—that it was so certified by the Son of God. Two great challenges have been met and, we believe, conquered. The first challenge is that Christ was not (at least for the time of the Incarnation) the inerrant Son of God. This we have shown to be not only blasphemous, but absurd. The second challenge is that Christ, being human, must have been capable of error and can be shown to have erred in teaching that the Bible is inerrant. This we have shown to be erroneous, because Christ's human nature (which indeed could have erred if it had been alone) was rendered incapable of error by virtue of personal union with the second Person of the Godhead, who is incapable of being contaminated by error and who therefore strengthened Christ's human nature so that (though agonizingly tempted) it never could succumb to sin or error. He who could never err unerringly said that the Bible cannot err. Therefore it is demonstrated beyond all question that the holy Word of God is as inerrant as is the holy Son of God.

The theory of accommodation often has been introduced as a solution to various textual problems. It is evident here that in my opinion these "problems" exist only in the minds of the critics. Suppose, however, that they do have substance; the theory of accommodation would only raise more problems— and grave ones. It would be another case of curing a headache by decapitation. If Jesus Christ knew otherwise, but in order not to trouble his hearers he "accommodated" himself to what he knew to be their erroneous views, how could he be absolved from "doing evil that good may come"? And would that not, in fact, have created a great deal more evil? If Christ accommodated himself in one case, why not in others? When could anyone believe he was saying what he himself thought, rather than what his audience wanted him to think? Strange behavior, for one who called himself the truth (John 15:26).

The Challenge of Circularity

It may be thought that we have presented a very powerful argument for the inerrancy of Scripture, except for one thing: The argument is circular. It appears to begin by assuming the inspiration of the Bible, and from that accepts the deity of Christ, and from his deity, in turn, proves the inspiration of the Bible. The divine Christ rests on the inspired Bible and the inspired Bible rests on the divine Christ—the famous vicious logical circle.

However, the argument, properly stated, is not circular. Its steps are as follows:

1. The Gospels, not assumed to be inspired, are generally recognized as highly reliable historical sources.
2. From these sources, even allowing for errors and dis-

crepancies, the picture of a miracle-working Christ
emerges.

3. Miracles can be performed only by God. As Nicodemus
   observes: "Rabbi, we know that thou art a teacher come
   from God: for no man can do these miracles that thou
   doest, except God be with him" (John 3:2 KJV).

4. Thus to use John Locke's expression, Christ's "credit as
   a proposer" of doctrine is established.

5. It is this Christ who teaches that he is the Son of God and
   that the Bible is the Word of God.

The Protestant Doctrine of
Biblical Authority Applied to Society

General Application

We now turn to the Bible and society. What is the
relationship between Scripture and the authoritative structures of the community? It seems self-evident and immediately apparent that if one believes what orthodox Protestants
profess to believe about the Bible, one must believe
everything it says and obey every command it gives. The
Westminster Shorter Cathechism opens with these two
questions and answers: "Q. What is the chief end of
man?   A. Man's chief end is to glorify God and enjoy him
forever.   Q. What rule hath God given to direct us how we
may glorify and enjoy him?   A. The Word of God which is
contained in the Scriptures of the Old and New Testaments is
the only rule to direct us how we may glorify and enjoy him."
Knowledge of and obedience to whatever is contained in the
Old and New Testaments is the way, and the only way to know
and serve God. So the relationship between Scripture and the
authoritative structures of the community is this: The
structures are authoritative by virtue of the Scriptures and
must function in accordance with them. The only authority is
God, and if he has spoken, that is the place where his
authoritative will for the individual, for the home, for the
church, and for the state is to be found.[18] In the words of the

prophet Isaiah, "To the law and to the testimony: if they speak not according to this word it is because there is no light in them" (Isa 8:20 KJV).

Particular Applications

Home. The most basic of all institutions is the family. Since the Bible teaches that children are to honor their fathers and mothers, parents must be in authority over their children and must be obeyed. Suppose father and mother disagree. Who are the children to obey? The Bible teaches that wives are to be subject to their husbands (Eph 5:22; Col 3:18). It follows, therefore, that if the mother is to obey the father, the children should also, in the event of an undesirable and much-to-be-avoided difference. This is the fundamental hierarchy of authority in the home.

But it is a limited authority. We have seen already that the mother has no authority if she herself disobeys her husband. It is also made plain in Scripture that if the husband disobeys God, he loses his authority and is not to be obeyed by either wife or children. This is indicated by the command that all authority and obedience be "in the Lord," meaning in accord with the express will of God (Eph 6:1). Christ, who teaches us to honor our fathers and mothers, says that if a man "hate not his father, and mother" he cannot be Christ's disciple (Luke 14:26). So although the individual is set in a certain authority pattern, this pattern derives from God. The individual is therefore constantly subject to God and must judge whether the higher authority is also subject to God. If a person judges that it is in fact not so, he must disobey man in order to obey God (Acts 4:19). Furthermore, since the commands of God are for men—not men for the commands of God—those in authority must administer their authority for the well-being of their subjects. Thus husbands who rule their wives must be controlled by love (Eph 5:25-26). Parents, in turn, must bring up their children in the "nurture and admonition of the Lord" and not "provoke" them to wrath (Eph 6:4). In a word, the father, who is head of the home, must use his authority "in the Lord" for the good of those for whom he is responsible; they in turn must obey him "in the Lord," but only insofar as their obedience is "in the Lord." One must add, for emphasis, that Scripture, not the arbitrary judgment of the individual, is the rule by which human authority is itself to be judged. Thus subordinates (for example, children) must conform to authority (parents) in the home, providing that authority does not violate the revealed will of God even though it be contrary to the children's own judgment. This promotes stability and order without slavishness or denial of individual integrity (because even when a person conforms, he does not necessarily approve the wisdom of the authoritative judgment to which he conforms).

State. The same pattern applies to all areas of human authority, but let us see its bearing on the Protestant citizen and the state. The classical biblical statement is contained in the words of Jesus: Render to Caesar what is Caesar's, and to God what is God's (Matt 22:21; Mark 2:17; Luke 20:25; also, Rom 13:1-2). First of all, the Bible makes it very plain that all authority is God's, so that the Christian renders obedience to Caesar because and only because God says he must. That being the case, whatever authority Caesar has cannot violate that which makes it authoritative—namely, the revealed will of God.

This explains why people who believed in the inerrancy of Romans 13:1 also could be involved in the American Revolution. They judged, rightly or wrongly, that the British authority had become tyrannical: Rather than being a "terror to evil works" and a "praise of the good," it had become a terror to good works and a praise of the bad. It was, therefore, no longer an authority operating according to divine command and had forfeited its right to rule. The general principle is that Caesar is to be obeyed in all his legitimate activities, legitimately pursued. Christ cites the levying of taxes; Paul, the using of punitive sanctions against law-breakers.

Church. Perhaps a concluding word should be said about ecclesiastical authority in the classical Protestant pattern. Every Protestant, theoretically at least, acknowledges the principle that "God alone is Lord of the conscience." Each must determine for himself the will of God—that is, the teaching of the Bible. If the person deems it contrary to an ecclesiastical deliverance, he is obliged by God to disregard the church. The Protestant Church teaches the individual to disobey her if she disobeys God.

It all begins with Christ's questions to his disciples, "Who do men say that the Son of man is?" and "But who do you say that I am?" (Matt 16:13, 14 RSV). When Peter, speaking for the apostles, said, "Thou art the Christ, the Son of the living God," Christ accepted that and proceeded to say, "Thou art Peter" *(Petros),* the confessor of the Christ the Son of God, and "upon this rock [*petra*] I will build My church. . . . I will give you the keys of the kingdom of heaven; and whatever you shall bind on earth shall be bound in heaven, and whatever you shall loose on earth shall be loosed in heaven" (16:18-19 NAS). This was the equivalent of giving authority to the whole church, which consisted of those who believed that he was the Christ, the Son of the living God. From Matthew 18:17, it is clear that those who will not obey the "church," or congregation, are to be excommunicated. So the pattern is this: Those who believe Christ to be God are to join together, forming a church with officers (first the apostles, and then ordinary officers, whom they have approved, to continue after they are gone). These officers teach, administer the sacraments, and dispense discipline, but are ultimately responsible to the congregation, as we have seen. The individual member may be excommunicated from the group, and the individual must accept this, unless he believes it involves a denial of Christ. So we see that the relation of the individual to mother church is parallel to the relation of children to their parents. They must obey ministers and other officers unless the regulations violate the will of Christ as revealed in the Scriptures, and this the individuals themselves must judge.

This ecclesiastical pattern was classically demonstrated in the life of Martin Luther. His study of the Bible led him to conclusions different from the teaching of his church. He accepted excommunication rather than abandon his interpretation, because he could see no error in it. When summoned before the emperor, at whose hand he could have been executed, he still maintained that unless "I am convinced by the testimony of Scripture or by manifest reasoning, I cannot and will not recant."[19] If his error could be shown him, he would recant and obey the commands of the church. But when they failed to convince him, neither pope nor council nor emperor could persuade him to conform.

According to Roman Catholic theory, the magisterium is responsible for the interpretation of Scripture, and if the individual's judgment differs, the individual must consider himself in error and conform to what is necessarily the correct interpretation. The real locus of the sixteenth-century Protestant Reformation was not, therefore, as so often represented, a conflict between authority of the Bible and authority of the church, but between the *individual* and the church, as to who is responsible for interpretation of the Bible. The Roman church said then, and still says—the church; the Protestant church said then, and still says—the individual. The Roman church claims an infallibility for the magisterium that Protestantism does not claim for the individual.[20] But right or wrong, the individual Christian must cleave to what he thinks the Word of God teaches; he cannot, any more than Luther, do otherwise.

It was thought by many that such individualistic Protestant ecclesiology would prevent any ecclesiastical organization from emerging and would amount to ecclesiastical anarchy. Obviously, it might have; equally obviously, it did not. If the Bible is what Protestants believe it to be—a unified revelation of the will of God—and if there is any integrity and competence whatever among its interpreters, one would expect them to see at least the main lines of Bible teaching. This is precisely what has happened. Though many denominations have appeared, there have been only a few theological systems and a few different church polities. The obvious possibility for variations within these systems and polities (since individual consciences may vary) have been exploited. To compensate for the unfortunate abundance of these variations is the fact that they reflect the individual freedom and integrity of personal conviction, though one cannot deny the presence of vanity, perversity, and willfulness, as well.

Such abuses never can be prevented in a free society, though the unity of the Bible and a basic tendency to integrity of private judgment is surely shown in the much more vast amount of agreement than disagreement.

Conclusion

What shall we say about the Protestant view of the Bible and authority? The Bible itself has already said it: "All Scripture is inspired by God and profitable for teaching, for reproof, for correction, for training in righteousness; that the man of God may be adequate, equipped for every good work" (2 Tim 3:16-17 NAS).

THE MISHNAH is the fundamental document of rabbinic Judaism. Composed in its present form near the end of the second Christian century, it is the first source to present itself as the authoritative codification of those practices that we today call Judaism, and as such, it serves as the basis for further discussion and development in later Jewish tradition. Thus one could argue that the Mishnah is Judaism's formative document, but the Mishnah itself makes no such claim; rather it, and hence Judaism as well, is presented as standing in relationship to Scripture. The Bible (written law) is consistently perceived as the source and legitimation for a tradition (oral law) that is ostensibly separate from it. The rabbinic contribution to Jewish thought and practice appears thereby to be interpretative, rather than creative. —F.E.G.

Scripture and Mishnah: Authority and Selectivity

JACOB NEUSNER
BROWN UNIVERSITY

WHEN WE TAKE UP THE QUESTION of the authority of Scripture for diverse expressions of Judaism, the answers are apt to be general and, while accurate, banal and uninformative. It is self-evident, on the one hand, that every expression of Judaism confesses the primacy of the Scripture's authority and, on the other, that it also says pretty much whatever it wants about Scripture. Proof for this obvious proposition lies in the diverse positions imputed to any one Scripture. So the role of Scripture in the communities of Judaism is to validate what people want to say anyway. The place of Scripture can be described pretty much in terms of opposites: paramount and subordinated, definitive and wholly secondary, source of truth and font of proof texts and pretexts. It furthermore is possible to demonstrate that the authoritative structures of the various communities formed of Judaism derived their principal laws and theologies from Scripture and also read into the program of Scripture whatever they wished. Community structures can be seen to be the formation of Scripture's precepts and also to be statements *upon,* not *of,* the meaning of Scripture.

These obvious facts are hardly surprising, for the diversity

A version of this essay appeared as "Scripture and Mishnah: Authority and Selectivity," in Jacob Neusner, *Method and Meaning in Ancient Judaism,* 2nd series (Chico, Calif.: Scholars Press, 1981) © 1981 Brown University.

of the communities of Judaism, from the formation of the
Torah literature in the time of Ezra to the present day, has
been possible only within the contradictory results of a single
principle of scriptural authority, as just outlined. One
community will find one thing in Scripture, another will
choose some other, and both will then be right in claiming the
authority of Scripture for what they say and do. A moment's
reflection on the florilegium of Scriptures important to the
Evangelists of the New Testament, in contrast to the
repertoire of those Scriptures that were clearly determinative
of the way of life and world-view of the Pharisees and earlier
sages of Rabbinic Judaism, makes the point full well. The
former found in apocalyptic prophecy the principal focus for
their biblical authority. Their work was to show, for one thing,
how the life and teachings of Jesus had been foretold of old
and had fulfilled Scripture. The latter, for their part, took up
and vastly expanded the laws of the Priestly Code, giving what
I believe to have been a quite accurate account of the original
requirements and meanings of those laws, an account which
also fulfilled Scripture—but different parts of Scripture.

It follows that when we analyze the theme of the authority
of Scripture in the diverse communities of Judaism, the
principal points of interest will appear in the details. These
details deal with the concrete facts about the way a given
community of Judaism made its choices of verses of Scripture
to be deemed authoritative. The details tell us the meaning of
the authority of those particular Scriptures, what the choices
imply about the larger *principles* of choice, and the traits of
reflection characteristic of the community that made the
choices. What we will learn about the authority of Scripture,
therefore, will not bring many surprises. What we shall see
about the potential of Scripture to generate and precipitate
fresh and remarkably profound and original thought about
Scripture itself, and about its authority, will, I think, be
consequential and suggestive.

I will place this question of authority and selectivity into
context with an account of one group in ancient Judaism—one
whose thought and life came to ultimate expression in the
Mishnah at the end of the second century of the Common

Era—and of the way that group reached an accurate grasp of the deepest meanings and implications of the Priestly Code of the sixth and fifth centuries Before the Common Era. This account of the context of authority and selectivity demands two things: first, that I lay out those facts that require explanation of the relationship between Scripture and the Mishnah; second, that I attempt to offer one plausible reason for the facts being what they are.

In this argument, I will first show how the Mishnah relates to Scripture. Specifically, I will indicate that the relationship of a given division of the Mishnah to the Scripture depends upon a prior choice, on the part of the framers of the Mishnah, of those parts of Scripture deemed to be of such special relevance as to require exegetical analysis.

Then I shall try to account for the principle of selection that drew the attention of the framers and philosophers of the Mishnah to one particular set of Scriptures. For this, I shall offer an essentially historical explanation.

The argument as a whole, therefore, will rephrase the issue of the authority of Scripture for the Mishnah in terms of concrete context and specific setting. So I hope to escape from the thrall of banality and generality on a topic so rich in potential for saying the obvious in plain or fancy ways.

From Scripture to Mishnah: The Issue of Authority

On the surface, Scripture played little role in the expression and formation of the Mishnah's ideas and system. The Mishnah rarely cites a verse of Scripture, rarely refers to Scripture as an entity, rarely links its own ideas to those of Scripture, and rarely lays claim to originate in what Scripture has said, even by indirect or remote allusion to a scriptural verse or teaching. So, superficially, the Mishnah is tradition, totally indifferent to Scripture. That impression, moreover, is reinforced by the traits of the language of the Mishnah. The framers of mishnaic discourse never attempted to imitate the language of Scripture, as did those of the Essene writings at Qumran. The very redactional structure of Scripture, found so serviceable to the writer of the Temple Scroll,[1] was of no

interest whatsoever to the organizers of the Mishnah and its
tractates, except in a few cases (the tractates of *Yoma,
Pesaḥim*).

Formally, radactionally, and linguistically, the Mishnah
stands in splendid isolation from Scripture. This is something it
was necessary to confront as soon as the Mishnah came to
closure and was presented as authoritative to the Jewish
communities of the Holy Land and Babylonia. It is not possible
to point to many parallels—that is, instances of anonymous
books received as holy—in which the forms and formulations
(specific verses) of Scripture play so slight a role. Other writers
commonly would imitate the Scripture's language; they would
cite concrete verses. Or they would claim (at the very least) that
direct revelation had come to them, so that what they said stands
on an equal plane with Scripture. The internal evidence of the
Mishnah's sixty-two usable tractates (excluding *Abot*), by
contrast, in no way suggests that anyone pretended to speak as
Moses did, write as Moses did, claimed to cite and correctly
interpret statements Moses made, or even was alleged to have
had a revelation such as that of Moses and so stand on the
mountain with Moses. There is none of this. So the claim of
scriptural authority for the Mishnah's doctrines and institutions
is difficult to locate within the internal evidence of the Mishnah
itself.

We cannot be surprised that, in consequence of this
amazing position of autonomous authority implicit in the
character of mishnaic discourse, the Mishnah should have
demanded in its own behalf some sort of apologetic. Nor are
we surprised that the Mishnah attracted its share of quite
hostile criticism. The issue then, in the third century, was
precisely the issue phrased when we ask about the authority of
tradition in Judaism: Why should we, standing in the early
third century, listen to this mostly anonymous document
which makes statements on the nature of institutions and
social conduct—statements we obviously are expected to
keep? Who are Meir, Yosé, Judah, Simeon, and Eleazar—
people who lived only fifty or a hundred years ago—that we
should listen to what they have to say? God revealed the
Torah. Is this, too, part of the Torah? If so, how? What, in

other words, is the relationship of the Mishnah to Scripture, and how does the Mishnah claim authority over us such as we accord to the revelation to Moses by God at Mount Sinai?

There are two important responses to these questions. First and most radical: The Mishnah itself constitutes *torah*. It too is a statement of revelation "to Moses at Sinai." But this part of revelation has come down in a form different from the well-known written part, the Scripture. This tradition truly deserves the name *tradition,* because for a long time it was handed down orally, until given the written formulation now before us in the Mishnah. This sort of apologetic for the Mishnah appears, to begin with, in *Abot,* with its stunning opening chapter which links Moses on Sinai through the ages to the earliest named authorities of the Mishnah itself, the five pairs, and on down to Shammai and Hillel. Since some of the named authorities in the chain of tradition appear throughout the materials of the Mishnah, the claim is that the statements of these people came to them from Sinai through the processes of *qabbalah* and *massoret*—handing down, traditioning.

So the Mishnah does not cite Scripture because it does not need to. It stands on the same plane as Scripture. It enjoys the same authority as Scripture. This radical position is still more extreme than those taken by pseudepigraphic writers who either imitate the style of Scripture or claim to speak within that same gift of revelation as Moses. It is one thing to say that one's holy book is Scripture because it is like Scripture, and another to claim that the author of the holy book had a revelation independent of that of Moses. These two positions, it seems to me, still concede to the Torah of Moses an analogical priority over those writers' own holy books. The Mishnah's apologists make no such concession when they allege that the Mishnah is part of the Torah of Moses. They appeal to the highest possible authority in the Israelite framework, claiming the most one can claim in behalf of a book which, in fact, bears the names of men who lived fifty years before the apologists themselves. That seems to me to require remarkable courage.

Then there is this matter of Scripture not being cited by the Mishnah. When we consider the rich corpus of allusions to

Scripture in other holy books, both those bearing the names of authors and those presented anonymously, we realize that the Mishnah claims its authority to be co-equal with that of Scripture, while authority is claimed for so many others only because they depend upon the authority of Scripture and state the true meaning of Scripture. And that fact brings us to the second answer to the question of the place of Scripture in the mishnaic tradition. It is the position that the Mishnah is contingent upon Scripture, the result of exegesis of Scripture.

The two Talmuds and the legal-exegetical writings produced in the two hundred years after the closure of the Mishnah take the position that the Mishnah is wholly dependent upon Scripture; that whatever is of worth in the Mishnah can be shown to derive directly from Scripture. So the Mishnah—tradition—is deemed distinct from and subordinate to Scripture. This position is expressed in an obvious way. Once the Talmuds cite a Mishnah pericope, they commonly ask, What is the source of these words? And the answer invariably is, As it is said in Scripture. This constitutes not only a powerful defense for the revealed truth of the Mishnah but also bespeaks a profound criticism of the character of the Mishnah. For when the exegetes find themselves constrained to add, they admit the need to improve or correct an existing flaw.

That the search for the scriptural bases for the Mishnah's laws constitutes both an apologetic and a criticism is shown in the character of a correlative response to the Mishnah—the *Sifra* and its exegesis of Leviticus.[2] This rhetorical exegesis follows a standard syntactical-redactional form. Scripture will be cited; then a statement will be made about its meaning, or a statement of law correlative to that Scripture will be given. Finally, the author of *Sifra* invariably states, Now is this not (merely) logical? And the point of that statement will be, Can this position not be gained through the working of mere logic, based upon facts supplied (to be sure) by Scripture? The potential power of *Sifra* lies in its repetitive demonstration that the stated position, commonly, though not always a verbatim or near-verbatim citation of a Mishnah pericope, is not only *not* the product of logic, but is and can be only the product of an exegesis of Scripture.

What is still more to the point, that exegesis is formal in its character. That is, it is based upon some established mode of exegesis of the formal traits of scriptural grammar and syntax assigned to the remote antiquity represented by the names Ishmael or Akiva. So the polemic of *Sifra* is against the positions that: First, what the Mishnah says (in the Mishnah's own words) is merely logical; and second, that the position taken by the Mishnah can have been reached in any way other than through grammatical-syntactical exegesis of Scripture. That other way, the way of reading the Scripture through philosophical logic or practical reason, time and again is explicitly rejected. Philosophical logic is inadequate. Formal exegesis is shown to be not only adequate, but necessary and inexorable. It follows that *Sifra* undertakes to demonstrate precisely what the framers of the opening pericopae of the Talmuds' treatment of the Mishnah's successive units of thought also wish to show. The Mishnah is not autonomous. It is not independent. It is not correlative, separate but equal. It is contingent, secondary, derivative, resting wholly on the foundations of the (written) revelation of God to Moses at Mount Sinai. Therein, too, lies the authority of the Mishnah as tradition.

If at this point in the argument we stand back and deal with our program of questions, we should offer the following answers.

First, tradition in the form of the Mishnah is deemed autonomous of Scripture and enjoys the same authority as Scripture, since Scripture and (oral) tradition are merely two media for conveying a single corpus of revealed law and doctrine.

• Or, tradition in the form of the Mishnah is true because it is not autonomous of Scripture. Tradition is secondary and dependent upon Scripture. The authority of the Mishnah is the authority of Moses. That authority comes to the Mishnah directly and in an unmediated way: The Mishnah's words were given by God to Moses at Mount Sinai and faith-fully transmitted through a process of oral formulation and transmission until they were written down by Judah the Patriarch at the end of the second century.

Or, that authority comes to the Mishnah indirectly, mediated through the written Scriptures. The Mishnah says the same thing the Scripture says, when Scripture is rightly interpreted. The authority of tradition lies in its correct interpretation of the Scripture. Tradition bears no autonomous authority, is not an independent entity correlative with Scripture. A technology of exegesis of grammar and syntax is needed to build the bridge between tradition, as contained in the Mishnah, and Scripture, the original utensil shaped by God and revealed to Moses to convey the truth of revelation to the community of Israel.

Or, matters could be very different. I hardly need to make them explicit.

These same either-or, yes-and-no answers of course are to be formulated to deal with the matters of a relationship between Scripture and the authoritative structures of the community, both discipline and doctrine, and the extent to which community structures are based upon or dictated by Scripture. If we regard the Mishnah as independent revelation—oral Torah, in the strict sense—then we must deem tradition to be a part of, but a distinct kind of Torah. If we regard the Mishnah as contingent, then tradition stands in a very close and comfortable bond with Scripture—Scripture's companion, complement, necessary consequence. So the Mishnah may be deemed to be (to invoke the appropriate metaphor), depending upon the position you take, the daughter of Scripture, or the wife.

Matters are not to be left with a mere description of opinions held by contentious third-century philosopher-theologian exegetes about a second-century holy book. Our generation has access to an independent stance. We can ask the question all over again, not through the phrasing of it from the third century. We may state the facts of the matter. We know the real relationship between the Mishnah and Scripture.

There are two sides to the question. First, we must speak of the principal components of the Mishnah, the bearers of its doctrine and ideas. Second, we must evaluate the claim of the Mishnah itself, asking not about its relationship to Scripture in general, but about its relationship to particular components of Scripture. So we conclude with the point with which we began, but we do so by turning the question around. From asking about Scripture and the Mishnah, we turn to discuss the Mishnah and Scripture: *What statement does the Mishnah make about Scripture?*

The Mishnah is formed of six divisions, divided into tractates. My studies of the relationship of each of the sixty-two usable tractates (omitting *Abot,* which has no *internal* relationship to Scripture, but a rich external one in its frequent citations) lead to the following simple generalizations.

First, there are tractates that simply repeat in their own words precisely what Scripture has to say, at best serving to amplify and complete the basic ideas of Scripture. For example, all the cultic tractates of the second division—that on Appointed Times—which tell what one is supposed to do in the Temple on the various special days of the year, and the bulk of the cultic tractates of the fifth division—on Holy Things—simply restate facts of Scripture. For another example, all those tractates of the sixth division—on Purities—which specify sources of uncleanness, depend completely on information supplied by Scripture. I have demonstrated in detail that every important statement in *Niddah,* on menstrual uncleanness; the most fundamental notions of *Zabim,* on the uncleanness of the person with flux referred to in Leviticus 15; as well as every detail in *Negaim,* on the person or house suffering the uncleanness that was described in Leviticus, chapters 13 and 14—all these serve only to restate the basic facts of Scripture and to complement those with other important facts.[3]

There are, second, tractates that take up facts of Scripture but work them out in a way those facts cannot have led us to predict. A supposition concerning what is important *about* the facts, utterly remote from the supposition of Scripture, will explain why the Mishnah tractates under discussion say the original things they do in confronting those scripturally provided facts. For example, Scripture takes for granted that the red cow will be burned in a state of uncleanness, because it is burned outside the camp Temple (Num 19:1-10). The Priestly Writers could not imagine that a state of cultic cleanness could be attained outside the cult. The absolute datum of tractate *Parah,* by contrast, is that cultic cleanness not only *could* be attained outside the tent of meeting, but that the red cow was to be burned in a state of cleanness exceeding even the cultic cleanness required in the Temple itself. The problematic that generates the intellectual agendum of *Parah,* therefore, is to work out the conduct of the rite of burning the cow in relationship to the Temple: Is it to be done in exactly the same way, or in exactly the opposite way? This mode of contrastive and analogical thinking—something either is like something else and therefore follows its rule, or it is different from something else and therefore follows the exact opposite of its rule—helps us to understand the generative problematic of such tractates as *Erubin* and *Beṣah,* to mention only two.[4]

And third, there are, predictably, many tractates that either take up problems never suggested by Scripture, or begin by making much of facts that are, at best, merely relevant to details of Scripture.

In the former category are *Tohorot,* on the cleanness of foods, with its companion, *Uqṣin; Demai,* on doubtfully tithed produce; *Tamid,* on the conduct of the daily whole-offering; *Baba Batra,* on rules of real estate transactions and certain other commercial and property relationships, and so on.

In the latter category are *Ohalot,* which spins out its strange problems within the theory that a tent and a utensil can be compared to each other (!); *Kelim,* on the susceptibility to uncleanness of various sorts of utensils; *Miqvaot,* on the sorts of water that affect purification from uncleanness, and many others. These tractates draw on facts of Scripture. But the problems confronted in these tractates in no way respond to problems important to Scripture. What we have here is a prior program of inquiry that makes ample provision for facts of Scripture in an inquiry that was, to begin with, generated essentially outside the framework of Scripture.

So there we have it: Some tractates merely repeat what we

find in Scripture, some are totally independent of Scripture, and some fall in between. Clearly, we are no closer to a definitive answer to the question of Scripture and tradition than when we described the state of thought on the very same questions in the third and fourth centuries. We find everything and its opposite.

But to offer a final answer, we must consider that fact. The Mishnah is not as remote from Scripture as its formal omission of citations of verses of Scripture suggests. It cannot, however, be described as contingent upon and secondary to Scripture, as its third-century apologists claimed. But the right answer is not that it is somewhere in between. Scripture confronted the framers of the Mishnah not merely as a source of facts, but as revelation. The framers had their own world to deal with. They made a statement within the framework and to the fellowship of their own age and generation. They were bound, therefore, to come to Scripture with a set of questions generated elsewhere. They brought their own ideas about what is important in Scripture. That is perfectly natural.

The philosophers of the Mishnah conceded to Scripture the highest authority. At the same time, what they chose to hear within the authoritative statements of Scripture will in the end form a statement of its own. To state matters simply: All of Scripture is authoritative, but only some Scriptures are relevant. And what happened is that the framers and philosophers of the tradition of the Mishnah came to Scripture when they had reason to do so. That is to say, they brought to Scripture a program of questions and inquiries framed essentially among themselves. So they were highly selective. Their program itself constitutes a statement *upon* the meaning of Scripture. They and their apologists of one sort hasten to add that their program consists of a statement *of* the meaning of Scripture.

In part, we must affirm the truth of that claim. When the framers of the Mishnah spoke about the Priestly passages of the Mosaic law codes, with deep insight they perceived profound layers of meaning embedded within those codes. What they have done with the Priestly Code (P), moreover, they also have done, though I think less coherently, with the bulk of the Deuteronomic laws and with some of the Covenant Code. But their exegetical triumph—exegetical, not merely eisegetical—lies in their handling of the complex corpus of materials of P. Theirs is a powerful statement *on* the meaning of Scripture, not merely a restatement *of* its meaning.

True, others have selected totally different passages of Scripture. Surely we must concede that, in reading those passages, those others displayed the same perspicacity as did the framers of the mishnaic tradition who interpreted the Priestly Code as they did. It is in the nature of Scripture itself that such should be the case. For after all, Jeremiah was a near contemporary of the framers of Deuteronomy (though so, too, were the authors of important parts of Leviticus and Ezekiel). The same Scripture that gives us the Prophets gives us the Pentateuch as well—and gives priority to the Pentateuchal codes as the revelation of God to Moses.

The authority of Scripture therefore is as we said in our rehearsal of the banal but accurate view. Scripture is authoritative—once we have made our choice as to which part of Scripture we shall read. Scripture generates important and authoritative structures of the community—including disciplinary and doctrinal statements, decisions, and interpretations—once we have determined which part of Scripture we shall ask to provide those statements and decisions. Community structures are based wholly on Scripture. But Scripture is not wholly and exhaustively expressed in those structures. Scripture has entirely dictated the character of formative structures of the Mishnah. But the Mishnah is not the result of the dictation of close exegesis of Scripture—except after the fact of choice.

Cosmopolitanism and Self-Identification: The Issue of Selectivity

The framers of the Mishnah made the choice they did and turned their principal attention to the Priestly Code of Leviticus and Numbers because the formative problem addressed and solved in the Priestly Code remained as vivid and chronic for them as it had been for those who first brought the code itself (and therewith the whole Pentateuch) to closure and redaction. In my judgment the particular structure of world-view and way of life both expressed within the Priestly Code and carried forward within the mishnaic code—that is, the world-view and way of life of the priests and the temple—was designed in response to a single definitive challenge. That world-view and way of life, moreover, in a profound and fundamental way, did solve that problem through the formation of the deepest structures of consciousness and culture. In consequence, the foundation of life much later on, in the confrontation with that same chronic and, in the first and second centuries, acute problem, could be laid—if asymmetrically—upon the bedrock of the Priestly Code. That fact accounts for the Mishnah's program of selection and exegesis. The sole problem, which would remain a problem for the heirs and successors to the Mishnah, would be to learn how to live in a building so far off the main line of Israel's material reality. But that is a problem to be solved when the legacy of the third and fourth centuries, the work of the heirs of the Mishnah and its continuators, has been subjected to the analysis of the history of religions. Thus far, I have reached only the end of the second century.

That formative and definitive problem addressed in the work of closure and redaction of the Priestly Code, and of the Pentateuch as a whole, may be simply stated. In the aftermath of the dislocation of Exile and the disruptive experience of return to Zion, a consciousness of identity had taken shape, and Israel now saw itself in the frame of a heightened reality. This sense of being special and distinctive, expressed in the certainty of Israel's distinctness from the other nations of the world, came into conflict with yet another fact of ordinary social and material reality. In the context of the economic and cultural life of the Middle East—a common economy and an encompassing culture of politics and thought emergent from that economy—of which the Jews around Jerusalem were an integral part, Israel was anything but distinctive and special. On the contrary, what we find happening in the Holy Land (wherever in Palestine that was, but certainly in Jerusalem) followed a standard and predictable pattern. Well it should,

since precisely those same factors that produced a codification
of the old laws and a statement of the old traditions in
Jerusalem were at work throughout what we must call a world
of modernization. Precisely that type of leader represented by
Nehemiah—that is, the *tyrannos*—is the sort of political figure
put forward throughout that known world of which Jerusalem
was very much a part.

So we discern a striking dissonance between Israel's
heightened sense of identity, engendered by the stunning
experience of Exile and return, on the one side, and on the
other, the sense of dislocation and disruption engendered by
the equally confusing experience of the breaking down of
barriers and boundaries among cultures. In a world of shared
economy, shared political and religious forms, shared social
and cultural structures, precisely who *was* Israel? This is the
question which became pressing at just that moment, and the
answer was not deemed self-evident.

The priests who took up and reworked the received
traditions and presented that Priestly Code and, with it, the
Pentateuch as a whole, supplied an answer to that question. It
was an enduring answer. Its power to persist derived from its
relevance to a lasting and chronic circumstance of dissonance.
When, in the aftermath of the messianic wars of the first and
early second centuries the established answer was dramatically called into question by the destruction of the Temple
upon which the answer had focused, it was time for a
restatement. The framers of the Mishnah presented that
restatement, and they did so in terms of those very scriptural
institutions and doctrines through which the original answer
had come forth. That is why, among all authoritative
Scripture, they chose the passages they did.

Let me now unpack this statement by returning to the
situation at the time of Ezra and Nehemiah, which we
conventionally call an age of *hellenization* but which, as we
shall see in a moment, we must deem also to be an epoch of
modernization.

Israel now was marked as distinctive by its preoccupation
with defining itself. In one way or another, it sought means of
declaring itself distinct from its neighbors. The stress on

exclusion of the neighbors from the group, and of the group from the neighbors, runs contrary to the situation of ancient Israel with unmarked frontiers of culture, the constant giving and receiving among diverse groups generally characteristic of ancient times. The persistent stress of differentiation, yielding a preoccupation with self-definition, also contradicted the facts of the matter. The people Israel was deeply affected by the shifts and changes in social, cultural, and political life and institutions captured by the word *hellenization*.

Perhaps, indeed, we may trace the preoccupation with self-definition to the context which yielded the later scriptural legacy of the Pentateuchal redaction, for it was in that protracted moment of confusion and change that Leviticus came to closure, and with it, the Pentateuchal heritage. As Morton Smith shows, the epoch of hellenization began long before Alexander and continued long afterward.[5] Greek military forces, Greek traders, Greek merchandise, and Greek ways penetrated the land of Israel; there were substantial Greek settlements before Alexander's conquest, and Greek influence thereafter intensified. Now, as we know, it is in the time of Nehemiah and Ezra that the Priestly Writers brought to completion and closure the collection of cultic traditions we now know as P. And, as Smith amply demonstrates, Nehemiah himself is the archetype of a Greek *tyrannos*.

One of the characteristic parts of the program of such a political figure was to pass measures, in Smith's words, "such as public works programs, cancellation of debts, release of persons enslaved for debt, confiscation of the property of their wealthy opponents, and redistribution of land."[6] The program of the *tyrannos* also included codification of the laws of a society, as a somewhat later response to social development. This whole political and legislative program was part of the common inheritance of the modernization of the Middle East even prior to Alexander.

The upshot of the codification and closure of the law under Nehemiah was to produce a law-code dominated by Priestly materials, the Pentateuch, which lay heavy emphasis upon the exclusivist character of the Israelite God and cult. Judaism gained the character of a cultically centered way of life and world-view, with both rite and myth aimed at the continuing self-definition of Israel by separation from and exclusion of the rest of the world. The purpose was to define Israel against the background of the other peoples of the Near and Middle East with whom Israel had much in common and especially to differentiate Israel from its neighbors in the same country.

The mode of differentiation taken by the Torah literature in general, and the Priestly sector of that literature in particular, was cultic. The power of the Torah composed at that time lay in its control of the Temple. The Torah literature, with its jealous God who cares about rather curious matters, and the Temple cult, with its total exclusion of the non-Israelite from participation and (especially) cultic commensality, raised high those walls of separation and underlined such distinctiveness as already existed.

When we confront the matter of the place of the Mishnah in the ongoing issue of the identity of Israel, we must place it in its historical context. Otherwise we shall lose sight of what is important in the mishnaic version of Israel's definition and miss the reason for its continuity with the Priestly version. For the Mishnah carries forward precisely those Priestly motifs which proved important in the time of Ezra and Nehemiah as the first encounter between Israel and what would be Israel's enduring ecological framework. That was the encounter between the pressing claim to be exclusive and to serve an exclusivist God, and the equally paramount facts of diffuse settlements in trivial numbers and diverse locations. These and related political and social factors, making for the very opposite of an exclusive and closed society within high borders, created a dissonance not ever resolved between social facts and the self-perceptions of Israel. Indeed, the very stress of the Torah literature on maintaining high and inviolable frontiers around Israel bespeaks the very oppo-site—a porous border, an unmarked boundary, an open road from group to group, down which not only ideas but also marital and other unions of people would and did travel.

As I have shown, the Mishnah takes up the perspectives of the work of the priests and Levites; it amply complements their part of the Torah literature and carries forward the great themes and theses of the Priestly Code. It is a Priestly document. That is why the Mishnah's principal themes and motifs, borrowed from the work of people of a much earlier age, must be placed into continuity, set upon the ecological continuum in which, in fact, they took shape.

The Mishnah presents a way of organizing the world that only the Priestly and Temple castes and professions could have imagined.[7] To point to obvious traits, we note that in its first division the document begins with the claim that God owns the Land. The land, therefore, must be used in a way consonant with its holiness. More important, what the land yields must be treated as belonging to God until the claims of God, the landlord, have been satisfied. These claims require that the calendar of the soil be set by the conduct of the cult in Jerusalem and that the produce of the land be set aside for the support of the cultic castes, priests, Levites, and their dependents.

The document proceeds to specify the appointed times of the year, those days that are out of the ordinary, by focusing upon two matters. First, the relevant appointed times are treated principally, or solely, in terms of what is done in the cult in celebration of those special days. Second, rules governing conduct on the appointed days in the towns and villages are so shaped as to bring village and Temple into a single continuum of sanctification. These are made into mirror images and complements of each other, so that what may be done in the Temple may not be done in the village, and vice versa. Just as the Temple is surrounded by its boundary, so the advent of the holy day causes the lowering of an invisible wall of sanctification on the perimeters of the village, as well. Third and fourth, two further principal divisions of the mishnaic system take up these matters: the conduct of the cult on ordinary days, in Holy Things; and the protection of the cult from dangerous forces, understood by the mishnaic philosophers as forces of disruption and death, in Purities. All this holds together. Uncleanness, which, above all, endangers the cult and must be kept away from the Temple, characterizes all lands but the Holy Land.[8] The lands of the Gentiles are

unclean with corpse-uncleanness. So death lies outside the
Holy Land, with consequent uncleanness. And life lies within
the Holy Land, with its locus and its apogee in the Temple and
at the cult.

These statements of four of the six divisions of the Mishnah,
of course, would not have surprised the framers of the Priestly
Code. Indeed, when we analyze the substantive character of
the mishnaic laws by their tractates, we find again and again
that they constitute important statements not only *upon*
Scripture, but also *of* what Scripture already has said. The
tendency of the mishnaic thinkers was to amplify, expand, and
extend the principles they found in the Priestly Code, even
while they were making an original and remarkably fresh
statement upon its contents. So in all, there is a close
continuity at the deepest layers of sentiment and opinion
between the Priestly Code and the Mishnah.

Why is it that the framers of the Mishnah choose just these
cultic and priestly matters for their painstaking and detailed
study? Two significant factors come into play here. First, we
must take into account the beginnings of the mishnaic system.
Second, we must repeat what we have said about the
fundamental ecological facts confronted by the priestly
system, which in later times down to the closure of the
Mishnah remained definitive to the situation of Israel.

Beginnings. The mishnaic system originated in the century
or so before 70 among lay people who wished to pretend to be
priests, or among priests who took so seriously the laws
governing their cultic activity that they concluded that these
same laws applied even outside the cult, or among both (as in
the Essene community of Qumran).

I believe that this is the point of origin of the mishnaic
system as a whole, for a simple reason. When we reach the
earliest layers of the system, at Purities, the givens of
discourse maintain a closely related set of positions. First,
cleanness with special reference to food and drink, pots and
pans, was possible outside the cult. Second, cleanness was
required outside the cult. Third, the cultic taboos governing
the protection and disposition of the parts of the sacrificial
meat that were to be given to the priests also apply to other

sorts of food. They apply, specifically, to ordinary food—food not deriving from or related to the altar—that is, food not directed to the priesthood. Fourth, the levitical taboos on sources of uncleanness therefore apply to ordinary food; and it follows, fifth, that one must be careful to avoid these sources of uncleanness or undergo a rite of purification if one has had contact with said contaminating sources. Finally, the direction and purpose of the system as a whole, in its earliest formulation, clearly was to preserve the cleanness of the people of Israel, the product of the land of Israel, the sexual life of Israel, the hearth and home of Israel. At the beginnings of the mishnaic system were, as I said, lay people who were pretending to be priests by eating their food at home as if they were priests in the Temple, and priests with so intense a sense of cultic cleanness that they did the same. So at the foundations were people who wished to act at home as if they were in the Temple, or who wished to pretend that they must keep purity laws at home because their home and its life lay within the enchanted circle of the cult.

Ecology. From the moment at which trade and commerce in goods and ideas broke down the walls that isolated one group from another, one region from another, the issue of the identity of each group and the claims each group might make to explain its distinctive existence proved pressing. Walls of another sort were now needed.

No one now had to ask what one group shared in common with all others. That was no issue—the answers in the cosmopolitan culture and economy were obvious. In the special case of Israel in the land of Israel, moreover, the dispersion among Gentiles within the Holy Land, the absence of contiguous settlement, the constant confrontation with other languages and other ways of life, along with the preposterous claims of Scripture that Israel alone owned the Land and that Israel's God owned the world—these dissonances between social reality and imaginative fantasy raised to a point of acute concern issues that, in other settings, were merely chronic and ongoing considerations.

Now when we ask why the Temple with its cult proved so enduringly central in the imagination of the Israelites, as indeed it did, we have only to repeat the statements that the priests of the Temple and their imitators in the sects were prepared to make. The altar was the center of life, the conduit from heaven to earth and from earth to heaven. All things were to be arrayed in relationship to the altar. The movement of the heavens, demarcated and celebrated at the cult as was the spatial dimension of the Land, marked out divisions of time in relationship to the altar. The natural life of the Israelite fields and corrals, the social life of its hierarchical caste system, the political life (this not only in theory, by any means)—all centered on the Temple as the locus of ongoing government; all things in order, in place, according to their genus and species, expressed the single message. The natural order of the world corresponded to, reinforced, and was reinforced by the social order of Israel. Both were fully realized in the cult, the nexus between those opposite and corresponding forces, the heavens and the earth.

The lines of structure emanated from the altar. And it was these lines of structure that constituted those high and impenetrable frontiers which separated Israel from the Gentiles. Israel was holy, ate holy food, reproduced itself in accord with the laws of holiness, and conducted all its affairs—both affairs of state, and the business of the table and the bed—in accord with the demands of holiness. So the cult was the font of sanctifying order. Holiness meant separateness. Separateness meant life. Outside the Land, the realm of the holy, lay the domain of death. For the scriptural vocabulary, one antonym for *holy* is *unclean,* and the opposite of *unclean* is *holy.* The principal force and symbol and the highest expression of uncleanness is death. The synonym for *holiness* is *life.* So in choosing their repertoire of scriptural passages, the framers of the mishnaic system, early and late, claimed to choose life.

Conclusion

This protracted account of scriptural authority in the Mishnah has carried us a long way from our point of departure. We began by asking about the authority of Scripture.

I pointed out that in the great religious traditions flowing from Scripture, there is unanimous agreement that Scripture is wholly authoritative, along with utter disagreement both on which particular Scriptures are authoritative and for what purposes they might serve. While that fact makes theology difficult, it precipitates just that sort of inquiry familiar to historians of religions. Once we realize that the important passages of Scripture in the mishnaic system prove, time and again, to derive from the Priestly Code(s), we want to account for that fact. The argument is that the Priestly system endured because it continued to deal with urgent questions of self-identification. In the two centuries in which the mishnaic system came to full expression and closure, then, a renewed inquiry into the potential of that same Priestly system was precipitated by a fresh experience of the same awesome sense of dissonance that had framed the issue confronted by the Priestly Writers and the revisers of the Pentateuchal legacy in the beginning. It is their Scriptures, in particular, that have played a critical role in Judaism. The passages formulated by them were chosen as authoritative. The authoritative structures of the community of Judaism imagined by the Mishnah rest wholly upon the Priests' Scripture. The Priestly Code forms the basis of and dictates the community structures of a large part of the mishnaic world-view and way of life. And the reason is that the authority of Scripture is secondary to the principle of selectivity exercised by those who first affirmed the authority of Scripture.

PART TWO
The Interpretation of Scripture

INTRODUCTION

ACCORDING TO Jewish tradition, Moses visited the academy of Akiva, a leading Jewish scholar of the second Christian century. Sitting in the back of the classroom, he was impressed with Akiva's ability to interpret parts of the Bible that he himself found difficult to comprehend. What was especially remarkable, however, was that when asked for the source of his teachings, Akiva explained that they were "law which Moses received at Sinai."[1]

This story is built on a paradox—that many of the teachings to which rabbinic Judaism ascribed biblical authority are not explicitly stated in the Bible. The preservation of such a story within rabbinic tradition itself demonstrates the rabbis' awareness of this contradiction. Such a tension is inherent in all the religious traditions with which we are presently concerned. Each rests on the authority of a book that is, by its very nature, unable to change; yet the traditions that emanate from it do change, so there evolves a distance between their doctrine and the text to which they appeal for legitimation. It is this distance between later practice and authoritative Scripture which explains why such diverse groups can hold the same text as authoritative. The Bible is never simply taken at face value. A literal and ordinary reading of the text would reduce it to antiquarian interest; conceived, however, as the Word of God intended for *all* generations, the Bible is subjected to an interpretative process so that the ancient words can be understood in the context of present reality. Whether the Bible is regarded as the fount of all truth or as only one way to determine God's will, there remains the task of finding within it the source of those doctrines and ideas for which a biblical mandate is claimed. This is the task of interpretation.

If the fact of interpretation testifies to Scripture's authority, the methods used are conditioned by preexisting attitudes about the role the Bible is expected to play; the process of exegesis thus reflects the exegete's own religious convictions. Within Christian tradition, for example, Scripture is seen as a witness to faith. Such an approach obviously tends to gravitate toward the values, whether theological or moral, that underlie a passage, rather than toward the narrative details that constitute it.[2] In contrast, the traditional Jewish perspective uses the Bible as a handbook for daily ritual, scrutinizing every passage for possible legal precedents. Christian fundamentalists seek also to derive scientific and historical insight from the biblical narrative.[3]

Having decided that the value in Scripture does not lie solely in its surface meaning, one needs an authority outside Scripture to locate and define the exact nature of the Bible's teachings. In the Roman Catholic tradition, this is designated *magisterium;* as we have seen, Judaism vested a similar authority in the rabbinate. The diversity of Protestant interpretations demonstrates that the lack of such an institutionalized authority can be problematic as well as liberating. If everyone can read the Bible and determine its religious meaning for him- or herself, then no one meaning will be normative for the community, and the assertion that Scripture contains an authoritative teaching becomes difficult to defend. Judaism confronted a similar dilemma as it developed interpretive techniques during the period of Hellenistic and Roman dominance, and the potential for abuse resulting from limited exegetical methods became increasingly clear.[4]

The process of exegesis is explicitly attested from the fifth pre-Christian century and is first known to have been accorded a status essentially equal with Scripture a few centuries thereafter.[5] Ever since, each religious tradition has regarded only *its* interpretation of Scripture as authentic. This rivalry was especially dramatic in the first century when Judaism was divided into a variety of sects, each claiming authenticity by virtue of possessing the correct interpretation.[6]

Methods of exegesis have varied both within and among various traditions. At times, allegory and typology have been regarded as appropriate means for understanding Scripture. Such approaches permit the exegete to transform one set of ideas into another by claiming that seemingly explicit biblical statements refer, in fact, to a different reality. The textual themes and motifs are thus regarded as more meaningful than specific details taken as a kind of code. A different interpretive stance focuses on the details of the text, attaching significance to idiosyncrasies of spelling and syntax, from which are derived truths not evident from the surface meaning. Such an approach probably played a critical role in the establishment of an official edition of the Hebrew Bible some two millennia ago. In any event, these techniques share with the allegorical mode an emphasis on a dimension of the text other than its surface meaning.

The variety of interpretive methods vividly demonstrates the role of hermeneutics in enabling the exegete to link authoritative Scripture with a reality that might appear to lie outside it. The centrality of the Bible on which such efforts are so clearly based is reflected, above all, in the notion that the Bible, by virtue of its being Bible, can have several meanings at the same time.[7] Thus the same biblical text can provide a lesson in proper behavior, impart theological truth, describe ancient events, and predict the future, all simultaneously! Many interpretative systems would add still further levels to the multiplicity of possible meaning in any one passage.

As we have seen, no religious group takes the Bible at face value, because no religious group practices its religion exactly as Scripture prescribes. Deviations from the seemingly plain sense of Scripture are explained in a variety of ways. Roman Catholicism and traditional Judaism appeal to a "tradition" that exists alongside the Bible. Reform groups regularly have claimed to return to the Bible (or its essence), which they regard their more traditional coreligionists as having ignored or misrepresented, even as they themselves engage in selective emphasis and interpretation. We can thus place the medieval Karaite and the more recent Reform Jews, both of whom deny the authority of the oral tradition now embodied in the written Talmud and subsequent legal literature, alongside classical Protestant perspectives. The process of interpretation is not, therefore, simply a disinterested academic exercise, but a critical link between the authority of God embodied in Scripture on the one hand and the teachings and practices of the religious community on the other, ensuring that the process of revelation remains a present reality, rather than becoming merely a fact of ancient history.

THE PROCESS of exegesis would eventually emerge as modern, scientific study of the Bible; at its beginning, however, interpretation was an attempt to harmonize, or perhaps better, to understand authoritative scriptural pronouncements in the light of changed circumstances. Already attested within the Bible itself, interpretation is an effort to trace the roots of religious teaching to a normative source. The diversity of Jewish approaches over the ages demonstrates the variety of purposes the Bible has been expected to fulfill and the wealth of techniques that have been applied to it within a single tradition. The extent to which such methods were deemed important attests not only to the distance between practice and theory, but also to the importance ascribed to the source of authority itself.
—F.E.G.

Jewish Biblical Exegesis: Presuppositions and Principles

MICHAEL FISHBANE
BRANDEIS UNIVERSITY

JUDAISM IS an exegetical religious culture par excellence, and the Miqra, the Hebrew Scriptures, is its foundation document and principal text. For more than two millennia, it has been reinterpreted for simple meaning, for spiritual/moral insight, and for legal applicability. Whether one turns to early halakhic (legal) or aggadic (moral) texts, to medieval homilies or arcane poetry, to philosophical theologies or mystical theosophies, to moral tracts or late legal codifications—the matter is the same: Biblical exegesis serves either as the explicit structural feature of the composition, or as the implicit religious foundation of the very possibility of composition.

The reason this is so is at once simple and the basis for the fascinating and sometimes paradoxical developments that constitute the history of Judaism. As with other book religions such as Christianity and Islam and, in certain respects, even Hinduism, Judaism places a sacred Scripture at the center of its religious life. For its part, the Miqra is the sacred textual source of religious authority precisely because it is rooted in a divine source. Its contents, accordingly, have come to constitute the prescriptive norms of all sanctioned behavior and mental attitudes. But such a semidogmatic notion of a comprehensive Sinaitic revelation did not develop in Judaism with one master stroke. Indeed, close examination discloses

Michael Fishbane's translations of Scripture are his own.

that the Miqra itself bears testimony to the fact that its diverse legal materials were recurrently perceived to be inexplicit, insufficient, or inadequate as a normative guide to all areas of developing religious life. The most striking aspect about the various innerbiblical solutions is that they are neither presented nor represented as independent exegetical traditions—complementary or supplementary to revelatory authority. But with the closure of the canon this situation necessarily changed.[1]

The range of innerbiblical exegesis which attempted to close the gap between the authoritative divine sources and their manifest insufficiency is surprisingly diverse. Within our Pentateuchal sources, one main tendency is operable: to preserve the divine authority of all regulations. But this tendency expresses itself in several forms. According to one type, where the law was unknown or inadequate, a new divine revelation was sought, received, and *added* to the divine corpus (cf. Lev 24:10-23; Num 9:1-14). In other cases, divine authority was safeguarded by the inclusion of supplementary addenda into the original law. Even where these expansions are signaled by explicit formulae, the fact is that the novum is presented as part of the revealed law, not as a human exegetical stratum. Similar considerations pertain to the book of Deuteronomy. While many of its laws are not attested to in earlier legislation, or develop features found in the Covenant Code (Exod 21–23), the rhetorical fiction of this book is that it constitutes Moses' repetition of the Sinaitic law.[2]

The overall tendency to preserve the integrity of the Sinaitic revelation continues into the latest biblical strata. For example, blatant contradictions with respect to the paschal offering in our Pentateuchal sources are harmonized and re-presented as Mosaic law (2 Chr 35:11-13). But a new feature is also at work. Second Chronicles 30:2-3 is clearly an attempt to reinterpret and apply an earlier revealed addendum to defer the Passover ceremony (Num 9:1-14), based solely on human authority. No recourse is made to divine authority *even though* the new legal situation is decidedly not identical with the older one.[3]

A number of considerations having later Rabbinic reflexes

thus already are noticeable in the biblical period: the concern to protect the divine authority of the laws; the tendency to obscure human innovations; the blending and consequent dehistoricization of historically diverse textual levels; and the gradual emergence of an explicit exegetical culture. Indeed, this latter feature tallies with other postexilic processes. Not only were Ezra and his levitical aides involved in the explication of legal obscurities (Neh 8)—they also engaged in polemical exegesis. Their attempts to sanction the exclusion of certain groups from intermarriage with the "community of the exile" (the returnees) clearly strikes a new chord: Group maintenance and integrity could be combated and assured via scriptural exegesis (cf. Ezra 9).

Two interrelated considerations supplement the preceding discussion. With the growing centrality of Torah and the necessity and importance of supplementary-clarificatory exegesis, a visible shift is made from presenting exegesis as a new or old divine revelation to presenting it as the product of human ratiocination. Indicative of this—and truly significant for future development—is the transmutation of the oracular verb *darash* into one indicative of exegetical *inquiry* (cf. 1 Kgs 22:8; Ezra 7:10).[4] Alongside these processes is the ascendent value of Torah study as a postexilic religious ideal, as well as the mediating role of exegesis in the application and ongoing authority of the divine law.[5]

From Antiquity to the Redaction of the Talmud (c. 200 B.C.E.–500 C.E.)

By the postexilic period, most of the procedures, tasks, and tendencies of later Jewish exegesis were well underway. The older sacerdotal structures of the preexilic period gave way during the Exile, so that new emphasis was placed—by the priests and, increasingly, the laity—on public teaching and interpretation of the Torah. In addition, the national decentralization brought on by the Exile sponsored diverse postexilic communities. These groups laid claim to the same scriptural authority, but differed radically as to its proper meaning and application. For "What is Scripture?" if not "the interpretation [*midrash*] of Torah" (*b. Qidd* 49b). Clearly the Torah required interpretation for the sake of its ongoing vitality and authority. But how was it to be supplemented? What was to constitute the proper reading tradition? What method of exposition would bring the ancient law and prophecies to their proper elucidation and application?

The deep crisis of religious continuity that underlay such questions was nothing short of ominous—as much for the immediate sectarian developments as for the history of Judaism generally. For at its root was the fundamental claim of the diverse postexilic communities that they were the true heirs of biblical Israel. On this matter, only exegesis could arbitrate. But as to the question, Which exegetical program and procedure was legitimate?—no definitive answer was at hand. Some groups claimed that their modes of scriptural exegesis would be eschatologically verified. But such divine confirmation *ex eventu* was no help in the present. In this context, the interpretation of Scripture took a new and fateful turn: It became the cutting edge of group boundaries, even as it provided the content of new religious behaviors, ideas, and hopes.

The Dead Sea Scrolls give paradigmatic expression to these issues. An initiate into this community was progressively introduced to its unique method of exegesis; so that to grow in knowledge and authority in this group was inextricably bound up with its claim to the true meanings of Scripture.[6] It is reported that the founder-teacher was granted divine guidance in the exposition of the laws of Moses. As a result, two Torahs were distinguished: the exoteric Torah, revealed to all Israel at Sinai, and an esoteric Torah, known only to the covenanters and constituting the basis of their legal behavior.[7] On the other hand, the secret meanings and applications of the ancient prophecies were also revealed to the teacher—as the remarkable *pesher* literature of this group attests. It was the covenanters' conviction that their legal-ritual life and future expectations would be vindicated in the imminent Final Days.

The crucial relationship between right interpretation and right observance cannot be underestimated. At stake was the "true meaning" of the divine Word. It is recorded, for example, that one early (proto?) Pharisaic group refused to share food with other pious Jews who did not conform to its ultrameticulous food regulations.[8] Related, is the following negation of the exegetically based food observances of R. Yochanan ben Zakkai by circles that sponsored different interpretative methods: "If this is how you have practiced," they said, "you have never eaten clean heave-offerings in your life!"[9] The contradictory legal constructions of Hillel and Shammai (and their followers) are well known (e.g., *m.Eduy* 1.1-3). They not only complained about each other's interpretations (*m.Yad* 4:6-8), but extreme divisiveness was often the result (cf. *b. Shab* 17a, 88b). Along different lines, the Sadducees mocked the Pharisees who "afflict themselves" (with the oral law).[10] The derogation and refutation of the religious claims of rival groups through a condemnation of their modes of exegesis is a recurrent feature in New Testament sources as well (Matt 15:1-3; Mark 7:1-3; Col 2:8; 1 Tim 6:3-4).

In time, one of these groups, the Pharisees, put forward a remarkable claim—one that was to be of inestimable significance for the history of Rabbinic Judaism. Their claim was that their particular exegetical tradition had Sinaitic origins; that it was divinely given to Moses at Sinai, side by side with the written Torah; and that it had been preserved through an unbroken chain of transmission. This opinion was nothing short of revolutionary. The mythicization and retrojection of Pharisaic exegetical claims back to Sinai gave normative sanction to *two* Torahs—one and inseparable—an oral Torah and a written Torah.[11] Indeed, if Judaism can be said to endorse a notion of progressive revelation, one would find it here, at least. Whatever a scholar would claim via exegetical diligence, it was said, had been given *already* at Sinai. When God spoke *"all* these words" (Exod 20:1 [italics added]) at Sinai, said R. Elazar ben Azariah, he spoke the exoteric Torah *and* the various—even contradictory!—words of human exegesis (*b. Hag* 3a-b). Thus oral Torah is a progressive unfolding of the mysterious plenitude of the original divine revelation. "Turn it [Scripture], and turn it again," says an early source, "for all is contained therein" (*m. Abot* 5:22). In a later self-serving legitimation—not one whit less remarkable, for all that—the notion of a continuous revelation found this formulation: "The Holy One, Blessed is He, speaks Torah out of the mouths of all rabbis" (*b. Hag* 15b).

But such formulations took time. Josephus, long before, had reported contentions between the Sadducees and Pharisees. While both groups accepted the divine authority of Scripture, the Sadducees rejected the exegetical traditions of the Pharisees.[12] It often has been claimed that the Sadducees held solely to the purity of the Sinaitic revelation and refused to supplement it in any way. This may be a misreading. Much more probable, given their own exegetical output, is that they rejected the Pharasaic attempt to find and authorize their exegetical tradition in the written Torah.[13] Be this as it may, even the Pharisees show a process of development from the independence of tradition to its rootage in Scripture. The various recensions of a famous story about Hillel are most instructive in this regard. It is reported that the sages were perplexed as to whether the paschal offering could be slaughtered on the sabbath—a matter on which Scripture was obscure, at best. The Talmudic sources present Hillel as repeatedly unable to convince his audience by means of his exegetical pyrotechnics and ultimately forced to legitimate his method of observance by reference to an oral tradition received from his teachers, Shemayia and Avtalyon. Only after establishing such a chain of tradition was Hillel able to introduce an exegetical method which could prove or establish tradition *from the words of the Torah itself.*[14] As this idea took hold and was variously legitimated, the revolution of Rabbinic Judaism was established. The one-time event of Sinai became an ever-recurring moment when the human words or exegetical tradition actualized the words of God at Sinai.

Throughout the tannaitic period—that is, up to the redaction and codification of law in the Mishnah (c. 200 C.E.)—the Miqra was the central preoccupation of Jewish exegesis. The earliest legal exegesis (the halakhic midrashim), as, for example, the *Mekhilta of R. Ishmael,* attest to a diversity of procedures bent upon deriving new applications from the old law as well as understanding the "plain sense" of the text (e.g., through stylistic or syntactical analysis). To be sure, not all the legal rulings put forward or legitimated by scriptural reference are exegetically derived. In some cases, these references merely serve mnemonic ends for the students. But it is nevertheless abundantly evident that exegesis served as an active instrument in the derivation of new law—both theoretical and practical—from the Miqra. There is testimony to the fact that Rabbinical jurists could and did turn to the pertinent scriptural passage as a guide for their concrete deliberations (cf. *Tos.Sanh* 9:1).

Diverse schools of Bible exegesis developed, and hermeneutical techniques became standardized. In this process, R. Yochanan ben Zakkai was the root of a many-branched tree. One chain of students, which began with R. Nehuniyah bar haQaneh, leads to R. Ishmael, who emphasized that exegesis of Scripture must follow common usage and meaning. The latter differed radically from his contemporary R. Akiva, whose method of utilizing every jot and tittle for exegetical derivations is ultimately traceable to Nahum Gimzo, Nehuniyah's contemporary and fellow student at the feet of Rabbi Yochanan.[15] In the chain of exegetical method leading from Nahum Gimzo to Akiva, a momentous development occurred: Hillel ordered hermeneutical *middot,* measures, into a rational sevenfold classification; R. Ishmael extended them to thirteen.[16] The categories embraced analogical, elucidative, logical, and restrictive considerations. There is, on the one hand, a strong formal resemblance to contemporary Roman techniques of interpretation; on the other hand, the impact of the methods and terminology of the Alexandrine scribes cannot be disregarded.[17] Quite certainly, the rationalization of methods of biblical exegesis at the turn of the millennium was part of a larger cultural enterprise which embraced the entire region. Classical antiquity was at an end, and its traditions were being reevaluated and reinterpreted. Homer and Bible gave way to Stoic philosophy and Rabbinic exegesis.

The intense preoccupation with Scripture was not limited to

legal matters. Not only do the oldest legal sources attest to species of aggadic midrashim (moral and homiletical), but this genre is abundantly preserved in the relatively early and great collections known as *Genesis Rabba* and *Leviticus Rabba* (compiled 300–500 C.E.). This literature—and the Talmud, too—is replete with evidence of an at-once playful and highly serious hermeneutical imagination. Philological and syntactical matters are repeatedly taken up; so, too, are matters of custom, moral behavior, and theology. With aggadic midrash, as with the legal, there is the strong presupposition that Scripture is a seamless web. The exegete is permitted and encouraged to move back and forth across its surface, connecting texts and reconnecting them, harmonizing the contradictory and bringing the seemingly discordant into patterns of new and surprising concordance.[18]

In all this, one fact is clear: Exegesis is a cultural product. Many rabbis commented on diverse verses, and sometimes on a sequence of them. But no extensive running commentary was produced by any one individual. Josephus began such a project in his *Antiquities,* but it was not completed. To the extent that we do have continuous commentary in this formative phase of classical Judaism, it is as a cultural product, as anthologies organized around the structure of Miqra and comprised of the opinions, observations, and sermonic précis of many scholars. And just this is a matter of immense significance. Scripture was the organizing prism of the people: It gave focus, structure, and, of course, authority to the ratiocinations, the theological speculations, the moral values, and the folk customs of the nation of Israel.

A counterdevelopment is nevertheless observable. While Miqra was authoritative for tannaitic halakhic and aggadic exegesis, a fork marks the path of the subsequent amoraic period (200–500 C.E.). As noted, the ongoing aggadic midrashim continued to respond to Scripture—perhaps primarily due to the latter's liturgical centrality. The biblically based halakhic midrashim gave way, however, to the authority of Mishnah. Certainly Miqra continued to be cited in the Talmud (now often called *talmud!*); but the Talmud sees its chief exegetical task as the elucidation and harmonization

of Mishnah.[19] A great shift occurred therewith. Inasmuch as
the formulation of halakha was the principal rabbinic activity
and value, this led to a deemphasis of Miqra and the role of
scriptural authority in legal exegesis. ("Do we need Scripture?
It stands to reason!" [b. B. Qan 46b]). This trend was fateful
for the whole course of Talmudic Judaism.

Concern with the peshat, the plain sense of Miqra, and the
derush, halakhic-aggadic exegesis, did not exhaust the
modalities of Jewish Bible exegesis at this time. Two other
types are found: the allegorical and the mystical.

If peshat and derush arise as a result of a crisis in
reading—insofar as the text appears opaque, insufficient, or
incomprehensive—this estimation is doubly pertinent with
respect to allegory. For the allegorical impetus does not arise
from the content of problematics of a text; it derives rather
from the encounter between an authoritative text and an
attractive and religiously approachable body of thought. It
may be for this reason that while there seem to be scattered
references to allegorizers in early Palestinian sources, there is
nothing comparable to the sustained output of Philo or his
like-minded contemporaries.[20] For while the work of these
men is undoubtedly a reflex of individual spirituality, their
private efforts nevertheless are symptomatic of a widespread
attraction to Stoic piety and thought among Alexandrian
Jewry. There was no comparable situation in Palestine.

Faced with a clash of values, biblical allegory—like any
other—performs a paradoxical twist: It reads one thought-
world in terms of another. The result is a mode of syncretistic
exegesis which harmonizes diverse thought-claims and
establishes them as diverse levels of meaning. Thus to the
degree that derush is a horizontal mode of exegesis—reading
the text and connecting citations across its surface—allegory is
a vertical mode. There is a surface sense to Scripture, and
there also is a hyponoia—a deeper, spiritual sense. Most
significant in all this, the biblical text remained the dominant
authority for the spiritual depths exegetically achieved—an
authoritative status all the more reinforced by the identification of Torah with Sophia, or Divine Wisdom. For with this

identification, the Stoic truths first exegetically attributed to Torah were now dialectically discovered to be inherent in its very supernal, a priori nature.

Philo's exegesis is altogether remarkable. Human personages such as Abraham and Sarah become figures of ethical/spiritual virtues; sacrificial rituals and legal prescriptions are read as a guide to inner piety; and narratives, such as those about the Garden of Eden and the sin of Adam, are transformed into spiritual patterns which the discerning mind might use to perceive its proper place in Universal Mind, the true Polis of Man. Correctly read, then, the biblical text was nothing short of a spiritual/philosophical document—an expression of divine wisdom given to humankind to guide its perfectability.[21]

But just such a spiritualization of the external sense of Scripture caused alarm. A tannaitic source, for example, warned against those who might "disclose the [inner] meaning of Scripture *with contra-halakhic results.*"[22] In this remark is expressed the real and potential danger that allegorization of the exoteric law would undermine its ritual, performative basis. Clearly sensitive to such dangers (and criticisms?), Philo emphasized that no spiritual meaning ever deprives Scripture of its plain sense. He was certainly aware that Judaism, as an halakhocentric religious community, could never allow the hard edges of the revealed Torah to be blunted. No hidden meanings in the text could be permitted to gainsay or otherwise relativize the history of Israel and the divine commandments. Bible exegesis was to be in the service of the "revealed things" (Deut 29:28) of God, not at their expense. This principle became, as it were, a watchword of faith.

The capacity of the biblical text to sponsor awesome and almost unimaginable levels of meaning is nowhere more evident than in mystical exegesis, whose main lines are observable from tannaitic times. Typical are the ancient mystical interpretations of the Song of Songs. These love lyrics were read as a *corpus mysticum,* disclosing theosophical levels in and descriptions of the Godhead. To enter the chambers of the beloved, for example, is to ascend into the recesses of the Divine Being; the physical form of the groom was understood to veil the actual structure of the Divine Anthropos![23] It is not, now, new spiritual depths of the Jew which are plumbed via Bible exegesis but, in point of fact, the illimitable depths of God himself. The face of Scripture is nothing less than the surface play of divine mysteries; it is the outer map, as it were, of mystical visions and journeys. All this the mystic knows from experience; his exegesis merely confirms it.

Such mystical exegesis was, of course, esoteric in the extreme and deliberately preserved in pious conventicles. As the textual record of national history and divine commandments gave way to an exegetically reconstructed religious community, and as this textual record simultaneously sponsored new spiritual/moral readings as well as insights into the very life of God, the previously cited adage "Turn it, and turn it again, for all is contained therein" becomes the epigram for the ore of Torah as hewn out by an exegetical community. It is a concept of Torah remarkably befitting a text revered as the very Word of God.

The Medieval Phase to the Onset of Modernity (800–1800 C.E.)

The four levels of scriptural meaning that developed in the early classical period anticipated their more sophisticated permutations in the Middle Ages. Indeed, the concept of a fourfold meaning of Scripture is actually referred to in Jewish mystical texts from the thirteenth century, no doubt influenced by contemporary trends in Christian exegesis. From the fourteenth century, these four senses were referred to as *PaRDeS* (paradiscal garden), an acronym for the *Peshat* (plain sense), *Remez* (implied or allegorical sense), *Derush* (halakhic and aggadic exegesis), and *Sod* (mystical sense) of Scripture.[24] The widespread use of the term *PaRDeS* in Jewish sources does not, however, mean that each level was equally valorized by all groups in all periods. But the acronym does signal a view of Torah and exegesis as the very source and method of all realizable Jewish truth.

The diverse levels of scriptural sense which culminated in *PaRDeS* developed differentially. On the one hand, aggadic *derush* continued unabated. Legal *derush,* however, became ever more removed from Miqra as the oral Torah became increasingly absorbed in its own internal processes. Herein lay the seeds of crisis; for with their attention drawn elsewhere, Rabbinite circles were ill-prepared to face the critique of scriptural "irrationalities" advanced by Islamic rationalistic polemicists and their Jewish and Zoroastrian protégés. Among the Jews, it was the Karaites who particularly decried the Rabbinite neglect of the written Torah. These B'nei Miqra, or Sons of Scripture, as they called themselves, rejected the Rabbinite claims of an oral Torah; they preferred to derive their halakha directly from Scripture by their own methods. Their attentive focus on Scripture, and the challenge of the halakha derived therefrom stimulated new Rabbinite emphasis on *peshat.* The *tafsir* commentary by R. Saadia Gaon (9th century), one particularly distinguished response to these several stimuli, focused on the plain sense of the biblical text.[25] Arabic lexicographical and comparative philological studies made their own marked impact on subsequent developments.

A highly sophisticated investigation of *peshat* was soon underway among the Jews of Moslem Spain. The great grammatical work of Jonah ibn Janah (11th century) is filled with acute exegetical observations. Building on the long-recognized phenomenon of ellipsis, for example, ibn Janah isolated numerous instances of haplography, transpositions of letters and words, and even dislocations of whole sentences. He even introduced the daring notion of "substitution," whereby Miqra "intended one thing but wrote another."[26] The task of the exegete was thereby doubly desiderated: to understand the words of the text and restore its original meaning. Ibn Janah's cogeners added many more penetrating observations, not stopping short of historical observations regarding the late-dating of passages traditionally viewed as preexilic.[27]

The work of R. Abraham ibn Ezra is characteristic of the Spanish trend toward rational lexicographical exegesis and attempts at systematic Bible commentaries. In the introduction to his commentary, ibn Ezra discusses the allegorical and midrashic approaches that preceded him and proclaims his own method: "I shall be unbiased concerning the Torah," he says, "and shall [first] investigate the grammatical form of each word with my full ability and then explain its meaning to what extent I am able." Since there are seventy "faces" to Torah, the literal approach does not displace the midrashic interpretation, he goes on, but when "it comes to the laws, rules and regulations," the opinion "which is in accord with the bearers of Tradition [the Rabbis]" must be relied upon. "For God forbid that we get involved with the Sadducean [Karaite!] contention which claims that [Rabbinic] Tradition contradicts Scripture and grammar."

Scriptural exegesis is thus a self-regulating task and must choose the method most appropriate to it. But it is also ultimately subservient to the halakhic basis of the community and must not undermine it. Similar considerations—as to method and program—are referred to by ibn Ezra's great Franco-German contemporary R. Samuel ben Meir (RaSH-BaM), who remarked, "Lovers of reason should fully comprehend that . . . no Scriptural verse ever loses its plain-sense, even though the principal aim of Torah is to teach and instruct us in the doctrines, laws and rules derivable by hints in the plain-sense of Scripture" (see his comment *ad* Gen 37:2). But not all Franco-German Jews were as devoted to the *peshat*. Rabbinic midrash was a far more weighty factor in these circles, although their commentaries were often the *locus* for instruction in Jewish-Christian theological polemics.[28] In these several ways, this community acknowledged the educational and religiocultural obligations of Jewish Bible exegesis.

Medieval Spain is also the scene of another development—philosophical exegesis. If, as stated, allegory is an exegesis born of a crisis between competing thought-worlds, the renewed recourse to *remez* by Jews who felt the keen challenge of Neo-Platonic and Aristotelian philosophy is more than understandable. And since Philo had long been lost to Jewish thought, the new conceptions that developed in Judaism seemed little short of revolutionary. The Bible was now perceived as a book capable of bringing the adept to an ultimate spiritual felicity, for it could guide one toward a rational, contemplative love of the God of the philosophers.

The work of Maimonides (12th century) is a paradigmatic expression of this overall trend. He not only begins his magisterial *Guide for the Perplexed* with lexicographical considerations, but actually devotes forty-seven chapters to a reexamination of the language of Scripture in an effort to reconcile it with philosophical truth. While drawing upon older considerations as to the appropriate use of metaphorical interpretation *(ta'wīl),* Maimonides put more emphasis on the distinction between the inner *(bāṭin)* and apparent *(ẓāhir)* levels of textual meaning then common in Islamic philosophical circles. This distinction, itself an inner-Islamic development of *ta'wīl* to include doctrinal matters, helped him resolve several issues at once. For not only was Maimonides well aware that the written Torah often presented God in anthropomorphic and anthropopathic images which ostensibly violated proper philosophical understanding; he was also highly conscious of the fact that even philosophy, due to the inherent limitations of language, would often need recourse to images (i.e., parables or similes). This gordian knot was deftly cut by the realization that though the masses tend to read the surface images of Scripture literally, they would not thereby be led astray from the Truth. As a divinely revealed teaching, the exterior level of Scripture is sufficient to guide the faithful to spiritual and moral excellence; but this level conceals a superior level, which establishes "the truth in all its reality."

The *apparent* meaning of Scripture thus gives way to the *inner* as one grows in wisdom. Increasingly appreciating the philosophical truths within these literary figures, one ascends in virtue and the love of God. Seen thus, the truths of religion and philosophy are concordant. A person moves from the one to the other—actually, from one *into* the other—while moving from the exterior religious content of Scripture to its philosophical core. Scripture is thus a bi-level structure which establishes a religious/moral community and instructs the reader in ultimate Truth. One sees Scripture according to one's depth of intellectual development. Speaking programmatically, Maimonides says in his introduction: "The key to the understanding and full comprehension of all that the Prophets have said is found in the knowledge of the figures, their general ideas, and the meaning of each word they contain." Responding to Proverbs 25:11—"A word fitly spoken is like apples of gold in vessels of silver"—the master explains that this is like scriptural truth:

> In every word which has a double sense, a literal one and a figurative one, the plain-meaning must be as valuable as silver, and the hidden meaning still more precious. . . . Taken literally, such expressions contain wisdom useful for many purposes, among others, for the amelioration of the conditions of society. This hidden meaning, however, is profound wisdom, conducive to the recognition of real Truth.[29]

Maimonides' method produced violent controversy in Franco-Germany. While he himself did not disclaim the plain sense of Scripture and wrote a code of halakhic observance, it was once again feared that focus on the inner, spiritual level of Scripture would subtly undermine the public spirituality of Judaism, based as it is on the performance of the divine commandments.

Nahmanides (13th century) was asked to mediate this acrimonious dispute, and his great prestige did in fact prove conciliatory.[30] He was a man of vast erudition and interests—a factor reflected in the new style of synthetic commentary he produced. Nahmanides' exegetical work entered into fruitful—if prolix—debate with the received opinions of his predecessors, from the Rabbinic sages to Rashi and ibn Ezra. But he did not stop there. Again and again, he drops hints about "the way of Truth," the mystical sense of Scripture (sod). Indeed, Nahmanides was more than marginally conversant with the new developments in Spanish mysticism that surfaced around Gerona in his day. His introduction to the Pentateuch actually presents a highly reflective mystical understanding of the written Torah: that it is at once a reflex of cosmic Truth and identical with the Divine Being.[31] The script of Scripture, he said, indeed the very discursiveness of its ideas and syntax, are an accommodation to the ordinary human mind. For one initiated into *raza dimehemanutha,* the mystery of the faith, as the Kabbalists called it, the letters could be reassembled into highly esoteric combinations, and so ever more directly express the nondiscursive "Infinite Source of all Origins."

The Book of Splendor, the *Zohar* (13th century), is the classical source of medieval Spanish Kabbala. While giving evidence of literal and figurative exegesis, its biblical expositions focus particularly on the luminous truths of *sod.* As noted, the early Kabbalists saw this as the fourth level of *PaRDeS*—hidden within the shell of outer meanings like the meat of a nut, the seeds of a pomegranate. In another image, *sod* is personified as the Shekhina—the indwelling feminine aspect of God—who is veiled in the exterior garments of exoteric textual sense. This divine Bride beckons *even through* the plain sense of *peshat.* For those who can respond, the textual tokens of her bidding lend exegesis a deep erotic drive and yearning—one that is not less than the love of God—to unveil Scripture and robe the Bride in the garments of mystical splendor.[32]

Insofar as the mundane Torah is, in truth, a condensation of God in his infinite Mystery, the Torah pulses with rhythms of the divine potencies that structure the cosmos. Exegesis thus begets entry into the mysteries and guides a spiritual journey into the sephirotic-emanationist structure of the Godhead. It is a subtle decoding of Torah, or better, a recoding of it, into the theosophical truth that the mystic has been privileged to see. Accordingly, every person and every event described in Scripture—even the most apparently meaningless, such as the genealogies of Genesis 36—veils the vitality of the Divine. And insofar as the sephirotic structure of the cosmos is perceived as a Divine Anthropos whose earthly reflex is the human, mystical ascent into the recesses of God is also descent into the corresponding depths of the self. "Out of the depths I have called unto you, Lord," says the psalmist—but actually, adds the mystic, one calls God out of his mysterious and hidden depths as one descends into the source of one's soul.[33] God dwells in the recesses of the soul as in the depths of all Being. The macrocosm and microcosm are thus one and concordant; and Scripture is the linguistic concordance, bridging the two realms. Biblical exegesis is here nothing less than an "opening" to Divine Reality.

Spanish theosophy was matched in Franco-Germany by its own brand of arcane Bible exegesis. Again, but in different ways, every letter of Scripture was accorded the utmost significance; only now, new meanings were also derived via numerological permutations. We read these exegetical musings with mixed feelings. Astonishment at the utterly fantastic lengths to which one might go to "discover" new meaning in Scripture goes hand in hand with wonder at the pious zeal that believed the Torah to be the source of all Truth. Here, as in all the levels of interpretation discussed hitherto, biblical exegesis was the most vital of religious tasks. It was the great resource of Jewish *homo religiosus* who undertook the arduous—and audacious!—task of enabling the God of Scripture to continue to speak and be realized as the living God.

The Beginnings of Modernity and Beyond
(1700——)

Among the many striking patterns in the history of Judaism is the conjunction of its transformative moments and renewed vigor in biblical exegesis. New spiritual developments or crises sponsored new views of Torah, revelation, and exegesis. And this holds for the modern world born from the wombs of Baruch Spinoza, Shabbetai Tzvi, and Moses Mendelssohn. Hasidism, the popular and late heir of Kabbala, produced astonishingly subtle rereadings of Scripture for those obsessed with exploring new levels of psychospiritual inwardness. Where the psalmist once cried "Do not abandon me in old age," the Baal Shem Tov is reported to have found a watchword against spiritual aging, against the decrepitudes of ennui and routine in divine service.[34] Such exegetical recodings went together with reworkings of the older theosophical structure of Kabbalistic interpretation; and the emergence of a new style of pneumatic exegesis gave charismatic authority to the biblical discourses—called Torah—of some early masters.[35]

The post-Enlightenment rationalist circles, on the other hand, turned to Scripture to confirm the existence of Jewish ethical precepts that would not be found lacking by the standard of Kant. One thinks, in this regard, of Samson Raphael Hirsch and of his program for the revival of an Enlightened orthodoxy. But S. D. Luzzatto walked an entirely different and more delicate path into the modern world.

In all these enterprises, however, Scripture retained its stature as authority and source of halakha; and biblical exegesis remained part of a larger cultural dynamic. But what happens when the textual source of authority breaks down and the supporting context for study shifts and becomes decentralized? What happens when the autonomous self becomes an arbiter of meaning; when the Bible is but one of many books making a spiritual claim; when one studies in the university or secular world and adopts methods that serve the self-centered interests of professional elites rather than the interests of communities of faith? For the Jew, as for moderns generally, these are great problems. Will whole areas of contemporary Jewry be able to perceive new power in Torah—if only as a source of wisdom, though no longer as a source of divine Truth; if only as the source of significant spiritual memory, though no longer as the resource of the Jewish spiritual heritage?

If an age when the transcendent Source has been fractured into humanized substitutes and idolatries of one sort and another, can Torah somehow reorient one to a transcendental point of reference? In an age of cant rhetoric, can biblical exegesis disclose new powers of speech and a living God beyond language? A positive response to these questions was one of the hopes and life tasks of Martin Buber. His great friend Franz Rosenzweig was no less aware of the crisis of spirituality and authority in modernity. He formulated the following hard hope and exegetical option for the modern Jew:

> Modern man is neither a believer nor an unbeliever. He believes and he doubts. And so he is nothing, but he is alive. Belief and unbelief "happen" to him and all he is required to do is not run away from what is happening. . . . Whoever lives in this way can approach the Bible only with a readiness to believe or not believe, but not with a circumscribed belief that he find confirmed in it. . . . For such a man the days of his own life illumine the Scriptures, and in their quality of humanness permit him to recognize what is more than human. . . . This humanness may anywhere become so translucid under the beam of a day of one's life that it stands suddenly written in his innermost heart. . . . Not everything in the Scriptures belongs to him—neither today nor ever. But he belongs to everything in them, and it is only this readiness of his which, when it is directed towards Scriptures, constitutes belief.[36]

THE BIBLE is not simply an important book, nor is it even the only authoritative entity for most Jewish and Christian institutions. The church and rabbinical bodies that perceive themselves as implementing biblical teachings exist in a creative symbiosis with the Bible. Defining the nature of this relationship is a difficult process, particularly in light of the competition between religious bodies and the challenge of alternative perspectives. Harmonizing these separate interests has been a long and difficult process, as evidenced in the history of Roman Catholic attempts to articulate the relationship between church and Bible.

—F.E.G.

The Bible in the Roman Catholic Church

BRUCE VAWTER, C.M.
DePAUL UNIVERSITY

IN CONCERT with most other traditional Christian bodies, the Roman Catholic Church has proposed, in its official formulations of faith, a view of Scripture as *norma normans et non normata* (a standard which sets the standard without being subject to any other standard) of belief. Also, in concert with the formulations of the other bodies, those of the Roman church still reflect, to some degree, even now, the theological controversies of the fourteenth to sixteenth centuries that culminated in Reformation and Counter-Reformation. The theological tensions reflected in the formulations have, in these ecumenical times, provoked difficulties for those respective bodies that wish to disembarrass themselves of polemics no longer useful. I am thinking, on the one hand, of the Faith and Order Conference of the World Council of Churches which grappled with the traditional *sola Scriptura* formula in its discussions at Montreal in 1963 and whose findings were published under the intriguing title *Tradition and the Traditions*. With that side of the problem I am, of course, not presently concerned. I am, however, concerned with the correlative problem that has been presented to the Catholic Church, with its traditional "Scripture *and* tradition" formula.

The concept of Scripture presumed in the Catholic formulations represents that of the medieval theologians, which was, in turn, an inheritance, broadly speaking, from the

Fathers of the Church of the third century onward. For the Fathers, Scriptures were, first and foremost, divine oracles— teaching communicated by God to men by means of human writers imbued with a prophetic spirit.[1] This concept owed something to the New Testament (the *theopneustos* of 2 Tim 3:16, esp.) but probably much more to the image of the mantic oracular prophet that had prevailed in the Hellenistic world and to the precedent of such figures as Philo of Alexandria, who had explicitly identified the biblical process with the divine possession of mantic prophecy. This tendency to equate the Bible with oracular revelation carried with it at least two other associated tendencies, which also were inherited by the medieval church and caused problems for it and for later generations, not excluding our own. The first was the prejudice against consideration of the Bible as human literature subject to the literary conventions of man. The second was the recourse to a multiplicity of scriptural "senses" in order to extract religious significance from a text that did not possess it obviously on the surface.

These were tendencies, not absolutes. Augustine, to take a random example, could quite straightforwardly assert that there were statements in Scripture *nulli saluti profutura,* having no bearing on salvation, and that by that same token, the Scripture was not to be bent to pretend to the teaching of biology or physics.[2] Such would be the basis for a later principle laid down by Aquinas, that scriptural writers had dealt with matters of profane science simply according to appearances, utilizing popular figures that even those who knew better still found convenient to employ for understanding.[3] Chrysostom, Augustine's contemporary in the East, could employ the concept of *synkatabasis,* condescension, an idea that pervades his writings, to account for adjustment of the divine authorship of Scripture to the human hearts, minds, and circumstances that eventually had produced it. Yet we know that when Theodore of Mopsuestia (c. 350–428)—one of the early Christian writers with whom a modern exegete would feel most comfortable—tried to systematize such practical conclusions in a theory that would have distinguished prophecy from other spiritual gifts that had gone into the production of Scripture, he was rewarded in 533 by a posthumous condemnation by the Second Council of Constantinople.[4] As for what commonly is called the allegorical or typological interpretation of Scripture (not to mention the "tropological" or other "spiritual" senses discerned in it), there is no doubt that from Philo through the Alexandrians and Antiochenes, down through the Middle Ages and into modern times, dissatisfaction with the historicocritical method of getting at biblical meaning has been motivated by reluctance to accept the plain sense that the biblical author intended his words to have.[5] I recognize that a present-day synchronic exegetical approach to the biblical text which relies heavily on the structures that emerge from comparative literatures may have a great deal to contribute to our understanding of the Bible. Such an understanding, however, I am sure can only supplement, never substitute for the diachronic study of a text that is a part of human history. Literature is a human phenomenon to be investigated in its own right, and religious literature is only one part of human literature. But on the other hand, some of the religions that have produced literature wish to be judged not on *what* they have written but on *why* they wrote it. I think that we are asked to view the Scripture first of all as a record of what God has done at determined points of time: This is the essence of historical revelation, that God has *acted* (the ṣidqôt Yhwh, "justices of the Lord" [Mic 6:5, etc.]). It was in this posture of enquiry that in the thirteenth century, at the height of the Middle Ages, Thomas Aquinas appeared on the theological scene.

Aquinas was one of those persons who appear every millennium or so—or in these times of geometric progression, perhaps every century or decade or so. He revolutionized contemporary theology, however, more than any Barth, Wellhausen, Bultmann, or Dalman ever has done in his own time. When Aquinas died on March 7, 1274, on his way to the Council of Lyons—forty-nine years of age and in ill health, summoned to the council by the Pope—he was under condemnation by the universities of Oxford and of Paris: The archbishops of both Canterbury and Paris, renowned theologians in their own right, had run athwart Aquinas on purely intellectual grounds. There was then no Inquisition or Holy Office or Congregation for Sacred Doctrine; Aquinas died as thoroughly rejected in high ecclesiastical circles as one could have been in the thirteenth century. Despite this, of course, and despite the fact that the influential Franciscans declared his teachings unacceptable in their schools, Aquinas shortly was canonized and declared a doctor of the church. He is now customarily termed the *doctor angelicus,* or *doctor communis,* the very standard of orthodoxy, particularly for those for whom any later Aquinas is an unthinkable prospect and whose acquaintance with him, in any case, is likely to be quite superficial.

It is not directly pertinent to our discussion, but indirectly very pertinent to note that Aquinas was the first of the medieval theologians to characterize *faith* as an *intellectual* virtue. This, totally apart from the fact that for Aquinas, no less than for Luther, there was a rigorous distinction between faith and reason. It was this theological position that put him into sharpest opposition with John Peckham, Archbishop of Canterbury, and Stephen Tempier, Archbishop of Paris—a position that was due to Aquinas' acceptance of Aristotelian realism in contrast with the Platonism and mysticism inherited from earlier theology. Our discussion is affected by the degree to which this theological determination reinforced the persuasion derived from the Fathers: to treat revelation, which was the object of faith, and Scripture, which was revelation in concrete form, as *doctrina sacra,* sacred teaching. Such an approach resulted in the fact that for Aquinas, *sacra doctrina, sacra Scriptura,* and even *sacra theologia* could be synonymous terms.[6] But by the same token, since Scripture was a teaching, it was not the text of the Scripture that was most important, but rather the meaning of the text—what it was understood to signify through the distillation of more than a millennium of Christian tradition. The text was involved, of course, both for what it plainly said and for what it plainly excluded. But what it plainly said was the same thing tradition had made plain, and of course, a doctrine became no less scriptural simply because tradition

had found better words to express the reality intended than
the scriptural text itself possessed. Thus Aquinas found it both
appropriate and scriptural to use, in relation to God, a term
such as "person," not found in the Scripture but also not
Scripturarum sensu discordans, contrary to the meaning of
Scripture.[7]

A theologian of the Middle Ages was primarily an expositor
of the Bible. Only after becoming established as proficient in
this area could one be presumed worthy to compose *sententiae*
or *summae* of various kinds. The tradition continued long:
Martin Luther's initial theological essays were commentaries
on the psalms, which he produced while still lecturing as an
Augustinian monk in his German university. (It might be
noted that, until quite recently, a nervous post-Vatican I
Roman Catholic administration had quite reversed this
ancient rule, requiring a candidate for a "biblical" degree first
to acquire one in "theology.") The Bible that the medieval
theologian presented was, of course, the Bible of Christian
tradition. It was the Bible, for all that—the only Bible that
existed. Yves Congar has put it accurately:

> The theological thought of St. Thomas, as of the Middle Ages, at
> least up to his time, was based essentially on the Bible and
> tradition. We can never stress too much the fact that in those days
> theological teaching was profoundly biblical. The ordinary lecture
> of the master was a commentary on Sacred Scripture. That is why
> the scriptural commentaries of St. Thomas represent his ordinary
> public teaching as a master.[8]

And, if one who has studied both Aquinas' commentaries
and his theological tractates may be permitted an added note,
it is in the commentaries (especially, I would think, in those on
Romans and Galatians, where he anticipated Luther's
doctrine of *sola fide*) that he is at his scriptural best, in contrast
with the fairly casual way he uses Scripture in his *Summa.*

If I seem to dwell unduly on the biblical orientation of
pre-Reformation Catholicism, I apologize, but do not repent.
It remains a fact that there is enormous ignorance of this
matter even among theologians and church historians. I will

not pursue it further, but only recommend to those who do not
know it the work of Beryl Smalley on *Study of the Bible in the
Middle Ages*.[9] There is also a little book of my own in which I
begin with Geoffrey Chaucer (a contemporary of John
Wycliffe and the Lollards) to suggest that the Bible was quite
as much a way-book in Catholic England as it became later in
Protestant England.[10] Only the circumstances were different.

. The circumstances, of course, were those produced by
history. If, in the words of an earlier Roman Catholic
enthusiast, the thirteenth was "the greatest of centuries," it
seems appropriate to agree with a modern historian's view
that the fourteenth century was indeed "calamitous."[11] The
melancholy story needs no rehearsing. It is a tragedy of
errors—political, civil, and ecclesiastical—abetted by numerous acts of God. What is most important for our consideration
is that, by reason of ecclesiastical schism, heresy, and
disruption, the notion that any authentic ecclesiastical
"tradition" regarding the Scripture had been safely handed
down from of old simply disappeared. There remained only
manmade "traditions" which had grown up about the
Scripture and which could easily be seen as being contrary to
it. When people came to believe that there was no longer a
reliable tradition resulting from the decisions of a thousand
years of Christianity as to the meaning of a scriptural text, the
way was open for any interpretation one wanted to make. Of
course, such a potentially anarchic situation did not always
occur: Various Protestant orthodoxies with traditions of their
own were soon established.

We come back to the *sola Scriptura* principle. It is certain
that no Fathers of the church, no medieval theologians of the
church, would have been uncomfortable with the formula *sola
Scriptura*. According to their lights, that is exactly what they
were dealing with. They were dealing with it, they thought,
when they took the Scripture for what they thought it meant,
as centuries of tradition had taught them its meaning. What
became incredible to them, but very credible to the
Reformers, for whom the church itself had become incredible,
was that the proverbial ploughboy with the vernacular Bible in
his hand was a match for the pope of Rome with all the

councils of the church behind him. We really should try to understand this position as the enormity it must have appeared in Catholic eyes in the fifteenth century. It was as though, in our time, a fresh translation of the United States Constitution, independent of judicial interpretation from 1789 onward, should be presented in 1989 as the basis of the establishment of an American Republic with all the authenticity attaching to that name, disregarding two centuries of history.

It should be noted that the Scripture that had been adapted by the church—the Old Testament, which it had inherited, and the New Testament, which it had created largely on the precedent of the Old Testament—was also exclusively a matter of tradition. As for the New Testament, Augustine's principle is well known: He would not have accepted the truth of the gospel, except for the authority of the Catholic Church. The determination of the Old Testament had been even more traditionally tied. The Christian Old Testament—which is not the Hebrew Bible—is a genuine creation of proto-Christianity, growing out of Judaism (Palestinian and Diaspora) into something new. That new something was, in one respect at least, standard Christianity. It is not necessary to take a stand on the accuracy of the Septuagint as a faithful translation of the Hebrew Bible (to the extent that it was, indeed, a translation of the Hebrew Bible) to come to the conclusion that in any case, translation or otherwise, the Septuagint was the Bible of the New Testament and of early Christianity. (At least three-quarters of the citations of the Old Testament in the New Testament are from the Septuagint. It is a well-known fact that in early Christian times, the Septuagint had become so "Christian" that the new translations of Aquila, Symmachus, and Theodotion were called for in the Greek-speaking Jewish community.) The Septuagint "canon," in any case, is in reality the Old Testament of the Christian church as it was eventually determined by the Council of Trent.[12] The "Protestant" canon of the Old Testament, ultimately a determination of copy editors rather than of biblical scholars, was the result of a misunderstanding which began with Jerome concerning the authentic text of "the Word of God," together with a lack of factual information about the historical process that had led to a collection of works which would be finally denominated as canonical.[13] The so-called Protestant canon of the Old Testament is ultimately a Renaissance construct based on insufficient knowledge of the past. In a rather different area, but out of a similar faulty reconstruction of the past, the Renaissance scholars popularized the *textus receptus* of the New Testament—the averaged, Byzantine text—which long enjoyed pride of place in Protestant Bibles in preference to the better text tradition that underlay the Vulgate Latin, and which has in recent times been replaced only with great difficulty.

And so we return to consideration of Scripture as the determinant of faith, Catholic or Protestant, as represented in the various formulations. *Sola Scriptura,* for reasons that now should be apparent, was a formula made impossible for Catholic orthodoxy by the Reformation movement. A century—even a half-century—earlier, it would have been possible, but now it had become, in Catholic eyes, little more than a slogan of Protestant intransigence. Hence the decree of the Council of Trent, in its Fourth Session of April 8, 1546, determined, first of all, that the source *(fons)* of

> all salutary truth and moral discipline [is] the gospel promised before by the prophets in the holy Scriptures, promulgated by the very mouth of our Lord Jesus Christ the Son of God, then to be preached by his Apostles to every creature [and that] this truth and discipline is contained in written books and unwritten traditions which were received by the Apostles from the mouth of Christ himself or by the Apostles themselves under the inspiration of the Holy Spirit [*Spiritu Sancto dictante*].[14]

In retrospect, this formulation certainly could have been happier. Had it put tradition in the singular rather than the plural, it would have been more pleasing to any present-day Catholics properly attuned, as they think, to the belief and profession of their church: that tradition is not a rival source of doctrine to that contained in Scripture, but that it is the interpretative envelope in which Scripture has been transmitted as *sacra doctrina*. However, as everyone must surely know, conciliar language is committee language, the language of compromise. The concept of tradition and of traditions was as much confused—that is, subject to variant interpretations—at the Council of Trent as it was in Montreal in 1963, where the words of Kristen Eynar Skydsgaard were remarkably like those of Trent:

> Naturally Luther agrees that the church existed before the Scripture, but he also insisted that the word of God itself already was before the church and before the written book. . . . The living word of God is before every Gospel . . . a word which first of all is not to be written down but to be preached. In the church it does not suffice that books should be written and read, but it is absolutely necessary that this word be spoken and heard. . . . Christ has not called us to write, but to preach.[15]

At Trent the concept of tradition(s) was variously understood: as traditions which were apostolical or merely ecclesiastical; as being on a par with or subordinate to Scripture; as interpretative of or supplementary to Scripture; as relating only to practice or to doctrine itself; and in many other ways. We should hardly expect this council, under the pressures it then experienced, to have accomplished in the sixteenth century successful ecumenical formulas which have not yet been produced by the twentieth. One formulation it did avoid—for whatever reason—was that which had been proposed in pre-Tridentine Counter-Reformation theology at the council itself and which subsequently would appear in some post-Tridentine theology—namely, that divine revelation was the possession of Scripture and tradition(s) *partim . . . partim,* partly in the one, partly in the other. This formula disappeared entirely in the deliberations of the council. And thus it appears that George H. Tavard is quite correct in his final assessment of the achievement of Trent as the most and the best that could be expected at that time of any ecumenical council:

Compared with pre-Tridentine theology, the decree of April 1546 makes it impossible to hold that new doctrines may still be revealed to the Church [the thought that postapostolic traditions could be intruded into the articles of faith]: the stress on apostolicity is too well marked to be compatible with such a view. It remains neutral on a notion of Tradition (in the singular), which would include Scripture and be identified with the life or conscience of the Church: the rationale of the Council precluded consideration of this problematic but did not gainsay the underlying theology. It finally respects the classical view: Scripture contains all revealed doctrine, and the Church's faith, which includes apostolic traditions, interprets it.[16]

Vatican Councils I and II, the two councils of the Roman church that have occurred since the Council of Trent, have added nothing essential to the determinations of that council (composed mainly of Italian and Spanish bishops, never more than a hundred or so) with regard to this vital question. The First Vatican Council did no more than reiterate Trent's definition of Scripture, interpreting that *Spiritu Sancto dictante* should be read in more modern terms: *Spiritu Sancto inspirante*.[17] In either case, of course, we are dealing with gross anthropomorphisms. "God dictates"—I need not remind you that dictation in the modern sense, or at least in the sense we like to think modern, when the one dictated to is totally passive to the dictator, is the product of a recent world of shorthand pads and electronics. "God inspiring" calls us back to an even earlier frame of reference, to the concept of a vital essence that can be breathed into a passive recipient. I will not enter here into the question of the mechanics of biblical inspiration. My only point at this juncture is to insist that Vatican I did nothing further than the Council of Trent, except to change its terminology slightly.

Nor did Vatican II much affect the question. Vatican II accepted the "new" terminology of *inspired* to characterize the sacred Scripture, but beyond this and the specific note that these books of Scripture contain "revelations without error" and attest to "God as their co-Author," nothing much more was said—certainly nothing more than had been suggested by both Protestant and Catholic theology in the interim.[18]

The only real question that arises, therefore, from the standpoint of the Catholic reader of Scripture is this: Who indeed determines the traditional meaning of the Scripture, the meaning that should appeal to us in an existential sense; the meaning that commands us to take action, that reveals to us the *Sachgehalt,* content, of the Word of God?

In the Catholic Church we talk about the magisterium, the teaching authority of the church, the ultimate determinant of what is to be believed and not believed—in these days, at least, what the pope and his bishops have determined to be the norm of faith. It was not so always. I have no intention here of invading the realm of the ecclesiastical historian, who will tell you that there was a time when an ecumenical council of the church could stand up against the pope and say him nay without recrimination. It is very obvious today that a pope can stand up against an ecumenical council and say it nay without recriminations. In the Middle Ages, the magisterium of the church referred to: the authority of the pope, which was always respected; the accumulated authority of the bishops, which was respected only slightly less because it was harder to garner; the *consensus theologorum,* the common agreement of those who were supposed to devote themselves professionally to the study of the meaning of revelation; and the *consensus fidelium,* the common belief of all Christians, against which deviations and heresies could be measured. All these constituted the magisterium of the church when there was, for all practical purposes, only the one church which was coextensive with the body of Christian believers.

None of these components of magisterium was judged to be absolutely imperative of itself. The famous formula of Vincent of Lerins: *quod semper, quod ubique, quod ab omnibus,* the commonality of Christian faith, was called into question long before John Henry Newman's *Essay on the Development of Christian Doctrine,* and certainly before Walter Bauer's *Orthodoxy and Heresy in Earliest Christianity.* "Athanasius against the world" of Arianism is a far earlier precedent. Theologians, as we have seen, could stand fairly well against a consensus of their peers, and yet almost within their own lifetimes be styled "doctors of the church." Pope could and did anathematize pope, council could anathematize council, and, for good measure, pope could anathematize council—and council, pope. Together, however, these components were constitutive of the beliefs of the church in regard to its constitutional documents, the sacred Scripture of the Old and New Testaments.

Historical circumstances have radically altered this rather free and easy approach to magisterium. Both the Reformation and a more respectable papalism which eventually developed in reaction to the Reformation resulted *within the Catholic Church itself,* and not merely with regard to those outside its fold, in the concept of an *ecclesia docens,* the teaching church, superior to the *ecclesia docta,* the church that is taught, the faithful.

There has been no doubt, in recent times at least, according to textbook theology, about who it is that constitutes this "teaching church." It is the bishops of the church and, more specifically, the bishop of Rome, speaking with or without the consultation of the other bishops, who, in practice, serve as his appointees throughout the Roman Catholic world. To be even more specific, the teaching church generally finds its exercise through the decisions of the largely anonymous decrees of the congregations or bureaus of the Roman curia, which officate in the name of the Holy Father, sometimes with and sometimes without his explicit advertence.

Actually, the situation does not affect individual Catholic consciences as much as one might think. The First Vatican Council on July 18, 1870, defined the infallibility of the Roman pontiff in matters of faith and morals under certain sharply defined conditions.[19] His decisions, it was decreed, should be regarded as definitive of themselves, and not from the consent of the church. This is what the textbooks call the extraordinary magisterium of the church. It would, I think, be difficult to find any contemporary Catholic theologian who would defend the proposition that the Catholic Church, either prior to or subsequent to the First Vatican Council, has ever submitted the Scripture in whole or in part to this "extraordinary magisterium" for any effect that would not find general agreement with most of those who consider themselves Christians.

We are left, therefore, in the main with the church's "ordinary magisterium," which, as I have said, in post-Reformation times has come increasingly to mean the utterances of the pope or of his surrogates in the Roman congregations. Especially in the nineteenth and twentieth centuries, there came into existence the papal "encyclical letter," a pronouncement made in the pope's own name and above his signature, carrying with it, no doubt intentionally, a greater than usual approbation of the Apostolic See. The encyclicals, as far as they have affected biblical studies, have been very liberal and enlightened. The *Providentissimus Deus* (November 18, 1893) of Leo XIII, for example, while it treated the newfangled "critical" approach to the Bible with some horror, at the same time recognized—against the fundamentalism of biblical inerrancy—that the biblical authors had intended to write nothing about profane matters *(nulli saluti profutura,* in the words of Augustine), but only saving truths; that therefore their observations on physical realities and the like must be judged in accordance with the opinions of their age. In a special paragraph, Leo noted that the same principle of interpretation might "especially be applied to biblical history."[20] When the largely unsung but profoundly influential Austrian Jesuit Franz von Hummelauer (1842–1914) took up this historical challenge, he succeeded only in provoking several decisions by the Pontifical Biblical Commission in 1905, under Pius X, which condemned all his views—the courtesy extended, however, of no reprobation by name.[21] (Mercifully, no encyclical on biblical studies was ever issued in the reign of Pius X.) The *Spiritus Paraclitus* of Benedict XV (pope 1914–1922), a pope hardly remembered today, was a truly pedestrian enterprise—little more than a series of commonplaces on Scripture, together with an affirmation that Pius X had not been wrong when he insisted that Leo XIII had never authorized any conception of biblical history as "relative" rather than "absolute." Both these terms were qualified as "so-called" and "according to common parlance," whatever this may mean.[22] Nothing further really happened in the papal area until the *Divino afflante Spiritu* of 1943, which was appropriately termed by French scholars *l'encyclique libératrice,* the liberating encyclical, which, among other things, endorsed wholeheartedly the Humme-lauerian principle that *"jede literarische Art hat die ihr eigentümliche Wahrheit,"* which was acceptably translated into the Latin of Augustin Bea as *"sua cuique propria est generi litterario veritas."*[23] The anathema and unacceptable of one age thus became the *doctrina communis* of another. Since 1943 there has been no additional papal encyclical expressly on the Scripture. It must be admitted, however, that the *Humani Generis* of 1950, an encyclical of the same Pius XII who had authored *Divino afflante Spiritu,* in the process of criticizing certain contemporary tendencies in the sacred sciences found it necessary to reprobate "in a special way" the "too free interpretation of the historical books of the Old Testament."[24] The mistake, the encyclical noted, was due this time to misinterpretation of a letter sent by the Pontifical Biblical Commission in 1948 to Cardinal Suhard, then the archbishop of Paris. This leads us to consider the other media through which the "ordinary magisterium" of the church has been exercised in respect to the Bible.

Since the Council of Trent, three Roman congregations or commissions have had to do with official ecclesiastical pronouncements regarding the Scripture. First, there was the Congregation of the Council, which initially was instituted to provide authentic interpretations of the decrees of the Council of Trent. It did not last long in this capacity; there is still a Congregation of the Council in the Roman curia, but it is concerned with other matters and has nothing more than the name in common with its predecessor. Second, there is a group originally called the Congregation of the Inquisition (not connected with the Spanish Inquisition); for most of its recent life, it was termed the Congregation of the Holy Office and now most recently has been renamed the Congregation for the Doctrine of the Faith. Its purpose was and is the preservation of the purity of Catholic doctrine; the change of names doubtless reflects in some measure the difference of approach to this preservation through the centuries.

Finally, there was the Pontificial Biblical Commission established in 1902 by Pope Leo XIII (who included among its first consultors both Franz von Hummelauer and also Marie-Joseph Lagrange, O.P., who had been equal sufferers under Roman scrutiny) partly at least in answer to a wave of protest that had greeted a response of the Congregation of the Inquisition in 1897 regarding the so-called Johannine comma (1 John 5:7). Could the authenticity of this passage be called into question? No, was the response of the Congregation, even though to every critical eye of the time it was already obvious that it was a Latin interpolation into the Greek text, inserted no earlier than the fourth century. Leo XIII intended to avoid future embarrassments of this kind' for church authority by assembling a corps of consultors who were competent to rule on such critical matters. But in 1903, Pius X began to rule, and from that time on the Biblical Commission outdid the Inquisition at its own game, piling up a collection of authoritarian decrees—on implicit citations in Scripture, on the species of scriptural historiography, on the Mosaic authorship of the Pentateuch, on the authorship of the four Gospels and Acts, and so on—in a total vacuum of naked authority isolated from the scholarly world. (It is to be remembered, of course, that in this same period appeared the decree of the Holy Office *Lamentabili* and the encyclical *Pascendi* in which the Modernist crisis was faced by the Roman Church.) Not until the time of Pius XII and under the secretaryship of J. M. Vosté, O.P., did the Biblical Commission resume the positive directions that originally had been intended for it. It should be acknowledged, however, that in 1927 the Congregation of the Holy Office did reconsider the 1897 decision on the Johannine comma, and it explained that its intention had not been to inhibit free and critical discussion of the text, but only to vindicate the teaching authority of the church against mere private opinion. As I once wrote, "Given the literary form of Roman curial documents, this amounted to a handsome apology for having made a precipitate and unnecessary intrusion into the arena of scholarly discussion."[25] Only in 1979, after all, did Pope John Paul II find it opportune to declare that the same

Congregation of the Inquisition had erred in its seventeenth-century condemnation of Galileo—a matter to which we shall return.

Most of the early decrees of the Biblical Commission were framed from the assumption of an adversary situation between church tradition and critical acceptation of the Bible. The more the critical view of the Bible prevailed in the western world, the less credible some of these decrees appeared as applicable to the Universal Church. In 1955 the Roman curia recognized this fact and, within its *stylus curiae,* corrected the bad situation that had developed. On the appearance in that year of a new edition of the *Enchiridion Biblicum* (a more or less official Roman collection of ecclesiastical documents pertaining to the Scripture), both the secretary and the undersecretary of the commission simultaneously published an identical article, indicating that in their minds those prior decrees, to the extent that they did not touch on essential matters of faith and morals, ought not to inhibit the free exercise and use of critical method and its results in coming to quite opposed conclusions.[26] Since that time the Biblical Commission has, by and large, not only refrained from negative inhibitions on critical biblical research but, on its own initiative, also has suggested avenues of research in which biblical science can and should assist in the *magisterium ecclesiae.* It has not, to be sure, suggested very many of these, nor have there been too many other invitations from the hierarchical church for exegetical assistance in its pastoral mission. Nevertheless, the climate of the present is vastly different from that which preceded the Second Vatican Council.

Thus for example, in 1964 the commission issued an "Instruction on the Historical Truth of the Gospels,"[27] which effectively distinguished the levels in the Gospel narratives that frequently are called the *Sitz im Leben Jesu* (the origin within the circumstances of the historical Jesus of Nazareth), the *Sitz im Leben Ecclesiae* (the area covered by form criticism), and the *Sitz im Evangelium* (the area of redaction criticism), and it invited exegetes to consider the implications of these distinctions as they affect the question of the historical character of the New Testament.[28] The substance of this instruction was accepted into the New Testament section of the *Dei Verbum* constitution of the Second Vatican Council.[29] In more recent times we have witnessed a ruling by a majority vote of the members of the commission to the effect that there is no peremptory argument to be extracted from Scripture that would prohibit the ordination of women to priestly ministry within the church, a position which, to say the least, has not proved acceptable to the higher exercise of the magisterium.[30]

It was probably this once quasi-adversary symbiosis of church authority with theology/exegesis that accounts for, or at least contributed to the involvement of the authoritarian levels of the Roman Catholic Church with a concept of total biblical inerrancy in the nineteenth and early twentieth centuries. This concept, as James Barr has correctly maintained, is essentially a Protestant concept—a more or less modern Protestant concept, for that matter—a reaction that emerged among people whose only guide of life, the Bible, plain and unencumbered by any traditional refraction, suddenly was found to be in apparent conflict with the revelation of a newfound science and history.[31] Some years ago Karl Rahner also raised the question: What is the point of proposing an infallible Bible in a church that professes to already have an infallible teaching authority in faith and morals?[32] I am less interested in Rahner's response than in the pertinence of his question.

The concept of biblical inerrancy is not to be confused with the venerable Jewish and Christian affirmation that the Bible is the true Word of God communicated without falsehood. *Falsehood,* not *error,* is the antinomy of the *truth* of the Bible that was sustained by the Fathers and the theologians of the medieval church.[33] As we have seen before, it was the conviction of these earlier generations of Christians that the Bible, throughout, was a document of divine revelation relating to salvation, not an encyclopedia of useful information concerning matters that could be ascertained through the natural means of human observation or record. Apparently purely "profane" *dicta* of Scripture either were researched for the "spiritual" religious sense that lay beneath their surface or were dismissed as *obiter dicta,* peripheral to the divine message, a natural accompaniment to it conditioned by the circumstances of the times.[34] It was not assumed that there was, apart from a salvific context, a biblical utterance about anything whatever that could be called inerrant.

The notorious Galileo case of 1633 is no exception to this rule, unless to prove it. Some years ago, I spent a bit of time looking at the exegetical principles employed by some of the most respected Catholic exegetes of the late sixteenth and early seventeenth centuries and compared them with those employed by Galileo.[35] Incidentally, in the case at hand, Galileo was not, as some secondhand apologists have tried to maintain, a mathematician who foolishly had tried to play the theologian without learning the rules. On the contrary, Galileo's exegesis (which was, by the standards of the time, entirely to the point and unexceptionable) differed in no respect from the exegesis of those who opposed him.[36] It was as hard then as it is now for me to avoid the conclusion that Galileo's ecclesiastical condemnation was a matter of contemporary convenience, in conformity with the judgment of Giorgio di Santillana *(The Crime of Galileo).* That is to say, it was the academic conservatism of the dominant Aristotelianism, more than anything religious, that decided Galileo's fate. Academe then spoke with a religious voice rather than with another, for this was the seventeenth and not yet the eighteenth, nineteenth, or twentieth century, but it was an academic voice for all that. The admixture of the academic with the religious is evident in the Inquisition's decree:

> The proposition that the sun is the center of the world and does not move from its place is absurd and false philosophically, and formally heretical because it is expressly contrary to Holy Scripture. The proposition that the earth is not the center of the world and immovable, but that it moves and also has a diurnal motion, is equally absurd and false philosophically and at least erroneous in faith.[37]

This was neither the first nor the last time the secular arm returned the compliment the church had frequently conferred upon it by impressing it into the service of doing its dirty work.

The fact is that in no council of the Universal Church, either before or after the Reformation, has the formula of inerrancy been applied to the Bible. The formula was applied, to be sure, by various popes and papal commissions, but only subsequent to Vatican I. By Vatican II, it was expressly rejected, though it appeared in its crassest form in the original draft presented to the conciliar fathers, and it clung there tenaciously until the fourth and penultimate redaction of what finally would emerge as the constitution *Dei Verbum*.[38] Through this process the original, truly fundamentalistic assertion that "divine inspiration by its very nature excludes and rejects every error in every field, religious or profane" yielded at last to the conclusion that, concerning inspiration, "it follows that the books of Scripture must be acknowledged as teaching firmly, faithfully, and without error that truth which God wanted put into the sacred writings for the sake of our salvation."[39] This was the voice of authentic Judeo-Christian tradition, rather than a reaction to the displacement of scriptural omniscience exploded by the Enlightenment or to the danger of exegetes' infection by the spirit of skepticism.

Another anomaly from which Roman Catholicism has been protected by its tradition is Marcionism, whether in its original or in its latter-day manifestations—namely, the position that Old Testament history and theology are irrelevant to Christian faith. This position, in modern times, without recriminations, I perceive to be characteristic of German rather than of other continental scholarship—certainly not of Anglo-Saxon. In any case, no doubt owing to the well-deserved acclaim of German scholarship, it is a much respected position in Protestant circles (and also, of course, in some Catholic circles, which are no less immune to the prestige attached to German scholarship). There are many chapters and verses I could cite, but I shall cite only one, a quite recent one. Franz Hesse, a truly distinguished biblical scholar, at the conclusion of an excellent commentary on the book of Job, finds it necessary to note that its sublime message is, after all, obsolete for Christians, since it appears in a part of the Bible that is not normative for Christianity.[40] Such a position would be impossible for one sensitive to the Catholic tradition, not only because of papal statements such as the *Mit brennender Sorge* of Pope Pius XI, which reaffirmed the *Heilspädagogik* of the Old Testament and was sent to the German bishops in the heyday of Nazi superstition;[41] but more important, because of an unbroken succession to which one feels he belongs, a succession that stretches from its earliest written records, perhaps in the Muratorian canon, down to its latest, such as the *Dei Verbum* of Vatican II.

Let us conclude. If the *norma normans* of Scripture on the official teaching of the church is to be measured ideally in terms of the immediate effect produced on it by the consensus of its exegetes, we are not as advantageously positioned in this present century as was the church of the Fathers or of the Middle Ages. The adversary condition between authority and scholarship still exists to some degree, manifested now not as much in repression of the one over the other as in the former's choice to ignore what the latter may be saying. Any number of doctrinal and moral issues presently troubling the church could be alleviated and not further confused were the "teaching" church only more receptive to the words of those who manifestly possess from the Spirit the charisma of teaching rather than of government. Still, in the long run there is much more reason to rejoice than to despair. The same issue of *L'Osservatore Romano* which reports the censure of Hans Küng also contains an allocution of the currently reigning Roman pontiff on the Yahwistic creation story of Genesis 2–3 which depends on an impeccably critical appreciation of the biblical text. The Council of Trent, which desiderated a restoration of a Latin Bible *quam emendatissime,* corrected to the extent possible, for the liturgical and doctrinal usages of a Latin church, has, in this last year, finally seen the realization of its aspirations in the appearance of a new Vulgate—an entirely new version done by an international corps of scholars from the original texts, mandated by Pope Paul VI and promulgated by Pope John Paul II. In turn, this has pursued a policy inaugurated by Pope Pius XII, who never cited a biblical text in Latin unless the translation was in accord with the original. And it would be hard to imagine, despite all the prognoses that dictated otherwise, a more satisfactorily scriptural emphasis in the official utterances of any Christian body than that which emerged in the decrees of the Second Vatican Counil. Such is providence, an even more trustworthy companion than scholarship.

PROTESTANTISM IS, by its very nature, more diffuse than either Judaism or Roman Catholicism. As a result, the diversity of approaches used to interpret the Bible within Protestant thought demonstrates well the pressures and problems of modernity itself. Challenged by the results of modern biblical scholarship, the original (historical) and religious meanings of Scripture have been driven farther apart, despite the initial belief of Protestant thinkers that the two were mutually reinforcing. This dilemma has led to a wide diversity of responses, ranging from an emphasis on theological significance to an attempt to prove the Bible's historical veracity. —F.E.G.

Protestant Attitudes Regarding
Methods of Biblical Interpretation

DAVID H. KELSEY
DIVINITY SCHOOL, YALE UNIVERSITY

THERE IS NOTHING more dangerous than attempting to generalize about Protestants and their religious beliefs and attitudes, especially in the United States. There are very many important ways in which they are not one Community. Perhaps nothing brings this out more sharply than a survey of attitudes concerning different methods of biblical interpretation. It is a confusing scene. Protestant denominations, for the most part, have no official or authoritative teaching concerning the proper methods of biblical interpretation. If they have adopted positions related to the issue at all, they are committed to doctrine about the *nature* of Scripture—its authority, inspiration, and inerrancy. On these matters some denominations do differ. It would be a natural assumption that differences about the nature of the Bible would imply fairly clear-cut differences about appropriate methods of biblical interpretation. But that does not in fact regularly seem to follow. Differences among Protestants concerning methods of interpretation do not seem to correlate tightly with broad theological differences between denominations. Nor do they correlate neatly with broad differences in historical tradition. Heirs to "sectarian" traditions, such as Baptists, do not consistently stand opposed to heirs to "established church"

David H. Kelsey has used the King James Version for biblical references.

traditions, such as Episcopalians. One is tempted simply to conclude that in the Protestant community, anything goes. Nonetheless, there do seem to be discernible positions, and some Protestants who are like-minded on this issue tend to rally in support of their own positions in passionate, vocal, and organized ways that cut across the lines of tradition and denomination that otherwise tend to separate them. When this happens, the immediate occasion is usually some controversy of the day: the teaching of the theory of evolution in public schools, proposals to ordain women, proposals to constitutionally grant women equal rights, aid by church groups to revolutionary movements in third-world countries, the ethics of abortion. The challenge for this essay is to identify specifically the theological issues and theological reasons for differing views on methods of biblical interpretation which persist through and underneath these more immediate and practical controversies.

We can begin to see some order in this perplexing picture if we note first the views of the sixteenth-century Reformers concerning the proper methods for biblical interpretation. After all, the overwhelming majority of American Protestants believe themselves to be standing in some sort of continuity with the Reformation in this matter. But then second, it will be important to note two quite different kinds of challenges to the Reformers' views. A major reason the present scene is so confusing is that some Protestants seem to be preoccupied with responding to one, and some to the other challenge, but few, if any, systematically address both. Thus in the third major part of this essay, we can begin to sort out a typology of current Protestant attitudes toward different methods of biblical interpretation.

Views of the Sixteenth Century

In 1567, Matthaeus Flacius Illyricus published *Key to the Scriptures,* which has been called "the first methodical examination of the proper interpretation of Scripture" by a Protestant. Flacius was well trained in the scholarly tradition of Renaissance humanism and was self-consciously attempting to work out the implications for biblical interpretation of Luther's theology. Flacius laid down four rules:[1]

1. Ascertain how the original readers of the biblical text understood individual words. And that demands a command of Hebrew and Greek. "Without that, O Reader, you are necessarily dependent on the judgment of others, or you must guess at the meaning"!

2. Ascertain how the readers understand the sense of the passage as a whole that is imparted by the words of the individual sentences. "Only so can one avoid getting a false meaning from badly constructed sentences."

3. Ascertain how the original readers understood the "spirit of him who speaks"—"the reason, the understanding, the judgment, and the purpose [or *scopus*] of the speaker."

4. Ascertain how the application of any given passage of Scripture is to be understood. "For Scripture divinely inspired is useful for teaching, for clarification, for correction, and for instruction in righteousness. . . . This understanding is assisted usually by assiduous and devout reading and especially by meditation."

The publication date of Flacius' *Key*—1567—is symbolically important. Three years after John Calvin's death, and four after the end of the Council of Trent, it stands at the end of the period in Protestant thought dominated by Calvin and Martin Luther. Thereafter, Protestant theology would be dominated by the need to respond, on one side, to the theological attack of Rome's Counter-Reformation, and to empiricist and rationalist schools of philosophy on the other. If we look at Flacius' rules in reverse order, we can see that they sum up the principle teachings of the Reformers about Scripture and that they demonstrate their own implications for rightly interpreting the Bible.

"Ascertain how the application of any given passage of Scripture is to be understood," because Scripture is divinely inspired. In affirming that God inspired the biblical writings, the Reformers were utterly traditional. They repeated Christian teaching of long standing.[2] However, it is important to note Flacius' association of Scripture's inspiration with the question of its practical application. It was characteristic of the Reformers' theology to hold together as one work of the Holy Spirit the inspiration of the writers of biblical books long ago and the illuminating and transforming of persons' lives today. It is in this connection that the Reformers did make a distinctive claim. Scripture *alone* is authoritative for faith today. The heart of the Christian gospel, as Luther understood it, is that fallen human life can be transformed only by God's love, or grace (*sola gratia*). This becomes incorporated into our lives not through anything we accomplish by way of works or self-discipline, but solely by trusting that God loves and forgives us—by faith alone (*sola fide*). And the good news that this is so comes only through Scripture (*sola Scriptura*). Indeed, for Luther, it comes only through Scripture used actively in preaching.[3] One does not know how the Reformers would have responded had someone asked whether scriptural texts are intrinsically inspired simply in and of themselves, even if it should happen that God did not use them to transform anyone's life at all. The possibility of separating the inspiration of Scripture in the past from its practical application to human life today never seems to have occurred to them.

Here there are at least three implications for the interpretation of Scripture. First, the same methods are to be used in interpreting Scripture for theological as for homiletical purposes. Theology deals with practical "wisdom" rather than with theory, with the general nature and basis of the life of faith to which people are called by Scripture. Correlatively, Scripture is authoritative as a "witness to faith." Second, inasmuch as all its writers were inspired by the same God, Scripture is a unity. All interpretation is to assume that the Hebrew Bible and New Testament together make an internally consistent whole. Third, because all Scripture is inspired, it can be trusted to interpret itself. An obscure passage always can be interpreted in light of a clearer one.

"Ascertain how the original readers understood . . . the purpose of the speaker." Implicit in Flacius' third rule is a distinction between the words of a text and its purpose, or *scopus.* Each paragraph has its point which one needs to grasp in order to make correct sense of otherwise awkward or obscure sentences. But every paragraph is part of a larger unit—a set of chapters, say, or an entire book—which has a point as a whole. Indeed, all divinely inspired writings have the same basic purpose; that is what constitutes them as a unity. Luther and Calvin were acutely aware of the diversity of literary genre and of apparent subject matter within the canon: narrative, poetry, law, wise sayings, letters, oracles, and so on. But they held that all these, in slightly different ways, were "witnesses to faith," a phrase which was, as we shall see, shot through with ambiguity. Luther held that all genuine Scripture declares or implies a tension between God's *law,* before which every person is a hopeless sinner, and God's *gospel,* which proclaims God's unconditional gift of forgiveness. Between them, law and gospel always point to Christ, in whom God at once judges and forgives humankind. Calvin tended to see the Bible as an extended narrative account of a single connected history of God's covenant with his people, first on the basis of a promise, which evokes hope (the Old Testament), and then on the basis of the fulfillment of that promise, which evokes faith (the New Testament) centering on Jesus Christ, to whom hope looked forward and at whom faith looks back. This contention about the singularity of the Bible's subject matter carried two implications for biblical interpretation.

First, it gave the Reformers freedom to be critical of some books traditionally considered canonical. Luther noted, on stylistic grounds, that the Epistle to the Hebrews could not have been written by Paul and, in any case, contradicts the Gospels by declaring that after a person has repented, should he sin again there can be no second repentance. He noted also that the Epistle of James has no internal coherence and contradicts Paul's letters; that the Epistle of Jude is a copy of part of Second Peter; and that in the Revelation of John, "Christ is not taught or known."[4] Luther printed these four books separately at the back of his German translation of the New Testament. Calvin had such a low opinion of the

Revelation of John that he declined to lecture or comment on it.

Second, the Reformers' stress on Christ as the subject of all inspired Scripture permitted them to acknowledge "errors" in Scripture. The historian Reinhold Seeberg has pointed out Luther's acknowledgment of errors by the prophets, untrustworthiness in the historical narrative in Kings in contrast to narratives of the same events in Chronicles, and the possibility of question about details in the Gospel narratives.[5] Calvin was especially conscious of ways in which New Testament writers sometimes misquote or even apparently misinterpret Old Testament passages (e.g., Paul's dubious interpretation in Rom 10:6 of Deut 30:12, "Say not in thine heart, Who shall ascend?"; Matt 27:9 refers to *Zechariah* when *Jeremiah* clearly is meant).[6] And in commenting on Genesis 1:14-16, where the moon is referred to as one of the two great lights (along with the sun), Calvin, cognizant that astronomers recently had proved Saturn to be a "greater" light than the moon, has no qualms in pointing out that Moses (whom he assumes to be the author) has no interest in astronomical accuracy.[7]

The Reformers stressed that in inspiring the authors of biblical writings, God "accommodated" himself, both to the limitations of our capacities to understand God and to the limits set by the writers' personalities and historical settings. Though they never would lie or deliberately deceive, they may have been mistaken on details. But they did not err in regard to the *scopus,* or basic point, of their message: the gospel of God's reconciling love. For the rest, wrote Luther, "When discrepancies occur in the Holy Scriptures and we cannot harmonize them, let it pass, it does not endanger the articles of the Christian faith."[8]

"Ascertain how the original readers of the biblical texts understood individual words . . . and the sense of the passage as a whole." Flacius' first two rules sum up the *grammatical-historical* method of interpretation to which the Reformers were committed. This method assumes that a text has *one* determinate meaning. It is significant that to find that meaning, Flacius refers us not to the intent of the author, which is too private to know, but to the original *readers* of the text. One uncovers the meaning by attending to how individual words were understood and what grammatical rules were used in a community that spoke that language at a particular time and place. This method had become the mainstay of the "humanistic" study of classical literatures that had marked the Reform and Renaissance of university education of the day, and in which both Luther and Calvin had been trained. It amounted to applying to the Bible the same methods applied to secular writings. And it involved a rejection of a common medieval method which posited *four* different sorts of meaning in biblical texts: a literal meaning, which the grammatical-historical method uncovers, and in addition, allegorical, moral, and anagogical (in reference to last things) meanings. The Reformers complained that this method permitted the interpreter to read into the text meanings that simply were not there.

It is usually said that, by contrast, the Reformers insisted that only the literal sense of Scripture is its true meaning. But *literal* needs to be understood carefully. What they had in mind was the "natural" sense of the passage. So if stylistic and grammatical analysis show that a passage would have been seen as a moral parable or as an allegory by its original readers, then its literal sense would be its moral or allegorical sense. It would be absurd to insist that it be taken in a flat-footed and unimaginatively "literal" way. This focus on the literal sense of the text, and the reliance on the grammatical-historical method for discovering it, carried two implications for biblical interpretation. *First,* Scripture could not be understood as a collection of atoms of meaning, each taken in isolation. Adequate interpretation must examine the relation of any text to its literary context and interpret parts in the light of the general thrust of the whole. *Second,* interpretation must rely on a grasp of the historical setting of the text: Even though there may be similarities in the meaning of a given word today and its meaning at an earlier time, one needs to be aware that over time, words do change in meaning. So for example, while we may use *peace* to translate *shalom,* one should not assume that what we mean by *peace* is identical with what someone in the eighth century B.C.E. meant by *shalom*.

Two Challenges to the Reformers' Views

By definition, Protestants are Protestant because they share basic theological convictions with the Reformers—in particular, three themes: Persons are redeemed by divine grace alone, as it is appropriated by faith alone, where faith is called into being and nurtured by Scripture alone. It is striking that in the Reformers' view of Scripture and the proper methods for interpreting it, they saw no distinction between the religious and the literal senses of a biblical passage. For them, the sense that is important for faith (we will call that the *religious* sense) is its literal meaning when taken in the context of the entire divinely inspired and internally coherent canon. But that is a position no contemporary Protestant can share. The Reformers' views on Scripture have been challenged by too many questions they did not anticipate and about which their explicit teaching proved too ambiguous to allow clear inferences to be drawn. As I shall show in a moment, there have been two different sorts of questions. One sort was raised by the very methods employed in explaining the "literal" sense of Scripture. The other was raised by reflections about the issues involved in the act of "interpreting" any text, religious or secular. Taken together, these two kinds of questions have tended to force apart Scripture's religious and literal meanings. The Reformers simply assumed the identity of these meanings, but it is now necessary to *show* just how they can be related. The diversity of opinion among Protestants as to the proper methods of biblical interpretation in relation both to preaching and to theology can be traced to the variety of ways they have responded to this issue.

The Reformers, equating Scripture's religious sense with its literal sense, had called the literal sense its *historical* sense. "Faith," Luther had said, "rests upon history."[9] Calvin would not have disagreed. Both would have meant that the Scripture, which is sufficient basis for saving faith today, is a witness to God's saving grace as it has been present in history.

Accordingly, from the Reformation period onward, Protestant scholars studied Scripture by methods that seemed likely to identify its historical sense. Initially, these were simply developments of methods used by the Reformers themselves. Thus there were efforts to establish critical editions of the Hebrew and Greek texts. When there were differences among several manuscripts of the same text, there were efforts to establish the most accurate version. There grew up a body of scholarship which compared various New Testament passages with parallels in classical Greek literature and in Hellenistic-Jewish literature. There were careful studies of the literary styles of biblical writers and of the literary structures of their writings. These were literary methods; they were not yet historical methods, strictly speaking. They were perfectly valid, of course—indeed, they are frequently employed by students of the Bible study, often under the name *rhetorical criticism.* In the late sixteenth and through the seventeenth century, they were usually employed on the theological assumption that the Old and New Testaments are divinely inspired and consequently are a single coherent whole. So it was thought proper to assume that the literary context of each individual passage of Scripture is, finally, the same as that of the entire canon. Any part of Scripture must be interpreted in its context, but that context is not only its immediate context in a particular book by a particular human author, but also the context of the entire Bible.[10]

However, as the eighteenth century progressed, the phrase "historical sense of Scripture" came to be very ambiguous. It could mean, as it had for the Reformers, "its sense to its original readers as witness to God's grace." But it also could mean "its sense as a witness to us concerning the historical situation in which it was written." A biblical writing, after all, emerged from a particular historical situation and so can be assumed to bear evidence about some features of that situation. The ambiguity in the phrase was not noted at the time, but subsequently has generated a great deal of confusion. The ambiguity was brought out by the rise of the discipline of critical history as a distinctive intellectual undertaking with its own methods of research and argumentation. The discipline developed slowly during the eighteenth century, but with rapidly increased sophistication and cultural importance in the nineteenth century. Biblical scholars simply assumed that the new methods developed by historians were obviously appropriate for discovering the Bible's historical (that is, literal) sense. But the historians' methods carried with them a religiously all-important implication concerning interpretation of Scripture. Although some scholars had been tacitly assuming it for some time, this implication came to explicit clarity among Protestant scholars only at the end of the eighteenth century in the writings of J. C. Eichhorn, a prolific and immensely influential biblical scholar: Biblical writings can be adequately studied as to their historical sense only if one totally *disregards* the question of their inspiration. Accordingly, an individual text is to be studied not in a literary context consisting of the entire Bible, but in the particular historical context in which it was written. If one wants to discover the historical sense of Scripture, then it is only on this basis that genuinely *historical* interpretation of biblical writings is possible—that is, interpretation using the methods of the professional historian.

The use of historians' methods to interpret the Bible has been immensely fruitful. On one hand, it has focused on the histories of each of the biblical writings themselves. On the other, it has emphasized reconstruction of the historical situation from which each writing came, relying on evidence provided by the biblical texts and, where possible, on evidence outside the Bible as well.

Reconstruction of the history of the development of individual biblical writings dealt first with the New Testament—the Gospels in particular—and then with Old Testament writings. When the theological assumption of the unity of the canon is disregarded, the focus falls on the distinctive features of each writing. The differences are more interesting than the similarities. For example, it had long been noted that the Synoptic Gospels—Matthew, Mark, and Luke—are interrelated in a confusing way. Although they overlap, reporting some of the same material, they report their shared material in different ways and in different orders. And they each include material not included by the others. The most fruitful hypothesis, called *source criticism*, was that they either depended on some common but now lost previous source, or that two depended in part on the third and in part on independent sources. The evidence to support any such proposal would need to come from within the texts themselves. Proposals of a common and now lost source were made and defended as early as 1776 by the philosopher G. E. Lessing.[11] In 1797, J. G. Herder argued for an oral source lying behind the first written texts of any Gospel.

In the twentieth century this same general line of argumentation has been developed in two additional ways. *Form criticism* sought to identify a variety of short literary units in the Synoptic Gospels—highly stylized parables, miracle stories, wise sayings, and the like—the sort of thing oral traditions of religious communities relatively independently of one another preserve over long periods of time. The historical hypothesis is that the authors—or better, editors—of each of the Synoptic Gospels strung these units on a thread of narrative like so many beads. The narratives were organized in ways guided by the editor's theological opinions and may not have been associated at all with the individual literary units in their original settings. *Redaction criticism* has focused on the evidence in the texts of a series of redactors—editors who revised traditions in the light of new historical situations and new theological viewpoints.

So too, the traditional Jewish and Christian belief that Moses had written the Pentateuch (Gen–Deut) was challenged in 1670 by the philosopher Spinoza. Late in the seventeenth century, Richard Simon attempted to work out a literary history of the Old Testament, tracing the process of the growth and change of its various books. This kind of historical work was continued for a century and culminated in Johan Semler's epoch-making work, *Abhandlung von freir Untersuchung des Canons* (1771-76), in which he argued that it is a major historical mistake to interpret the Old Testament canonical writings as though they were a unified and closed whole. This opened the way to the first really thoroughgoing use of historians' methods in study of the Old Testament, Eichhorn's *Introduction,* which simply ignored the questions of the inspiration and canonicity of Old Testament writings. At the end of the nineteenth century, Graf and Wellhausen developed the hypothesis concerning the development of Old Testament writings that has, with modifications, continued to guide Old Testament research and exegesis ever since: that the present text of the Pentateuch is the result of a series of editings and reeditings, in which three and even four different texts were synthesized at widely separated points of time (viz., E and J, written during the period of the monarchy; D, which reworks the earlier two and adds new legal material [e.g., Deut] some time toward the end of the seventh century B.C.E.; and P, written in the fifth century B.C.E.). At the beginning of the twentieth century, Hermann Gunkel developed a theory about the nature and function of the oral sources that lie behind these documents, which has become widely accepted as a corollary to the Wellhausen hypothesis.

Reconstruction of the historical situations from which individual biblical writings originate first focused on the "historical Jesus." Attention to the diversities among the Synoptic Gospels raised doubt about the reliability of any of them as a record of Jesus' life. This led to a distinction between the religion *of* Jesus and the religion *about* Jesus. This distinction was drawn and ably defended (not, to be sure, to everyone's satisfaction) by the end of the eighteenth century.[12] And that in turn opened the way to efforts to reconstruct the historical Jesus, or perhaps better, the historian's Jesus—that is, an account of what could be affirmed with some degree of probability about the life of Jesus on the basis of a critical sifting of the available evidence. The first account of Jesus "that at essential points is historical" was published in 1829.[13] Early in the nineteenth century it was pointed out that it is a mistake to take the Gospels as either competent or incompetent histories. They do not belong to the genre of history at all. They are proclamations, confessions of faith that make reference to historical events which they do not attempt to chronicle. Probably more shocking, it had been persuasively argued that at the heart of

Jesus' teaching, and of the world-view of the earliest church, were vivid eschatological beliefs—expectations that history soon would end in most dramatic ways and that the final judgment of all humankind would commence. The New Testament, at least, was claimed to be culturally and intellectually very alien to modern readers. In the eighteenth century similar efforts were begun to reconstruct the earliest Christian communities. It was claimed that evidence showed important differences between the points of view of Christian communities in Palestine and those in the Greek-speaking parts of the Empire; and between communities in Jerusalem and those in Galilee. Both the quest for the historical Jesus and the quest for the most primitive Christianity continue to be flourishing enterprises, the former relying on form-critical methods and the latter on increased knowledge of the social history of the ancient world and of the sociology of religious groups.

Efforts at reconstruction of the history of ancient Israel and Judah developed greatly in the latter part of the nineteenth century with the rise of the discipline of archaeology. Archaeological research has been guided by evidence in the historical sections of the Hebrew Bible and also has been a way to attempt to confirm the accuracy of those narratives. In the eighteenth century there was a similar effort to confirm the Genesis prehistory narratives of Creation, Eden, and the Flood. The rise of modern geology in the nineteenth century, with its vision of an earth vastly older than had been imagined, and Darwin's powerful hypothesis of the evolution of the species, with its vision of a continuity of all forms of life, requiring enormous amounts of time to develop the complexity we now know, brought that to an end. It shifted attention instead to investigation of the function of those stories in the common life of ancient Israel, where they were reedited into the continuous narrative of the election and creation of the people of God.

The methods historians employed in formulating these hypotheses and the mounting arguments to support them generally relied on some important assumptions. Two may be noted here. One is the so-called *principle of analogy*.

Historians can assess the probability of a claim about an event analogous to other events that are familiar and well attested. For instance, a claim that a physical miracle has occurred—in particular a resurrection from the dead—must be declared beyond the competence of historical assessment. This does not by itself amount to a denial or decisive disconfirmation of the claim on historical grounds; it amounts, rather, to a disqualification of historians' methods as irrelevant to the case. But by the same token, it means a disqualification of the claim from the range of phenomena called historical. So if one is trying to find the historical sense of a biblical passage which reports such a miracle, one cannot hope to profit by using historians' methods. If historians' methods are taken to be the proper way to interpret the historical sense of the text, the most one can obtain is a reconstruction of the life and world-view of early Christian communities and, especially, the role such stories played in their common life. To be sure, the principle of analogy has not been without critics. Not all biblical scholars who attempt to use historians' methods agree to recognize the principle as a criterion of adequate historical argument. And theorizers about historians' arguments have continued to criticize it, even then they share the theological judgments of quite radical biblical scholars. But the great majority of scholars seem to have assumed the validity of the principle.

A second assumption was widely shared by historians, theologians, and philosophers: that the literal or historical sense of a text is its *referent.* Perhaps the classical formulation of this notion was provided by the eighteenth-century philosopher Christian Wolff.[14] Wolff held that there are two ways to interpret an unfamiliar concept: One can give a verbal explanation (*Worterklärung*) in which one describes the concept by listing some of its distinguishing characteristics— one gives the concept, in other words; or one can explain the subject matter to which the concept refers by showing how the object signified by the concept is possible *(Sacherklä-rung)*—one discusses the object behind the concept. Words are signs of thoughts; thoughts represent objects. One understands a concept only if one has known the object. If one does not know the object, no amount of verbal explanation (*Worterklärung*) will help. Now, most biblical scholars and theologians in the eighteenth and nineteenth centuries assumed that interpretation of the literal sense of Scripture meant that one must come to know its "object," the reality that lies behind it and to which it refers. And as we have seen, they assumed that historians' methods provided the right way to come to know that object.

When used to interpret Scripture, both the asumptions and the results of historical methods tended to drive apart the literal and religious senses of Scripture. The very notion of a "religious sense" in Scripture assumed, for Protestants, that Scripture contains a single meaning, which is by itself sufficient for faith. The object that is the referent of the religious sense is God's saving grace in history, notably in Jesus. The unity and coherence of the multitude of biblical writings referring to that object is a result of their having been written by identifiable prophets and apostles who were inspired by the same self-consistent and truthful God. The religious sense of Scripture was held to be one with its literal, or historical, sense. But there turns out to be an ambiguity in the word *history,* and when it is taken in the sense of "critical history," the results seem to undercut both the unity of Scripture and the sufficiency of Scripture for faith. Historians' methods fragment the canon. They disconfirm the notion that books taken to be canonical were in fact written by identifiable prophets or apostles or even, in some cases, that they were written by any one person at all (rather than by, for instance, a series of editors). These methods exhibit a welter of differing theologies in Scripture, a variety not easily reconciled. When it is assumed that the meaning of a text is its referent, they also raise a question about Scripture's sufficiency for faith. For the records are shown to be unreliable, and the referent is shown to be both harder to come to know and much odder than had been supposed. That raises the question whether these methods need to be supplemented by others that can help us winnow out something that faith can rely on. And the assumption of the principle of analogy finally separates the text from its object altogether, in at least one way that is crucial for Protestants. It declares the resurrection of Jesus of Nazareth, an event central to the religious sense of the New Testament, to be beyond the competence of the methods one needs to use to uncover the historical sense of the texts. No group of Protestants today escapes the need, which the Reformers never faced, to come to terms with this irony.

There is also another reason that Protestants today cannot simply restate the Reformers' views on biblical interpretation. A second kind of challenge to those views was presented by reflection on what is involved in the interpretation of any text. The result was that the very idea of interpretation itself was reinterpreted. The new understanding of *interpretation* was largely the work of Friedrich Schleiermacher, the founder of modern Protestant theology. Although he published his views early in the nineteenth century, they did not become influential until the turn of the twentieth. As we have seen, in the eighteenth century, interpretation of a text was a matter of letting the subject matter to which it referred control the interpreting mind, which, ideally, was receptive and passive before it. This involved two steps. First, following the sort of rules Flacius had laid out in the sixteenth century, one engaged in the grammatical-critical task, ascertaining how the passage would have been understood by its original readers. Second, one engaged in the historical-critical task: accounted for the fact that the text was written in the first place and traced the history of its development; explained the nature of the object referred to by the text (*Sacherklärung*); and, if that were a series of historical events, assessed the degree of correspondence between the document's report and the putative facts. Once the "literal" meaning of a biblical passage was explicated in this way, there was yet another step. Because there was a large time gap between the original setting of the text and the situation of the interpreter, one still needed to show the religious application of the text in the present. This understanding of interpretation remained dominant into the eighteenth century.

Schleiermacher, however, contended that verbal exegesis plus subject matter explanation do not add up to *meaning*.[15]

Interpretation finally is an art in which the life of the interpreter actually confronts and, in a way, penetrates the life of the writer. Any discourse is an expression of a process of thinking within its author. The act of interpretation involves a reversal, moving back from the discourse to the thought process it expresses. Consequently, interpretation has two sides. The first is a grammatical moment which parallels the traditional grammatical-critical step: One tries to understand the passage, with its own stylistic uniqueness, as an individual use of an entire language (e.g., Latin) that is universally and publicly used by a given society (e.g., Roman society). The second side involves one in an attempt to understand the creative process of the author that is expressed in the discourse. This is an art and involves an element of intuition or divination. The two aspects are dialectically interrelated, and the interpreter oscillates between them. Each serves to guide and check the other, and neither is ever completed once and for all. The result is that the interpreter relives the author's creative thought process that is expressed in the passage being interpreted, so that, as Schleiermacher once put it, one understands the discourse "first as well as and then better than its originator." Clearly, in this kind of interpretation, the interpreter is not merely a passive receptor but makes a major contribution out of his own life. By the same token, in this kind of interpretation, there is no distinction between the explication of a discourse's meaning and the application of it to one's life. To understand is to have one's life shaped in the very same way the author's life was shaped in the creative process finally expressed by the discourse.

The contrast between these two ways of understanding the interpretation of a document parallels an ambiguity in the Reformers' claim that Scripture is a "witness to faith." The Reformers understood faith to be a state or condition of certain human subjects. As such, it could be called a mode of subjectivity. On the other hand, just as sense experience, for example, is *of* something, so faith is always *in* something. Faith is in relation to an object. So, to say that Scripture is a witness to faith might be to say that it is a witness by faith to its "object"—namely, to the grace of God in history. That is the way the phrase is understood, at least implicitly, when interpretation of the literal sense of Scripture is understood in the eighteenth-century way. But to say that Scripture is a witness to faith might be to say that Scripture is discourse which gives expression to a mode of subjectivity; then interpretation is understood as Schleiermacher suggested.

As we have seen, when the task of interpreting Scripture is understood in the eighteenth-century way, the historical sense of the texts is explicated, but with the threat of totally divorcing it from its religious sense. When the task of interpreting Scripture is understood to involve all that Schleiermacher said it does, the religious sense of the text is grasped. It is grasped so immediately, indeed, that one therewith comes to participate in the inward movement of faith oneself. But this is done at the cost, it seems, of the texts' historical fact-claiming. Here too, in a way, religious and historical senses have been driven apart.

Current Protestant Attitudes

As we have seen, developments in biblical scholarship between the Reformation and the twentieth century exposed the fatal ambiguities in two formulas that were basic to the Reformers' insistence on the identity of Scripture's religious and literal senses: Scripture is a witness to faith; Faith rests upon history. The bewildering variety of opinions among contemporary Protestants as to the proper methods for biblical interpretation can be charted as diverse responses to the challenges these ambiguities pose.

The views of Protestants for whom this is an important question can be classified by a typology ordered on two coordinates. The horizontal coordinate, as it were, consists of the two senses of the phrase *Scripture is a witness to faith*. And the vertical coordinate consists of three different ways the sentence *Faith rests upon history* can be understood.

"History" as Sacred History

1. For some Protestants, *Scripture is a witness to faith* means that Scripture is a faithful witness to faith's object, the grace of God in history. However, while the history in which grace is present is part of world history, it is beyond the grasp of ordinary historical methods. It is a sacred history, knowable only by revelation received in faith. It has a sort of reality that is different from ordinary empirically describable historical events. If a miracle is an event contrary to and unexplainable by empirically based laws, then this is a "miraculous history." Here *Faith rests upon history* means that faith hangs or falls on whether, independent of Scripture, the sequence of events called sacred history actually took place. The Bible was written as part of that sacred history, and large sections of it report that history. Its meaning is that to which it refers—its subject matter. And that is either the objective reality of "sacred history" or the truths and moral laws derived from it.

Accordingly, these Protestants believe that Scripture is unlike any other writing—its authors were all inspired by God, and consequently, what they wrote is inerrant. There is room in this position for some disagreement over whether God's inspiration took the form of dictating the individual words each author used, or only the truths, which they then put into their own words. In any case, they feel that Scripture is without error in everything it says, regardless of the topic. Of course, this holds true only of the original texts, or autographs, written by the original authors themselves. During centuries of copying and recopying, errors have crept into the texts we now have. This amounts to a very strong reaffirmation of the sufficiency of Scripture as the basis of faith. It is a position rooted in the late sixteenth century, when Protestant theology was shaped as a response to the Roman Catholic Counter-Reformation. Part of the Catholic challenge was whether Scripture, by itself, was not too obscure and apparently inconsistent to be sufficient as a basis for faith. Does it not need, Rome asked, some authoritative interpretation?—which is precisely what the Roman Catholic Church's oral tradition could provide. To make their rebuttal as powerful as possible, Protestant theologians stressed that Scripture was perfectly capable of interpreting itself and that in its original, it was without error.

In the course of this polemic exchange, the Protestant

theologians and their Roman opponents came to share an important assumption about theology and faith. Theology is not as much reflection on practical wisdom for Christian living (as it had been for the Reformers) as a kind of theorizing. And *faith* in one sense of the term—as *personal trust*—is understood to depend on *faith* in a second sense—as *intellectual assent* to the truth of certain theoretical doctrines revealed by Scripture. Insofar as they shared these views, both Protestant and Roman Catholic theology in the late sixteenth century are usually described as Scholastic theology. In the intervening centuries, basically these same themes have been restated with increasing sophistication. They are widely held today and are defended by those theologians who stand in both Lutheran and Calvinist traditions and who usually are characterized as "conservative."[16]

There are clear implications here in regard to acceptable methods of biblical interpretation. Various methods of critical textual study are admissable and important since they go as far as they can toward recovering the original versions of the texts. And literary-critical methods are indispensable. But historians' methods of interpretation, which require, precisely as part of the method, that belief in the inspiration and inerrancy of Scripture and the unity of the canon be set aside, are simply inappropriate for such a text as the Bible.

2. The same attitudes toward the use of historians' methods of biblical interpretation are held by other Protestants, for whom *Scripture is a witness to faith* means that Scripture expresses the feelings and experiences of the person of faith. For these Protestants, too, the "history" that faith is based on is "sacred history." But sacred history is seen more as the history of miraculous transformations of persons' subjectivities, of lives reborn and hearts strangely warmed. Scripture expresses that transformation. It is the basis of faith today because it elicits the same experience of rebirth and warmth in people today. It is inspired and inerrant in regard to all topics on which it touches. Its literal and religious senses are the same—the sacred history of personal transformations to which it refers. To interpret Scripture is to grasp this subject matter, and that is done by using grammatical-critical methods and by opening oneself to the experience to which it refers. But given Scripture's inspiration and the superempirical status of the history it reports, historians' methods of interpretation are not appropriate.

These views are rooted in a movement called Pietism, which arose as a reaction to the high intellectualism of sixteenth-century Protestant Scholasticism. It stressed that Christianity is a religion of the heart, rather than of the mind, and focused theology on the experiential, rather than the theoretical aspects of faith. Nonetheless, it shared with Scholasticism the view that the religiously significant meaning of Scripture is its referent and that that referent is a nonempirical "history," located in world history but not identifiable with the history that the professional historian is able to grasp with his tools. This tradition, too, continues to be a vital one in Protestant thought and is represented by theologians who are heirs to the major American evangelical tradition, stressing the centrality of conversion and religious experience.

Both these "conservative" traditions keep the religious and historical senses of Scripture united by identifying the meaning of Scripture with a history, and then by understanding that history as something the professional historian is not able to study with critical-historical methods.

"History" as the Critical Historian's Reconstruction

1. For other Protestants, *Scripture is a witness to faith* means that Scripture is a witness to faith's object, Jesus of Nazareth, as he "actually lived." The history on which faith is based is history as reconstructed by the historian, using standard historical-critical methods to sift and organize the available historical evidence. "Faith" is the conviction that Jesus is the most adequate paradigm, or model, of the power of God's love to sustain life in the midst of evil; and that Jesus was the most complete instance of a human who lived in full trust in that love. Application to today is made by stressing that Jesus' life, as much if not more than his verbal message, was at once an example of utter trust in God and a call to us to live in such radical faith. It is of utmost importance to faith that Jesus' life actually did exhibit such trust; hence the quest for the historical Jesus also is of utmost importance.

The New Testament Gospels are the most direct witnesses to Jesus' life. But they are not eye-witness reports and so, at best, provide only indispensable evidence from which to reconstruct that life "as it actually was." But they do point to that life as the proper object of faith. The rest of the New Testament also witnesses to this object of faith, but somewhat more indirectly, by preserving ways in which earlier generations of Christians stated their convictions about Jesus. The Old Testament, from this point of view, is important because it provides the necessary background against which to understand the cultural and religious traditions that shaped Jesus and the way he was understood by his contemporaries.

Here religious and historical meanings are identical, in that they refer to the "historians' Jesus." To be sure, the historically reconstructed life of Jesus does not, by itself, generate faith—that is, the conviction that he is the most adequate model of God's love and of human trust in that love. It is necessary for the historical reality of Jesus to occasion a moment of inner illumination in which one unexpectedly finds one's otherwise incoherent life shown to be inwardly coherent. This is a moment of revelation. But it does not find different or additional meaning in the texts beyond that which is ascertained by historians' methods. It is rather a moment of application of that meaning to one's own life. And it depends on the historians' methods to interpret the texts and reconstruct the actual life of Jesus.

In rough outline, this attitude toward methods of biblical interpretation is rooted in certain nineteenth-century "liberal" Protestant theologies and is reflected in the viewpoints of the heirs to that tradition within Protestantism today.[17]

2. The same affirmation of historians' methods of interpretation as the best way to discover Scripture's religiously important sense is made by other "liberal" Protestants, for whom *Scripture is a witness to faith* means, rather, that it expresses faith as a mode of subjectivity.

In the nineteenth century, this was usually understood in

moral terms. To have faith was to have one's behavior guided by a moral vision and by moral principles expressed by Scripture. Historically, this is rooted in Immanuel Kant's contention that the New Testament expresses abidingly valid morality in a historically conditioned symbolism that must be interpreted allegorically.[18] It is not that the biblical writers necessarily intended to write allegories. But, as theologians later in the century argued, historical-critical study of the texts is indispensable because it can show how their stories and thought-patterns functioned in and for the religious communities to which they belonged. And it shows basically a form of moral life coming to naïve expression in what modern "enlightened" people would call myths and legendary narratives.[19]

On the contemporary scene, Rudolf Bultmann's proposal for demythologizing Scripture is a variation of this position, stated in existentialist categories.[20] Although his viewpoint has important parallels with the older "liberal" position, Bultmann is to be classified as a dialectical theologian and not as a liberal. As we shall see, he rejects both the liberals' equating of faith with a moral form of life and their quest for the historical Jesus. For Bultmann, "faith" as a mode of subjectivity is not understood in moral categories, but as "authentic self-understanding." One's self-understanding is the way one relates to oneself—the way one disposes of oneself or handles oneself in the world. It is authentic when it is marked by freedom from every preoccupation with proving oneself and by freedom to respond in service, in one's full particularity and uniqueness, to the neighbor's needs. The central Christian claim is that such authenticity comes as a response to kerygma—the gospel. The gospel is, at heart, the presentation of a possibility for our lives, a possible mode of self-understanding. We are called upon to appropriate it for ourselves, to live as those loved and affirmed by God.

This possibility is often expressed in Scripture, in literary units that are, in fact, mythic. Proper interpretation consists of recognizing them for what they are (their authors' expressions of faith's self-understanding) and then of restating the self-understanding in ways modern people can comprehend.

Historians' methods of interpreting texts, especially form-criticism, are indispensable means of ascertaining the religious sense of these texts. Not because they are the way to reconstruct the life of the historical Jesus (Bultmann held that to be virtually impossible), but rather because they identify the literary units that express self-understanding and recover the way such units functioned in the communities where they were first used. They enable us to reconstruct "Christian subjectivity" as it actually was at the beginning of the Christian movement. This is most important since it is normative for Christian self-understanding today. Other more radical theologians have argued that these texts understood in this way would have important religious sense, even if the historical Jesus in fact turned out not to have exemplified this particular form of self-understanding himself.[21] In both cases, whether more radical or less, the task of interpreting Scripture's religious sense is understood in Schleiermacher's way. Its religious sense is the lived experience or self-understanding it expresses. Its religious and historical meanings are held together because only by the historian's methods can the significant literary units that make up the text be identified and their original function of expressing religious self-understandings be recovered.

"History" as Narrative

For a third group of Protestants, the history upon which faith rests is neither a special sacred history nor the historians' history; it is the narrative that constitutes the greater part of the biblical writings. Here there is an important change in ideas about ways to probe the meaning of Scripture. There is a rejection of the assumptions shared by the first four types of Protestant attitudes. The meaning of a text is not equated with that to which it refers. One does not find the meaning by uncovering the subject matter behind the biblical narratives, whether understood as sacred history or as historians' reconstructed history. Rather, the narrative itself *is* the meaning. To find that meaning, one must attend to the structure and movement of the narrative itself. It may be helpful to consider an analogy. The meaning of a traditional realistic novel is not a character or a group of characters outside and independent of the novel's narrative. One does not interpret the novel adequately by attempting to reconstruct them. And that is not because those characters possess a privileged kind of reality for which historians' methods are simply inadequate. It is rather because one can only discover the meaning of the novel's narrative by attending precisely to the details and structure of the narrative itself. It is through these that the narrative renders its characters and their interrelationships.

So too, in this view, with Scripture. Taken as an extended narrative, it renders an agent—God the self-revealing, God as Word. More exactly, it renders that agent in its interrelationship with human agents; and it renders human agents in their subjective response to God. It renders the history of their relationship, which is often characterized as a covenant. And therein it renders each of them in their differences from each other and in the asymmetry of their relationship toward each other. As the narrative presents it, God is always the leading partner in the relationship, never apart from his covenant partners, but always the initiator in all their interactions. This dynamic ongoing relationship can be only narrated; it cannot be systematically described. On this view, Scripture is simultaneously a "witness to faith" in both meanings of that ambiguous phrase. It renders both that which is faith's object, God the Word, and that which is faith's subjectivity, the way of being human that marks God's covenant partners. This history is the basis of faith today, in that "faith" is a response by which one so thoroughly appropriates the history as to see oneself and the world rendered in it; one comes to live "in" it.

Something like this view of Scripture probably is implicit in a very great deal of Protestant preaching, even that done by persons whose explicit theology locates them in one of the other four types. An enormous amount of preaching consists, in one way or another, of "telling the story," or parts of it, as a way to put persons' lives in a fresh light. This view itself has been given relatively little explicit formulation. The major exception, and it is monumental, is Karl Barth's *Church*

Dogmatics, especially the volumes on Christology, in which much of the material seems both to explicate this view and to employ it in doing theology.[22]

This stand holds a curious middle position among the other four types. As we have seen, it is totally different in one major respect: It rejects the view that the meaning of biblical texts is the subject matter to which they refer, and the corollary—that to reach Scripture's meaning, one must explain that subject matter. However, it shares with the liberal and existentialist types (Critical Historian's Reconstruction, 1 and 2) a rejection of the idea of a sacred history, which is basic to the conservative and evangelical types (Sacred History, 1 and 2). The reasons for the rejection are partly conceptual and partly theological. On one hand, it is argued, the concept of sacred history trades on an ambiguity in the word *history.* If the term *history* means anything, then historical realities are spatial and temporal and can be studied by historians' methods. What cannot be so studied cannot be called *history,* except in a meaningless use of the word. Adding *sacred* cannot correct that. On the other hand, the "history" is said to be the history of God's grace in human affairs. That claim is theologically subverted if it is denied that that grace is a spatial and temporal actuality. If it is, it can be interpreted by historians' methods. But if it is not, then grace is not truly part of human experience either. For human experience is, by God's creative act, always and inescapable, spatial and temporal.[23] Consequently, this fifth position holds that historians' methods are perfectly appropriate methods to use in helping to interpret Scripture. That is imporant because it brings with it full acknowledgment of the diversity and reciprocal tensions that exist among the canonical writings. Belief in the inspiration of Scripture cannot serve as the basis of biblical interpretation, nor can it impose limits on the range of legitimate methods of interpretation.

On the other hand, this position shares with the first two more conservative positions (Sacred History, 1 and 2) the contention that the biblical writings do constitute a canon that has a kind of unity. It is, to be sure, a different sort of unity from that assumed by the more conservative traditions. It is not the unity of logical coherence. It is rather a unity-in-dialectical-tensions. It is like the unity of a multitude of independent eyewitnesses at a trial more than the unity of a logical system. Although they differ and even contradict one another, they do, all taken together, give the only rendering we have of the characters of whom they speak. The grounds for this contention do not lie in the results of critical historical study of the texts. That would show only the undeniable diversity among the texts. It lies rather in the faith commitment of the Christian interpreter. It is as though it were an integral part of Christian subjectivity to construe this group of Hebrew and Greek writings as a kind of "whole" whose wholeness is constituted by its being an extended narrative.

Given this view of the canon's unity, the historians' methods, while not excluded, may turn out to be of minimal value. They serve to point up the diversity in the Bible. They help make the interpreter supremely aware of the way biblical writings are constructed out of smaller and heterogeneous units, and of the complexity of the ways in which they are interrelated. But the methods of historical critical study of the Bible do not, for this position, provide special access to its meaning—that is, to a reconstructable history outside and independent of the texts. So while they are not to be rejected, their helpfulness in discovering the religious and literal meanings of the texts is limited.

With this view of the canon, this position has its own way to hold together the religious and historical senses of Scripture. It is grounded in the faith-commitment of the interpreter. More exactly, it is grounded in faith as a way of taking life, taking it whole—faith as a "total interpretation." In this case, the *sort* of wholeness that life is seen to have is found precisely in the biblical narrative. So to interpret a text's historical sense—that is, as a narrative rendering God as an agent in his interrelationship with us as his covenant partners—is simply to interpret its religious sense.

Finally, it is important at the end of this survey to note that the ways in which a very great many Protestants go about interpreting the Bible escape the net of this typology altogether. Many religiously active Protestant lay people and clergy are largely indifferent to the issue of holding together Scripture's religious and literal meanings. Their practice is untouched either by the challenge of historians' methods or by that of opposing theories of interpretation. Along with all other Protestants, they interpret biblical writings mainly by using literary methods that would have been recognized and approved by Reformers and Renaissance Roman Catholic scholars alike. They are methods deemed as appropriate for preaching as for theology.

These people simply assume that the Bible is in *some* way the inspired Word of God. They are more concerned with learning how to live in its light than with formulating just how it is inspired. They do not necessarily reject historical-critical methods outright, and they have no theological stand concerning their appropriateness or inappropriateness. They simply ignore them. And when controversies arise, they tend not to be involved in any of the recognizable types of attitude on those matters with which less irenic Protestants identify.

Such simple believers may well be the salt of the earth. But their position should not be romanticized. Simple believing can also be complacent and self-satisfied. There is one thing that can be recorded in favor of raising people's consciousness about the importance and complexity of these issues: Grappling with them has a remarkable power to shake one out of dogmatic slumbers.

PART THREE
The Relevance of Scripture

INTRODUCTION

BORROWING FROM the terminology of classical rhetoric, Augustine asserted that God accommodated himself to the limitations of human comprehension; just as a parent necessarily speaks in words a small child can understand, so too, God's revelation in the Bible is presented in a manner appropriate to the audience addressed.[1] This is exemplified by the Incarnation in which the divine presented itself in human form. Jewish tradition contains a similar perspective in its observation that "the Torah speaks in human language."[2] These assertions are the necessary response to a growing recognition that Scripture appears to reflect a very specific time and place. Originating within the ancient Near East, the Bible seems to be in dialogue with that environment, not our own. Its poetry draws on ancient imagery; its polemics are directed against Canaanite idolatry. And the New Testament addresses itself most often to the concrete concerns of the early church, many of which have since ceased to be of direct importance.

The problem for religious thinkers is exacerbated by the fact that most contemporary religious communities rely on sources of truth in addition to the Bible. Biblical authority is upheld, but alongside that of other sources characteristic of our time. We choose most often, for example, to accept the positions of contemporary philosophy, the methodology of modern science, and the moral sensitivities of our age, even though conflicts with the Bible result. We must deal, therefore, with many facts: that we believe God to be all-good and all-powerful; that physicists and geologists can present proof that the universe is billions of years old; and that we are inclined to attach great worth to the individual—even though each of these facts deviates to one degree or another from the biblical point of view.

If our modern perspective offers its own set of "truths," which are not always in agreement with biblical teachings, contemporary religious thinkers have been understandably reluctant to choose between them. To be sure, there are those who reject outright the authority of the Bible precisely because they hold it to be an ancient document written by ancient people for an ancient world; others honestly admit that a commitment to the Bible forces them to deny any claims that are at odds with its statements. But most thinkers and the traditions they represent seek to find a middle course.

One route to compromise is through exegesis. We have already seen many nonliteral methods of interpretation, among them various allegorical theories such as those offered in an attempt to demonstrate why, for example, so erotic a book as the Song of Songs should be included in the Bible. Similarly, phrases like "the rising of the sun" are explained as metaphors, just as the seven "days" of creation can be understood as a poetic allusion to seven aeons. Oftentimes such positions rely on careful analysis of language elsewhere in the Bible where the nonliteral sense is more evident.[3]

A second approach to resolving the seeming contradiction between modern thought and the biblical text argues that only part of the Bible is true. Some would accord greater authority to certain sections—the Christian notion of a "canon within the canon" or the Jewish emphasis on the Torah; others look to levels of meaning, such as the doctrine of accommodation, with its implication that the underlying message is more truly divine than the specific words.

A third approach looks beyond individual texts to the thrust of biblical perspective as a whole. So seen, the meaning of any specific text is absorbed into a broader context, which is

Scripture's teaching. Thus the famous "eye for an eye" passage would not be treated simply as a statement of equivalent retribution, but against the backdrop of other ancient civilizations where it appears as an advance over more dire punishments.[4] The problems with other troubling doctrines can be minimized similarly by emphasizing the general purpose of a biblical teaching rather than its specific regulations.

While modern perspectives have created difficulties for contemporary religious communities, it should be recognized that careful reading and scholarly insight can also resolve apparent problems which are, in fact, the result of misunderstanding. It has been pointed out, for example, that Genesis does not present Eve as having seduced Adam and that her actions are in many ways more praiseworthy than his.[5] Comparisons of Pentateuchal law with that of neighboring societies has clearly demonstrated the values and priorities that make the biblical perspective unique.[6] Still, the resolving of some specific difficulties does not eliminate the problem itself. As long as we inhabit a world different from that of the ancient authors, we cannot expect to eliminate the possibility of "embarrassing" passages in Scripture; and if the Garden of Eden is not one of these, then perhaps we should consider the wars of Joshua or Paul's observations regarding women. The problem is not a finite collection of specifics, but rather the more general quandary of defining the Bible's role in shaping modern religious teaching.

Various approaches to this question are described in the following sections. In evaluating them, one should bear in mind several observations that have already emerged. Foremost among these is the centrality of the Bible, a position no tradition considered here is willing to abandon, despite the variety of problems it raises and the difficulty of defining precisely what that centrality means in practice. The Bible is perceived as the source of religious traditions. Modern Jews, for example, probably would be surprised to learn that a holiday such as Hanukkah is mentioned nowhere in Jewish Scripture, just as Catholics may not always realize that the

Immaculate Conception of Mary is not mentioned in their Scripture.[7] For us, the discovery that the Bible does not mandate all contemporary practices, or that it is, in fact, used selectively, is by now hardly surprising. As we have seen, the process of reconciling conflicting biblical texts and attitudes can be traced back to the time of Deuteronomy and the Chronicler. A developing community, as part of its dynamic, uses a common language to express its links both with its own past and among its diverse constituencies. Reliance on the Bible provides that common language and thereby contributes to the community's sense of identity.

It is also now clear that many of the problems we have examined confront all forms of both Judaism and Christianity and that the solutions often are similar. Many times, divisions within one tradition parallel those found within another, inasmuch as the paradox with which we began confronts Christian and Jewish thought alike—namely, that each of these religions is very different today from the religion it once was, as a necessary result of centuries of adaptation to ever-changing circumstances and problems. The reconciliation of this change is accomplished by expressing present values and commitments in terms of an ancient source. As the adult looking back in amazement at his or her baby pictures must confront the radical difference between the original and the present self, so too, Jewish and Christian thinkers see a vast gulf between the traditions' original and present realities. The appeal to Scripture serves to bridge this gulf as the traditions seek to find in what they once were the seeds of what they now are. That these strikingly different traditions share, for the most part, the same Scripture points clearly to their common origin. But like brothers and sisters who are raised by the same parents and draw from a common gene pool, they still must make their way in separate worlds far different from that into which they were born. Coming together in reunion, they may note surface similarities; but these cannot hide the years of individual experiences and aspirations which have also contributed to making them what they are. Christianity and

Judaism have developed and matured separately, even while cherishing their common biblical origins. If harmony of perception thus is sometimes difficult to achieve, this may attest not to the resistance of those striving to achieve it as much as to the difficulty of the task itself.

*WHEN JUDAISM WENT through its own
"Reformation" in early nineteenth-century Europe, the
appeal, like that among the early Protestants, was to the
Bible and, in particular, to the prophets who exemplified
the kind of religiously grounded ethical commitment that
was of primary importance to the reformers. Among the
justifications offered was the claim that the Bible's ritual
regulations were intended only as a means to communicate
a more important message to ancient man. From this point
of view, ethical monotheism was conceived to be the
essence of Judaism; and for many of those "moderns,"
old-fashioned customs interfered with the appreciation of
these more enduring Jewish values. The selectivity this
demonstrates is, of course, characteristic of the way most
traditions utilize the Bible; it emerges most explicitly in the
perspective of those who openly admit Scripture's human
origin and stress only those passages that conform to their
own sensitivities and concerns.   —F.E.G.*

The Hebrew Scriptures
as a Source for Moral Guidance

SHELDON H. BLANK
HEBREW UNION COLLEGE—
JEWISH INSTITUTE OF RELIGION, CINCINNATI

LET IT BE SAID that in our denomination, as Reform, progressive, liberal Jews, we read the Bible as a human document—human, but with deep insights and basic moral and spiritual values. We read the Bible reverendly, but we deal with it selectively, and it is in this manner that I will be treating it here. This approach permits us to appreciate much of what we find in these Scriptures and, at the same time, harbor reservations about certain other parts and persons, admitting that not everything or everybody in the Bible is wholly admirable. There are passages to which, approaching the Bible selectively, I shall not be pointing with approval and pride—actions and themes not germane to our topic: "The Hebrew Scriptures as a Source for Moral Guidance."

The Bible speaks with assorted voices. The moral tone is one among others—a persistent tone, but not without competition. There are indeed records of violence and deviousness. Cain slays Abel. A Shechemite rapes Dinah and, through deceit and trickery, her Hebrew brothers take massive revenge, receiving only the mildest of rebukes. With the apparent approval of the narrator, Jacob drives a hard bargain with his older brother and, abetted by his mother,

---

Sheldon Blank's biblical quotations are taken from the New English Bible, the Torah, and the Prophets, and sometimes are paraphrastic renderings of the Hebrew text.

dupes his aged father and robs the brother of a rightful blessing. With endless slaughter, the Israelites dispossess the inhabitants of the divinely promised Land.

No, we do not applaud and sanction every reported action of our people in Bible times, as, for example, the alleged atrocities committed by Judah and its king Amaziah as these are recounted in a passage in Second Chronicles (25:11-12): "Then Amaziah . . . led his men to the Valley of Salt and there killed ten thousand men of Seir. The men of Judah captured another ten thousand men alive, brought them to the top of a cliff and hurled them over so that they were all dashed to pieces" (NEB). The event is simply reported in these words as a bit of history. The suspiciously round and bloated figures (10,000, twice over) do lend a legendary cast to the account. But were it all sober reporting, we still would not look upon the doings with patriotic pride and admiration.

As with the narratives, so with the laws. We would hesitate to accept at face value the so-called *lex talionis,* the law of retaliation, the eye-for-an-eye principle (Exod 21:24). We might express our reservation in one or another form. We might simply say that times have changed, and with them our mores, and that we have other ways of dealing with cases of mayhem in our courts today. Or, as the Rabbinic sages did in Talmudic times, we might interpret away the offensive nature of the law by deciding that it only meant payment of compensatory damages commensurate with the severity of the injury. Or again, in a more sophisticated manner, we might explain the presence of the *lex talionis* in the Bible as scholars have done—an attempt to modify in humane fashion a more barbarous custom prevalent in the ancient Near East, by which injuries might be avenged "seventy-sevenfold."

Consider, as well, the *ben sorer umoreh,* the "wayward and defiant son who does not heed his father or mother, and does not obey them even after they discipline him" (New JPS). When, according to the law in Deuteronomy (21:18-21), his mother and his father lodge a complaint against him and he is judged guilty, the penalty is capital punishment: "The men of his town shall stone him to death." (If we look for them, we can find horror stories even in the Bible.) Let me assure you, however, that this is not now common Jewish practice (either Reform or Orthodox) and I venture to say that it never was. For what it may be worth, we note that the Talmud ascribes to an ancient sage the view: *lo' hayah velo' 'atid liheyot,* "It never was and never will be." "Why then is the law in the Torah?" they ask. And they say, "One may profit from the gruesome warning" (*b.Sanh* 71a).

No, as Reform Jews, we do not insist on the binding nature of every "law of Moses from Sinai."

One further reservation before we take up our question itself: We cannot go the whole way with the Bible in the matter of the position of women. Without question, the Bible pictures a patriarchal society, with descent reckoned through the male members of the family, from father to son.

In general, the role of women in the Bible, with a few important exceptions—Sarah, Rebecca, Rachel and Leah, Deborah, Ruth, and Esther—is minimal. The E.R.A. would have had short shrift in that early mideastern culture. But, to be sure, in antiquity—and not in the Bible alone—the patriarchal pattern was normative.

So, reservations aside, we now ask, In what ways and to what degree are the Hebrew Scriptures a source for moral guidance?

We probably will agree that the Bible is potentially such a source and that it has in fact been a moral influence in the western world. Has it not passed as the very Word of God? Remember with me, if you will, how the prophet Jeremiah describes the experience that sent him on his prophetic way: "The Lord put out his hand and touched my mouth, and the Lord said to me: 'Herewith I put my words into your mouth'" (1:9 New JPS). In the same manner, introducing the Ten Commandments, Moses, reputedly the greatest of the prophets, reminds his people: "I stood between the Lord and you at that time to convey the Lord's words to you" (Deut 5:5 New JPS). That is the pattern. God puts his words into the mouths of his prophets. Their speech passes as the Word of God.

One need not labor the point. The thought is many times

repeated and pervasive. The Bible speaks with divine authority: "Thus saith the Lord." This observation has a bearing on our question.

The words endured, and through millenniums they were read and taught and absorbed into the psyche of the western world. Children learned the Bible at the knees of their parents; older, in church and synagogue and school, they heard the Bible expounded and preached as sermon or midrash or lesson, until it became a part of their nature—like the new covenant "inscribed in their hearts." So, whether because even now we look to the Bible as the authoritative Word of God and therefore consciously adopt it obediently as our guide, or because it has entered our genes, so to speak, or helped to shape our superego and so is a subconscious element in our moral judgment, the Hebrew Scriptures have become a source for moral guidance.

Consider with me then the nature of this source within the Scriptures, and in particular within the Law, or Pentateuch, and the Prophets—and first, the prophets.

We recognize two major types of authentic prophets: prophets of challenge and prophets of hope. They differ markedly in their approach, but this they have in common— that the human condition shaped their messages. Sensing God's response to the then prevailing human condition, some prophets met man's despair with encouragement and hope; others met man's arrogance with rebuke. To a people defeated and assailed with self-doubt, captive and degraded, the unnamed prophet of hope during the Exile offered a sustaining therapy of promise and mission. But to the affluent unscrupulous lords of Samaria and Jerusalem, such eighth- and seventh-century prophets of challenge as Amos and Isaiah, Micah and Jeremiah, spoke grim words of judgment and warning. Yet the two types of authentic prophets had one agonizing need in common: the need to lead their people, whether by encouragement or by rebuke, into the way of life. That was the common denominator: Their people's survival was both task and goal.

But it is to the thin-lipped prophets of challenge, who came with grim threat and warning, that we look for moral guidance. Survival—the way of continuing life—was much on the mind of these prophets, as indeed it is on our own minds today. They looked toward Assyria, and in turn to Babylonia, to the foe that loomed from the North, and they asked, Would God indeed be adrift without Israel? We look at the proliferation of nuclear weapons and waste and nuclear power plants and plutonium, and we ask, Will there be a twenty-first century? And many of us would say with the Hebrew prophets, It is a human choice.

Review with me some familiar examples of the method and message of the prophets of challenge. In the eighth century, in a three-link chain of propositions, Amos put the matter clearly. He first phrased the human choice for that day's Israel as a two-word classic: *dirshuni viḥeyu,* Seek me and live (5:4b). Resolve the syntax of the two imperative verb forms *(seek me* and *live)* and hear God pleading with his people: If Israel is to survive—and that is God's ardent desire—his people must seek him. This is a clear statement, and yet not clear. The substance of the concept "seeking God" eludes us. How is one to "seek" God? And Amos does not help us with his next words; they only say what that seeking is not: "Do not seek Bethel, nor go to Gilgal, nor cross over to Beersheba" (5:5 New JPS). God is not asking for the annual pilgrimage to such shrines as Bethel, Gilgal, and Beersheba or the cult observances there. "Seeking God" is not that, but something else. God does not care much for "religion."

The second link, the prophet's second proposition (5:14 New JPS), is more helpful: *dirshu ṭov ve'al ra' lema'an tiḥeyu,* Seek good and not evil, that you may live (and that the LORD, the God of Hosts, may truly be with you as you think). So, in God's words through Amos, "seeking God" is "seeking good." Clearer, but are we satisfied?

"Good" and "evil" are abstractions, as even Amos must have sensed, because he continues at once with his third proposition, as clear as one could wish (v. 15 New JPS): "Hate evil and love good, and establish justice in the gate; perhaps the LORD, the God of Hosts will be gracious to the remnant of Joseph." *Haẓigu vasha'ar mishpaṭ,* establish justice in the gate—we know what that means. When *gates* are associated with *justice,* a Bible passage refers to the courtroom. The city gate was the forum where elders met to sit in judgment. There, indeed, we should find justice.

By this three-part progression, "seeking God" comes to mean "seeking good." And "seeking good" comes to mean regard for the rights of one's fellows, concern for the victims of rapacity and violence, the poor and the weak, widows, orphans, strangers—no white man's court, no rich man's privilege, an end to bribery and venality—in a word, *mishpat,* justice.

At about the same time, Isaiah brought an identical message. In stacatto phrases he listed the demands:

> *hidelu harea', limedu heytev;*
> *direshu mishpat, 'ashru hamos;*
> *shifetu yatom, rivu 'almana.* (1:16b-17 New JPS)

> Cease doing wrong, learn to do good;
> seek justice, correct oppression;
> secure the orphan's right, take up the widow's cause.

As for Amos, so for Isaiah; their standards are the same: Seeking God is doing good, and that "good" is the pursuit of justice.

Both prophets use the figure of the plumb line. To Isaiah, as to Amos (7:7-9), God says, "Justice is my taut line, righteousness the weighted plumb line" (28:17). Apply that standard to their people, and the two prophets agree: Measured by the standard of social justice, contemporary Israel had failed the test. That society was a condemned structure, condemned by its obliquity. Remote was the prospect of survival, and the two prophets screamed their warnings.

Directness, simplicity, pertinence characterize the prophetic word. The prophets had their targets and their aim was sure. An Amos pointed an accusing finger at a group of Israelite grain dealers gossiping in the sanctuary at Bethel:

> Listen to this, you who devour the poor of the land, thinking: "If only the new moon were over, so that we could sell grain, the

sabbath, so that we could offer wheat for sale, using an ephah that is too small and a shekel that is too big, tilting a dishonest scale, and selling grain refuse as grain. We will buy the poor for silver, the needy for a pair of sandals." The Lord swears by the Pride of Jacob: "I will never forget any of their doings." (8:5-7 New JPS)

Equally direct and sinister, an Isaiah might enter the home of a merchant prince in Jerusalem, look about him and say, "Your house is richly furnished with stolen goods; I pity your victims." (If you do not find these very words in Isaiah's third chapter, v. 14, you will pardon my paraphrase.) Speaking for God, the prophet might then ask, "What is this that you do, crushing my people and grinding the face of the poor?" His was no amiable parlor talk, and one may doubt that Isaiah was welcomed again—"A preacher should stick to religion."

Contemplating the inevitable consequences of the prevailing greed and injustice, Isaiah must also cry, Woe! "Woe to those that add house to house, field to field, until they dwell in solitary splendor" (5:8). On the same theme, at about the same time, Micah denounced unscrupulous land-grabbers in like terms: "Woe to those who plan iniquity and design evil on their beds; when morning dawns, they do it, for they have the power. They covet fields and seize them, houses, and take them away. They defraud men of their homes, and people of their land" (2:1-2 New JPS).

The prime woe-sayer was Isaiah. "Woe!" he said. "Woe to the winos and the carousers!" (5:11-12 New JPS). "Woe to those who are so doughty—as drinkers of wine, and so valiant—as mixers of drink" (5:22). Woe to those "who vindicate him who is in the wrong in return for a bribe, and withhold vindication from him who is in the right" (5:23). Woe to "those who write out evil writs and compose iniquitous documents, to subvert the cause of the poor, to rob of their rights the needy of my people; that widows may be their spoil, and fatherless children their booty" (10:1-2 New JPS). The indictment is simple and direct.

So far, in search of moral guidance from the Hebrew Scriptures, we have been drawing on words from the prophets. We could as well have quoted the Torah, or Law, the so-called five books of Moses, the Pentateuch. Amos' confrontation with the business-minded grain dealers at their service in Bethel brings to our mind the principle laid down in Deuteronomy, the law book of Moses:

> You shall not have in your pouch alternate weights, larger and smaller. You shall not have in your house alternate measures, a larger and a smaller. You must have completely honest weights and completely honest measures, if you are to endure long on the soil that the Lord your God is giving you. For everyone . . . who deals dishonestly is abhorrent to the Lord your God. (25:13-16 New JPS)

Did Amos buttress his rebuke on some such tradition óf a divine law revealed at Sinai? Or alternately, is the formulation of the law in Deuteronomy the precipitate of prophetic agitation? Do not ask whether the Law or the Prophets came first. At this distance that relationship is not significant. But do observe that there are many parallels between them. Priority is not an issue; the significance lies in the fact that both the Law and the Prophets contribute massively to the body of material that affords us moral guidance.

For some reason, for which I presume psychoanalysts have an explanation, the word *morals* in our western culture is associated mainly with sexual behavior, and I suppose there can be little doubt that our own sexual mores have been dictated largely by Bible precepts, found for the most part in the Law, or Torah. Numerous laws dictate proper behavior between the sexes. The law against adultery is one of the Ten Commandments, where we also find the prohibition, "Thou shalt not covet thy neighbor's wife." Incest and rape, homosexuality and bestiality, even transvestism, are specifically forbidden. To be sure, much of what is said in the Law and the Prophets about sexual morals probably stems from Israel's reaction to the fertility cult practices of the neighboring Canaanites. But whatever cultural factors helped shape these biblical precepts, the precepts have indeed largely shaped our healthy western sexual mores. And the Jewish family was stable in Bible times, even as we like to think it is today.

Although the Bible does not speak with a single voice, there is, as we have seen, a resolute, clear, and persistent moral overtone—the voice of Moses in the Torah and that of the challenging prophets among the *nevi'im*. These voices resoundingly demand entry into the heart of the oppressed and impoverished, the slave and the stranger.

Consider the frequent biblical expressions of solicitude for the stranger, the *ger*. Repeatedly in Deuteronomic legislation, as in the hortatory sections of Deuteronomy, the stranger appears, along with "the Levite who has no hereditary portion," the fatherless, the widow, as equally deserving of charity and consideration (e.g., 14:29; 16:11; 24:14, 17, 19, 21).

Mention of the stranger in such a context frequently calls forth the exhortation, "Remember that you were a slave in the land of Egypt."

So, for example, included in the Deuteronomic version of the Ten Commandments is the sabbath command (5:12-15 New JPS): "You shall not do any work—you, your son or daughter, your male or female slave, your ox or your ass, or any of your cattle, or the stranger in your settlements, so that your male and female slave may rest as you do. Remember that you were a slave in the land of Egypt and the Lord your God freed you from there."

Examples are numerous:

> You shall not wrong a stranger or oppress him, for you were strangers in the land of Egypt. (Exod 22:20 New JPS)

And again:

> You shall not oppress a stranger for you know the feelings of the stranger, having yourselves been strangers in the land of Egypt. (Exod 23:9 New JPS)

Or these:

> When a stranger resides with you in your land, you shall not wrong him. The stranger who resides with you shall be to you as one of

your citizens; you shall love him as yourself, for you were strangers in the land of Egypt. (Lev 19:33 New JPS)

You must befriend the stranger, for you were strangers in the land of Egypt. (Deut 10:19)

Our Jewish home service for the Passover echoes this thought: "Generation after generation, each person must regard himself as if he personally had gone forth from Egypt." It says, "he personally." I am charged—I personally—to identify empathically with a victim from another age: to suffer with him the pain of oppression, exult with him in the breath of freedom, eternally remembering that I too was a stranger and a slave in the land of Egypt and that the Lord my God freed me with an outstretched arm.

Will you accept my suggestion that here we have a paradigm—a moral paradigm? Sensitized by history, we answer to the needs of the "huddled masses." Moved by a sensitive nature, we adopt the needy and the victimized as objects of personal concern.

A paradigm. Note the kinship with the words that Jesus called the second greatest commandment (Matt 22:39): *ve'ahavta lere'akha,* and you shall love your neighbor; *kamokha,* [he is] like you—your counterpart (Lev 19:18). As with the stranger and the slave, identify with your *rea',* your neighbor; *kamokha,* he is like you.[1]

The paradigmatic "Remember that you were a slave in the land of Egypt," and its companion piece, "Love your neighbor, he is like you," form high spots in the moral code of the Hebrew Scriptures.

According to the order of the books in the Hebrew Bible, the *ketuvim,* Writings, come last, after the *nevi'im,* Prophets. The Writings include such books as Psalms, Job, Proverbs, and smaller books—the Song of Songs, Ecclesiastes, and others. Our survey of the moral element in Scripture would be incomplete without a sampling of such material in these books—an example from the Psalms, and one from the masterpiece among the books of Wisdom, the book of Job.

If we ask, What (according to the Bible) is the basic

religious demand? What indeed does the Lord require of us?—almost as a reflex, we answer with the prophet Micah, "Only to do justly, to love mercy, and to walk humbly with your God."

In Psalm 15, a psalmist-educator asks the same rhetorical questions in poetic form and proposes quite similar answers. He begins his moral proposition with a search for the essence of his religion:

> Lord, who may stay in Your tent,
> who may reside on Your holy mountain?

And his ready answer is:

> He who lives without blame,
> who does what is right,
> and in his heart acknowledges the truth;
> whose tongue is not given to evil;
> who has never done harm to his fellow,
> or borne reproach for [his acts toward] his neighbor,
> for whom a contemptible man is abhorrent,
> but who honors those who fear the Lord;
> who stands by his oath even to his hurt;
> who has never lent money at interest,
> or accepted a bribe against the innocent . . .

For this teacher of righteousness, the author of this psalm, the ethical dimension is not simply the essence of religion; it confers stability:

> The man who acts thus shall never be shaken. (New JPS)

The thirty-first chapter of the book of Job offers a similar compendium of social ethics. In the most emphatic terms Hebrew rhetoric affords, Job denies that he has breached the moral code in any particular. As a rhetorical device, he violates the "word taboo" and specifies the almost universally suppressed details of those curses he takes upon himself if, as he means convincingly to deny, he has indeed committed any of the listed offenses. It is this list that concerns us. In good part, as phrased in the New English Bible, it reads as follows:

I swear I have had no dealings with falsehood
and have not embarked on a course of deceit. . . .
If my heart has been enticed by a woman
or I have lain in wait at my neighbour's door . . .
if I have ever rejected the plea of my slave
or of my slave-girl, when they brought their complaint to me . . .
if I have withheld their needs from the poor
or let the widow's eye grow dim with tears,
if I have eaten my crust alone,
and the orphan has not shared it with me . . .
if I have seen anyone perish for lack of clothing,
or a poor man with nothing to cover him,
if his body had no cause to bless me,
because he was not kept warm with a fleece from my flock,
if I have raised my hand against the innocent,
knowing that men would side with me in court . . .

These conditions, these "if" clauses, make up the greater part of the complex protasis of Job's involved oath of clearance. Assuming the operation of a principle of retributive justice, if he had been guilty of any of these offenses, he could have understood it, then, if such disasters befell him, as he then stipulates in the conclusion, the apodosis of his oath:

[If I have been guilty of any of these offenses]
may another eat what I sow,
and may my crops be torn up by the roots! . . .
May my wife be another man's slave,
and may other men enjoy her. . . .
May my shoulder-blade be torn from my shoulder,
my arm be wrenched out of its socket!

The picture seems to be taking form. In the early strata of the Law and the Prophets, basic moral principles were laid down. God is just, and justice is his prime demand—not justice as a vague abstraction, but as applied in the daily affairs of men, to strangers as well as to the home-born.

By the end of the prophetic movement—after the Babylonian captivity, which scholars speak of as the formative period of the religion called Judaism—the pieces could be assembled as a pattern. Through the voice of the late anonymous author of a chapter near the end of the book of Isaiah, God speaks, condemning gestures of fasting and self-mortification in favor of moral living:

> Is not this what I require of you as a fast:
>   to loose the fetters of injustice,
>   to untie the knots of the yoke, to snap every yoke
>   and set free those who have been crushed?
> Is it not sharing your food with the hungry,
> taking the homeless poor into your house,
>   clothing the naked when you meet them
>   and never evading a duty to your kinsfolk? . . .
> If you cease to pervert justice,
> to point the accusing finger and lay false charges,
>   if you feed the hungry from your own plenty
>   and satisfy the needs of the wretched,
>   then your light will rise like dawn out of darkness
>   and your dusk be like noonday;
>   the Lord will be your guide continually. (Isa 58 NEB)

It is fairly clear, this description of the kind of moral living that would satisfy divine demands and make survival possible. But let us look now, first in one direction, then the other. First, look back at the words of the eighth- and seventh-century prophets and their abundant parallels in the laws of Moses. Note that this late chapter in Isaiah reads like an individualized precipitate of the moral demands of those earlier sources. A religious Jew will build his life according to this pattern prefigured in the Law and the Prophets.

Now look forward at the somewhat later life-pattern drawn by the authors of Psalm 15 and Job 31—the psalmist's picture of the one who may reside securely on God's holy mountain and, too, Job's self-portrait as a moral and deserving man—and again observe the broad similarity with the description of God's moral demands in Isaiah 58. Isaiah 58 forms a link between the earlier prophets and lawgivers, and the passages from Psalms and Job.

The conclusion seems to be justified: By the dawn of what is known as Judaism, in the early postexilic period, a model and a standard had evolved. If I were to dramatize the thought, calling this development the birth of the social conscience of western man, that would be an overstatement—and yet not wholly wide of the mark.

With all the proper reservations, we may say that there has been, and to some extent still is a kinship between prophetic religion and historic Judaism, with its current manifestation in Reform. With roots deep in the soil of the Hebrew Scriptures and nourishment from developing Rabbinic tradition down the ages, Reform Judaism has a powerful commitment to social justice and human rights. The Hebrew Scriptures have served us as a source for moral guidance.

Early in its history, near the beginning of the nineteenth century, Reform liked to call itself, perhaps somewhat arrogantly, Prophetic Judaism. Our commitment has been both individual and institutional. As for individuals, to be sure, the intensity of this commitment has varied from person to person; but it is statistically evident, I should think, that Jews, be they Reform, Conservative, or Orthodox, are disproportionately well represented on the rosters of sponsors of liberal causes in the interest of humanity. Jewish philanthropists, too, give liberally of their means to share with the needy and relieve the world's hunger.

This is not said with self-praise and complacency. With self-reproach, we admit to ourselves that we do too little. Our moral sense still draws nourishment from Bible soil, and the Bible word still disturbs us. The Bible serves as a motive force, a call to nobler living.

RATHER THAN VIEWING the Bible as a divine instrumentality, one can perceive it as a collection of those documents in which the believer sees God's will. From this point of view, Scripture becomes an expression of the Community's own ideals and aspirations, codified in those books accepted as authoritative. As the Community itself continues to exist and develop, it looks back to the spirit of the Bible—to the whole, rather than to individual, isolated texts—to help it confront new problems and concerns. For Roman Catholicism, with its clearly delineated organizational structure, this is a particularly appropriate means to see in Scripture an integration of its adherents' diverse perspectives, out of which a common set of priorities and commitments can be identified.   —F.E.G.

Catholicism as an Integrationist Perspective

RICHARD P. McBRIEN
UNIVERSITY OF NOTRE DAME

THE CATHOLIC CHURCH does not have an official position on the applicability of Scripture to modern life. Its understanding of the relationship must be inferred from the way the church addresses other important theological relationships and from the ways it actually uses Scripture for moral guidance.

There is no doubt that the Catholic tradition has always insisted upon the close connection between the Bible and human existence. The Catholic view, however, consistently has excluded two extremes: the left-of-center position which implies that Scripture is, for all practical purposes, a charter for social and political revolution (i.e., the biblical Word of God speaks only of liberation from economic oppression); and the right-of-center position which insists that the biblical Word of God has nothing at all to do with social, political, or economic issues, except perhaps as a pointed critique of conventionally liberal approaches to such issues.

This tendency to see virtue always as standing between two extremes (*in medio stat virtus*) is entirely characteristic of Catholic approaches to theological questions. For the Catholic tradition, the premise is never faith *or* reason, but reasoned faith, and faith illuminated by reason.[1] It is never

---

Richard P. McBrien has used The New American Bible for his Scripture references.

nature *or* grace, but nature radically transformed by grace, and grace building on nature and presupposing it. It is never law *or* gospel, but law informed by the gospel, and the gospel as a law of love and responsibility. It is never authority *or* freedom, but authority in the service of freedom, and freedom dependent for its exercise—even its very survival—on the protection of lawful and just authority. It is never divine initiative *or* human effort in the coming of the kingdom of God, but divine and human collaboration for the sake of the kingdom. And for the Catholic, neither is it Scripture *or* tradition, but Scripture as a privileged form and expression of tradition, and tradition, among other things, as the gradual unfolding of the church's understanding and interpretation of the biblical Word of God.[2]

The same kind of integrating approach characterized the work of Catholic bishops at Vatican Council II. When providing an official title for the major pastoral constitution *Gaudium et Spes (Joy and Hope),* the council fathers were faced with a choice between "The Church *and* the Modern World" and "The Church *in* the Modern World."

The former reflected a sectarian and Protestant view of the church as a small, often beleaguered community surrounded by an alien and hostile world. Such a community's charge is to remain pure and undefiled and to keep its own members faithful to the gospel. The world must become the church. The church, on the other hand, has no mandate to remake the world. Indeed, the World Council of Churches meeting in Geneva in July 1966 *did* use the conjunction *and* in the very title of its conference on Church and Society, in order to stress the opposition, or "paradoxical tensions," between the two.

The adoption of the preposition *in* reflected a Catholic view of the church. The church is not the non-world; rather, it is that part of the world which proclaims and celebrates the Lordship of Jesus and the coming of the kingdom of God. The church is called upon to convert both itself and the rest of the world. Sin and virtue know no ecclesiastical boundaries. Sin is in the church and in the world at large. The church must face and confront it everywhere. But virtue also is in the church and in the world at large, and the church must sustain and celebrate it everywhere.

The Second Vatican Council, therefore, adopted the only course open to it if it intended to remain faithful to the long tradition of Catholic theological and social thought. *Gaudium et Spes* is, in fact, known by its official title, the *Pastoral Constitution on the Church in the Modern World.*[3]

A church with so fundamentally an integrationist rather than a sectarian orientation understands and uses sacred Scripture accordingly. The biblical Word of God is not simply a word about this material world, nor is it simply a word about the next utterly spiritual world. The biblical Word of God is addressed to us in this world, but always for the sake of the kingdom that is the destiny not only of each of us as individuals, but also of the whole world. It is a world that God created, loves, redeemed, and has destined for future glory.

This Catholic integrationist perspective informs all that church's views. Catholics, unlike sectarians of every sort, insist upon the universality of this saving love and redemptive activity of God in Jesus Christ (1 Tim 2:4; 4:10). Salvation is for all, even if they never can bring themselves to confess the Lordship of Jesus, for it is not the one who says "Lord, Lord" who will enter the kingdom of heaven, but he and she who do the will of God (Matt 7:21).

The Integrationist Perspective as Kingdom-Oriented

This integrationist approach, rooted in the Catholic understanding of sacramentality, is nowhere more evident than in the Catholic tradition's view of the kingdom of God.[4]

It also must be said at the outset that no reality or symbol is so central to the Christian faith as the kingdom of God. It was the heart and core of Jesus' proclamation and ministry, and it is therefore the key theme (we might say the *integrating* theme) in all moral discourse and action.

If one is to understand how the Catholic tradition interprets sacred Scripture and applies it to the modern world, one must understand how the Catholic community perceives the reality of the kingdom of God.

Again, the Catholic approach, articulated so forcefully at Vatican II, excludes the two extremes: the one, which assigns no significance at all to human effort; and the other, which sees the kingdom as the natural culmination of human effort. The council rejected both views: "Earthly progress must be carefully distinguished from the growth of Christ's kingdom. Nevertheless, to the extent that the former can contribute to the better ordering of human society, it is of vital concern to the kingdom of God."[5]

First, what is the kingdom of God? Second, what does it have to do with the church and with its reading of sacred Scripture?

The kingdom of God is the reign, or rule, of God. God reigns, of course, wherever God's will is operative. As Christians, Catholics believe that the will of God has never been more fully disclosed than in the person, the proclamation, the ministry, and the death and resurrection of Jesus Christ. Catholics do not insist that the will of God is available only in Christ. Rather, it is in Christ that the will of God is focused, or italicized.

The kingdom of God therefore comes into being wherever the gospel of Jesus Christ is realized, even if only implicitly (see Matt. 25:31-46). To use slightly different terms: The kingdom of God is the redemptive presence of God—reconciling, renewing, healing. And it is the presence of God as the power which makes community possible.

The kingdom is both process and end product. It is a *process* in that God is ever present—ever struggling, so to speak—to break through the barriers of sin. The final kingdom has not yet been achieved. We are still on the way. We are a pilgrim people.

The kingdom of God is also a *product*—that is, even though it is still essentially in process and therefore unfinished, it is also present here and there, already fulfilled, however tentatively and imperfectly, in various persons, groups, institutions, and the like.

This kingdom of God, which is at once a process by which God reigns and a product of God's reigning presence, possesses a threefold temporal character. It is a past, present, and future reality.

The kingdom of God has entered our history in the *past* wherever there has been genuine obedience to the will of God and, flowing from that obedience, a genuine transformation of individuals, groups, and institutions. The kingdom of God already has been disclosed in a new and definitive manner in Jesus Christ.

The kingdom is also a *present* reality. Our God is not a distant God. God's powerful presence touches us and our world even now. The God of sacred Scripture, who intervened on our behalf in the past, is the living God, the God who still effects new life and reconciliation.

Finally, the kingdom of God is a *future* reality. It is the coming reality, the reality that is *not yet*. The final kingdom of God will be given and manifested in all its glory at the end when Christ will hand it over to the Father (Matt 24:36; 25:31-46; 1 Thess 5:2; 2 Thess 2:1-8; Rev 20:11-15; 22:12, 20).

The whole work of Christ is unintelligible apart from his proclamation and practice of the kingdom of God.[6] And so, too, is the mission of the church, which embodies and carries forward this work of Christ sacramentally. Just as Jesus came to proclaim the kingdom of God in word and in celebration (one cannot discount the importance of his feasting with sinners as a sign of the kingdom's universality, for example), so must the church. And just as Jesus personified the kingdom in his very person, so must the church corporately personify it in its very community. And just as Jesus established and expanded the kingdom of God by his works, so too must the church commit itself to the coming of the kingdom.[7]

When the church reads sacred Scripture, therefore, it is not reading some alien document which comes from outside or from "above" and speaks of realities foreign to the church's consciousness and experience. The Bible is the church's own collection of works. It is the church that, over the centuries, has determined which books were inspired and which were not; which should belong to the canon, or official list, and which should not. Furthermore, the Bible is preoccupied always with the kingdom of God—with the redemptive activity of God on our behalf and with God's summons to us to participate in this historic redemptive process.

To respond to this call, however, we first must acknowledge our own need for the healing and forgiving presence of God. We must see how, in fact, we have managed to block and frustrate the divine presence in ourselves and in those around us. This means that each of us is called to a change of heart, to a new consciousness, to conversion (Mark 2:10, 17; Acts 2:38).

The Bible tells always of the kingdom of God, of its demands upon us, and of its promise of fulfillment in the end. Can the church, therefore, fail to recognize that the Bible is the church's own reflection on the kingdom of God and on its moral requirements? How else did the Bible come to be awritten, except as the attempt of Israel and of the church to formulate their awareness of the presence and the call of God in history?

And since the kingdom of God is as broad and as overarching as the whole cosmos, and since the will of God is sovereign over all that is or ever was or ever will be, there is no moral issue—of an individual or social nature—that is not somehow related to our understanding and practice of the kingdom.

Does the Catholic Church draw upon sacred Scripture for its ethical judgments and pronouncements? Of course it does, and of course it must. This is not to claim, on the other hand, that the manner in which it interprets and applies the scriptural message always meets the highest standards of biblical and theological scholarship. On the contrary, the Catholic Church too often in the past has used Scripture merely as an arsenal of proof texts with which to support arguments and conclusions already arrived at long before the Bible was taken in hand. Nor has fundmentalism been foreign to the Catholic experience, least of all today, with the emergence of various forms of charismatic and/or evangelical Catholicism. But these are aberrations, recognized as such by Catholic scholars and pastoral leaders alike.

Scripture and the Modern World:
Applications of the Integrationist Perspective

I will provide here specific examples of Catholic moral teaching which draw upon and apply sacred Scripture in the realm of both individual, or personal, morality and social morality.

First it must be said that sacred Scripture does not provide ready-made solutions to world problems. When Catholics turn to the Bible for guidance on matters of individual and social morality, it is not with the expectation that this inspired source will yield specific answers to specific ethical questions. Instead, one discovers a universe of values, providing a context within which particular moral issues can and must be addressed.

Here again the Catholic tradition steers a middle course between one extreme, which sees no relationship at all between the biblical message and the modern world, and another, which sees the Bible as a blueprint for the moral reconstruction of individuals and the world alike.

Catholic Social Doctrine

The church's social doctrine is to be distinguished from the social implications of the gospel. The social doctrine is a clearly discernible body of official teachings on the social order in its economic and political dimensions. It is concerned with the dignity of the human as created in the image of God, with the rights and duties which protect and enhance this dignity, with the radically social nature of human existence, with the nature of society and of the state, with the relationship between society and state (balancing the principle of subsidiarity and the principle of socialization), and with voluntary associations (e.g., labor unions) which serve as a buffer and a bridge between state and society.

Catholic social doctrine, as such, did not exist before the end of the nineteenth century, which is not to say that the Catholic Church expressed no official interest in or concern for the world outside the sanctuary until Pope Leo XIII's encyclical, *Rerum Novarum* (On the Condition of the Working Man), in 1891. But not until that time did the church begin to articulate in a consciously *systematic* manner a theology of social justice and all that it implies. This is not to say that this theology was well integrated with the rest of theology, particularly with ecclesiology. It was not. Little attention, in fact, was paid in the social teachings of Leo XIII, Pius XI, and Pius XII to the forging of a clear link between the social ministry of the church and the nature and mission of the church. That link was not forged until Vatican II.

Catholic social doctrine is not a blueprint for the reform of the world. It is rather a broad theological and philosophical framework of social analysis. Thus far, it has been developed in three stages.

Stage one consisted of the church's response to the problems posed by the Industrial Revolution. The key texts are Leo XIII's *Rerum Novarum* and Pius XI's *Quadragesimo Anno* (Reconstructing the Social Order), 1931. The principal issues are the role of government in society and in the economy, the right of laborers to organize, the principle of a just wage, and a Christian critique of both capitalism and socialism.

Stage two emerged during the Second World War and continues to the present (overlapping with a third stage). It is the *internationalization* of Catholic social doctrine: It confronts the growing material interdependence of the world and seeks to provide a moral framework for the political, economic, and strategic issues facing the human community. The key texts are those of Pope Pius XII—Pentecost message, 1941, and Christmas addresses, 1939–1957; John XXIII— *Mater et Magistra* (Christianity and Social Progress), 1961, and *Pacem in Terris* (Peace on Earth), 1963; Paul VI—*Populorum Progressio* (The Progress of Peoples), 1967; the Second Vatican Council—*Gaudium et Spes (Pastoral Constitution on the Church in the Modern World),* 1965; and the Third International Synod of Bishops—*Iustitia in Mundo (Justice in the World),* 1971. The principal issues are the political and juridical organization of the international community, the demands of international social justice in determining the rules and relationships of international economic policy, and the moral issues related to warfare in a nuclear age.

Stage three is represented by Pope Paul VI's apostolic letter *Octagesima Adveniens* (The Eightieth Year), 1971, reaffirmed to some extent in his apostolic exhortation *Evangelii Nuntiandi* (On Evangelization in the Modern World), 1975; and Pope John Paul II's *Redemptor Hominis* (Redeemer of Humankind), 1979. The keynote is sounded in *Octagesima Adveniens* as it addresses "new social questions." It examines the acute issues faced by the postindustrial societies that have been so transformed by technology and its effects, especially in the area of communications and mobility. On the other hand, the papal letter returns to the theme of the way postindustrial and developing societies are related internationally. The document focuses on the forms of organization that compete for primacy in society and on the intellectual currents that seek to legitimate other kinds of social and political orders.[8] This broader political approach is carried forward in Pope John Paul II's encyclical, which speaks of our alienation from the products and byproducts of technology—environmental pollution and destruction, the arms race, the widening gap between rich and poor, increasingly sophisticated methods of torture and oppression, wasteful attitudes and practices, inflation, and modern methods of warfare. The most essential issue today is the right of citizens to share in the "political life of the community" in service of the common good, whether national or international, and in service of the individual, whose dignity in Christ is the foundation and linchpin of the whole social and political order. "Thus the principle of human rights is of profound concern to the area of social justice and is the measure by which it can be tested in the life of political bodies" (sec. 17, par. 7).[9]

The Second Vatican Council, although still very much a part of stage two, prepared the way for the expansion of Catholic social doctrine to include the political dimension as well. Among the fundamental principles the council stressed, especially in its *Pastoral Constitution on the Church in the Modern World,* are the dignity of the human created in the image of God (12), the dignity of the moral conscience (16), the excellence of freedom (17), the social nature of human existence an of our destiny (24), the interdependence of person and society (26), the need to promote the common good for the sake of human dignity (26), respect for persons (27), the fundamental equality of human beings as the basis of social justice (29), the value of all human activities because of the redemption (34), the rightful autonomy of temporal realities (36), and the missionary responsibility of the church to attend to this constellation of values and principles (*passim,* esp. 40-45). The same insistence on human freedom is sounded in the council's *Dignitatis Humanae (Declaration on Religious Freedom),* a freedom that belongs not only to individuals but to groups (4) and that always is subject to the common good (7).

The social mission of the church is even more explicitly articulated in the synodal document *Iustitia in Mundo (Justice in the World):* "Action on behalf of justice and participation in the transformation of the world fully appear to us as a constitutive dimension of the preaching of the gospel, or, in other words, of the church's mission for the redemption of the human race and its liberation from every oppressive situation" (intro., par. 6). And later the same declaration applies the principle to the church itself, for "anyone who ventures to speak to people about justice must first be just in their eyes" (3, par. 2). The church, which is the sacrament of Christ, is called upon by missionary mandate to practice what it preaches about justice and rights.[10]

No complete inventory of all these documents is possible or practical. Accordingly, we shall concentrate upon perhaps the most significant of the texts, the Second Vatican Council's *Pastoral Constitution on the Church in the Modern World.* Here we find frequent and straightforward appeals to sacred Scripture for a fundamentally positive and activist approach to the modern world.

The church, like Jesus Christ, is called to serve, not to be served (John 18:37; Matt 20:28; Mark 10:45). But if the church is to function as a servant community, it must always be prepared to read the "signs of the times" (an obvious biblical reference) in light of the gospel.[11] This, of course, is the crucial sentence. The council explicitly teaches that the church must be ever attentive to the connection between our responsibilities in the world and the demands of the gospel itself. Farther on, it insists that the tendency to split the two "deserves to be counted among the more serious errors of our age" (43).

The foundation of Catholic social doctrine is, as we have suggested, the dignity of the human person, a theme that recurs with renewed emphasis in the official pronouncements and homilies of Pope John Paul II. The council summarized the church's teaching on human dignity in the first chapter of the *Pastoral Constitution* and drew frequently upon various biblical passages to support that teaching: Genesis 1:26-31, Wisdom 2:23, Sirach 17:3-10, Psalm 8:5-6, and more. One need only consult the text and footnotes to see how deliberately the council relied upon sacred Scripture. In no significant subsection are biblical references absent.

This is also the case as we proceed to chapter two and the social nature of human existence—on our God-given vocation to be a community, on the demands of the common good, on reverence for one another, on love of one's enemies, on human equality, and on the Incarnation as the basis of human solidarity.

The same biblical emphasis is carried forward into the third chapter, on the value of human activity throughout the world. This is especially important when the chapter turns directly to the question of the remaking of the earth (39). Although we do not know the time or the manner in which the earth and humanity will be transformed (Acts 1:7; 1 Cor 7:31), we do believe "that God is preparing a new dwelling place and a new earth where justice will abide" (2 Cor 5:2; 2 Pet 3:13) and that such a renewed earth "will answer and surpass all the longings for peace which spring up in the human heart" (1 Cor 2:9; Rev 21:4-5). Eventually, all creation will be unchained from its bondage to sin (Rom 8:19-21). The text, this time without specific support, insists that while we must carefully distinguish between earthly progress and the growth of the kingdom, nonetheless what we do here is "of vital concern" to the coming of the kingdom.

Just as there is continuity between the biblical message and human responsibility in and for the world, so there is continuity between what we do here on this earth for the sake of the world and what God will do at the end of history, when the kingdom will be given in all of its fullness: "For after we have obeyed the Lord, and in His Spirit nurtured on earth the values of human dignity, brotherhood and freedom, and indeed all the good fruits of our nature and enterprise, we will find them again, but freed of stain, burnished and transfigured." The kingdom that Christ will hand over to the Father will be "a kingdom of truth and life, of holiness and grace, of justice, love, and peace" (39).

The council appeals directly to the prophetic tradition to support its basic argument that there is indeed a direct connection between our work in and for this world and God's will for the world. "Long since, the prophets of the Old Testament fought vehemently against this scandal [the tendency to divide the two realms] and even more so did Jesus Christ Himself in the New Testament threaten it with grave punishments" (43; biblical refs. are to Isa 58:1-12, Matt 23:3-23, Mark 7:10-13). "The Christian who neglects his temporal duties," the council concludes, "neglects his duties toward his neighbor and even God, and jeopardizes his eternal salvation."

The *Pastoral Constitution* moves then into its second major part, in which it attends to specific moral issues: marriage and the family, economic development, war and peace, participation in the political process, international cooperation, and so forth. In no instance does the council suggest that the Bible offers detailed or even specific answers to these vexing issues. But neither does it suggest that the Bible has nothing to say about them. On the contrary, the document refers again and again to various biblical texts to strengthen its arguments and to support its conclusions.

Moral Questions of an Individual Nature

All Jesus' moral teaching is concentrated in the one commandment of love: love of God and love of neighbor

(Mark 12:28-34; Matt 22:34-40; Luke 10:25-28). On them, all the Law and the Prophets depend (Matt 22:40). Apart from the Great Commandment, Jesus did not speak explicitly about loving God. He did say that we should not offer sacrifice to God unless and until we have been reconciled with our brother (Matt 5:23-24) and that we cannot ask forgiveness for our sins unless we are ready also to forgive those who sin against us (6:12). But it would be wrong to equate love for God entirely with love for neighbor. Religious acts such as prayer also belong to the love of God (Matt 6:1-15, 7:7-11; Mark 14:38). On the other hand, "religious" access to God through prayer cannot finally be divorced from the principal sacramental encounter with God in one's neighbor. The great picture of the Last Judgment in the parable of the sheep and the goats (Matt 25:31-46) offers a classic illustration of this principle.

According to John, Jesus gave himself as an example of unselfish love for others. He humbled himself to wash the feet of the disciples (13:4-15). He insisted that he was in their midst as one who serves (Luke 22:27), who gives his life as a ransom for many (Mark 10:45), and who thereby leaves a new commandment: "Love one another. Such as my love has been for you, so must your love be for each other. This is how all will know you for my disciples: your love for one another" (John 13:34-35). But such love is not to be reserved for one's friends. The disciple of Jesus is commanded also to love the enemy (Luke 6:27-28), to renounce revenge (6:29). We are to avoid judging and condemning others (6:37) and be careful not to dwell on the speck in our brother's eye while missing the plank in our own (6:41-42). All this is summed up in Paul's classic hymn to love: "There are in the end three things that last: faith, hope, and love, and the greatest of these is love" (1 Cor 13).

The early church of the New Testament period understood itself as being a "new creature" in Christ (2 Cor 5:17), bound to manifest and realize in its own life the commandment of universal love.

There is an awareness, too, of being a new community in the Spirit, the new people of God. Christian existence, therefore, is corporate existence. We are called to a life of brotherly and sisterly love. We are all one in Christ, whether Jew or Greek, slave or free, male or female (Gal 3:28). We are one body, the Body of Christ (1 Cor 12:13, 27). The ethical significance of this is drawn out in Romans 12:4-8 and Colossians 3:11-17. We are to be clothed with mercy, kindness, humility, meekness, patience. We are to bear with one another and to forgive as the Lord has forgiven us. We are to put on love, which binds the rest of the qualities and makes them perfect. Christ's peace must reign in our hearts. We are to be grateful and do everything in the name of the Lord Jesus. In short, we are "to live a life worthy of the calling [we] have received" (Eph 4:1).

As for the Law, it is summed up and fulfilled in this one saying: "You shall love your neighbor as yourself" (Gal 5:14). The gospel is a new law, a perfect law of freedom (Jam 1:25), the law of love (2:8). Jesus himself is the new Law (John 1:17). "His commandment is this: we are to believe in the name of his Son, Jesus Christ, and are to love one another as he has commanded us" (1 John 3:23). If we love one another, "God dwells in us, and his love is brought to perfection in us" (4:12). On the other hand, "If anyone says, 'My love is fixed on God,' yet hates his brother, he is a liar. One who has no love for the brother he has seen cannot love the God he has not seen" (4:20). In any case, "perfect love casts out all fear" (4:18).

Unfortunately, the Catholic Church did not always remain faithful to its own highest ideals. Much of its moral theology deteriorated into a crass legalism.[12] Thus too many Catholic moral analyses and prescriptions either prescinded entirely from sacred Scripture or used the biblical texts in a frankly fundamentalistic, and certainly uncritical way. Complex questions concerning marital fidelity were simply resolved by recourse to the text "What God has joined together let no man put asunder" (Mark 10:9), while missing the really progressive thrust of that teaching—the insistence that a woman was not to be treated as if she were property, to be disposed of at the whim and desire of her husband.

The same tendency to draw a hasty conclusion on the basis of superficial reading of texts has characterized traditional Catholic moral reflection on such controversial matters as homosexuality.[13] In the case of contraception, of course, there simply are no texts, so no pretense to biblical support was ever made. It was necessary to root the position in extrabiblical notions of natural law and in the ecclesiological principle that tradition is a separate authoritative source of divine revelation, equal to sacred Scripture itself.

On the other hand, a more biblically oriented moral theology had begun to develop within the Catholic Church in the nineteenth century. In his *Christian Moral Teaching as Realization of the Kingdom of God* (1834), Johann Baptist von Hirscher (d. 1865) established himself as one of the pioneers in the effort to disengage moral theology from its customary casuistry and legalism and to reconnect it with doctrinal theology and the renewal of biblical studies. Understandably, therefore, he and others like him called for a return to the central New Testament notions of conversion and discipleship. But their general sense of Scripture was often uncritical.

Although the more legalistic approaches to moral theology continued to flourish, the more integrated, biblically grounded theology carried greater weight into the twentieth century, particularly in the works of Joseph Mausbach (d. 1931), Otto Schilling (d. 1956), Fritz Tillmann (d. 1953), and Theodore Steinbuechel (d. 1949). For them, the law of love, the ethos of the Sermon on the Mount, is the heart and soul of moral theology. When two other German theologians, Joseph Fuchs and Bernard Häring assumed teaching positions at the Gregorian University and at the Alphonsianum in Rome respectively, a wider dissemination of this evolving German theology was assured. Its effects can be seen outside Europe in the writings of Charles Curran, one of Häring's first American students. Another major influence on recent Catholic moral thought was Gerard Gilleman, whose *Primacy of Charity in Moral Theology*, along with Häring's *Law of Christ*, were among the most widely read books in Catholic seminaries in the years just before and during Vatican II.[14]

But even into the 1950s, this broadly based development on the continent notwithstanding, moral theology in the United States, for example, remained oriented toward the preparation of confessors. The emphasis was on the individual act, to determine whether it fell into the category of sin and, if so, whether the sin was mortal or venial. Stress still was placed on obedience to law: divine law, natural law, human law. The "good" was what is commanded by law. Therefore conformity with law was the fulfillment of the good. Analysis of moral action still tended to abstract from the concrete circumstances and situation of the moral actor. The manuals in use in the United States and other countries were based on an understanding of an essentially unchanging human nature. This was the so-called *classicist* approach. Classicist moral theology was largely unbiblical, unsacramental, and unintegrated with the great doctrinal themes of Christ, grace, the Holy Spirit, and the church understood as the Body of Christ and the people of God. It should be noted, however, that the classicist approach always enjoyed the favor of official teaching before the council, particularly in the various moral pronouncements issued during the pontificate of Pope Pius XII (e.g., the "Instruction of the Holy Office on 'Situation Ethics,' " 1956).

That official situation changed with Vatican II. In its *Decree on Priestly Formation,* the council urged the renewal of moral theology: "Its scientific exposition should be more thoroughly nourished by scriptural teaching. It should show the nobility of the Christian vocation of the faithful, and their obligation to bring forth fruit in charity for the life of the world" (16). In general, moral theology should be "renewed by livelier contact with the mystery of Christ and the history of salvation." Elsewhere in its two major constitutions, the one on the church and the other on the church in the modern world, the council proposes an ideal of Christian existence that goes well beyond the observance of law and juridical norms. Every member of the church is one of the people of God, and insofar as the whole church is called to be the sacrament of Christ, the whole church also is called to holiness.[15] This consists of following Christ, which leads to the perfection of love. This is at once a love of God and a love of neighbor—these two kinds of love cannot be separated.[16]

Conclusion

The Catholic Church has no official position on the applicability of sacred Scripture to modern life. One can readily infer, however, from the way the church draws upon the Bible in the formulation of its moral teachings that it assumes that such a relationship does exist. But the Catholic tradition, in spite of lapses to the contrary, does not propose that Scripture yields specific, much less detailed answers to a broad range of moral questions, at either the individual or the social level. Rather, the biblical message provides a universe of values that serves as a context within which and against which moral judgments can and must be made. Among these values are the dignity of the person and the love of neighbor. These values, in turn, generate moral responsibilities: the building of community, the creation of just economic and political structures, reverence for life of all kinds, and so forth.

For some, the Catholic integrationist perspective goes too far. In their minds, the Bible and the Christian tradition generally have nothing to contribute to moral reasoning. For others, the Catholic integrationist perspective does not go far enough. In their thinking, the Bible is indeed a blueprint for moral reconstruction at every level and stage of human development. It is not an unfamiliar (or an uncomfortable) experience for the Catholic tradition to find itself situated somewhere between the extremes.

REDUCED TO its simplest terms, the single issue confronting all traditions is captured in the observation that biblical teachings do not always accord with our own sensitivities. This problem is not, of course, particularly new; the Bible itself contains passages seemingly uncomfortable with positions described elsewhere in Scripture. Throughout the centuries any number of approaches have been proposed for resolving this dilemma; underlying them all remains the fundamental question of the nature of the Bible and its proper role within a given tradition. Is it an accurate record of God's revelation, or is it the expression of human aspirations? Are its contents binding by their very nature, or are they a source of symbols and language to fulfill our own religious inclinations? While such problems are not new, they become particularly vexing for those whose commitment to the Bible is as deep as their concern with the problems of modernity.   —F.E.G.

Ancient Scripture in the Modern World

KRISTER STENDAHL
HARVARD DIVINITY SCHOOL

IN THE PRECEDING SECTIONS there has been a good deal of commentary on principles and styles of interpretation. David Kelsey showed well that while the question of scriptural interpretation and application is of great significance, it has not, in the Protestant tradition—or in the Catholic—been laid down in official principles of a truly doctrinal nature. Actually, Kelsey shows that different methods of interpretation can combine with quite different types of theological attitudes and stances.

When a certain type of interpretation hardens into something that becomes a test of orthodoxy, it is triggered by specific issues. Certainly what we in American Christendom call fundamentalism is quite impossible to understand unless we couple it with the controversy about science, evolution, and Darwinism; that controversy became the magnet that caused the metal filings, so to speak, to shape themselves in the pattern we call fundamentalism. This is an important observation because it can be shown that hermeneutics (principles of interpretation) usually have something to do with the issue people were especially preoccupied with when they formulated their hermeneutics. The Scopes trial, the place of women in society and church, the question of

---

Krister Stendahl's biblical references are based on the Revised Standard Version and his own understanding of the Greek.

abortion, liberation theology, reflections on the Holocaust are some contemporary issues of that kind. They bring people's principles of interpretation into a higher degree of consciousness within the various communities of faith.

In the Protestant community this is so in a special way because one of the things that characterizes all those communities we call Protestant is that they never have created a clear place for the role of tradition in their *theological* structure. In the Roman Catholic scheme of things, it is obvious that the Bible, in a certain sense, is "back there," and we are connected with the apostolic tradition through the continuity of the church. There is a development, a clarification, an interplay between Scripture and tradition that can be described in various ways, and Richard McBrien has offered one way to do just that.

In one respect the Jewish tradition is unique among all the religious traditions. In the ongoing history of interpretation in the matter of halakha—that is, binding decisions as to right action—it records both the minority and the majority opinion, and the minority opinion is recorded without a final anathema. This is the ultimate symbol of an ongoing and open enterprise of interpretation.

Protestantism, due to the issues at the time of its birth, never has managed to express such a linkage, but tends to claim—one way or another—to read the Bible straight: "We go to the Bible." It is obvious that we do not. In certain ways, to be sure, traditions of interpretation and understanding are operative, but there is no really good way within Protestant structures of theology to give form and shape and full, open, honest dignity to the process of interpretation. Thus there is always a certain biblicism—the kind of attitude that makes it difficult to understand how Protestants can be anything other than Seventh-day Adventists. (For is it not quite clear in the Bible which day is the Sabbath? There can be very little confusion about that, and there is no indication whatsoever in the Scriptures that there was a command to move the day of rest one day forward.)

But somehow we manage. We accept de facto the development of the Christian tradition; but we are afraid to make it verbal and formal lest direct access to the Scriptures be cut. That gives a special flavor to Protestant interpretation and to its anger with opponents. The heat of the discussion has much to do with this direct approach, symbolized in another way by the woman who said that "if the King James Version was good enough for Jesus, it is good enough for me." This reminds us of the strange fact that even with concepts of verbal inspiration, Protestantism never has developed a myth about how translations came into being. Along with the fully developed idea that the Septuagint (the Greek translation of the Hebrew Scriptures) is a truly dependable translation, goes the myth about seventy scholars having translated it. They worked in soundproof booths, and when they compared their translations in the evening, they found that the wording was exactly the same—thereby proving beyond a doubt that this is an inspired translation.[1] It is interesting to note that Protestantism, with its zeal for and trust in the translation, never developed attempts to sanctify the translators or the translation. For two motifs came into conflict—the holiness of the Scriptures and the need for the vernacular—that is, the evangelical zeal of the Protestant tradition.

I have understood that I am to take a somewhat different aspect than my predecessors. I will do so, but with some personal memory and bias. A few years ago when I was in Germany for some discussions, a woman who had seen my bibliography asked me a question about something to which I had never given much thought. She said, "I looked at your bibliography, and it seems there are two things you are constantly mentioning, constantly thinking about, and constantly writing about—women and Jews. How come? And what do women and Jews have in common for a New Testament scholar?" Actually, that is not so difficult to answer. From a New Testament scholar's point of view, these are two rather striking issues on which the Christian tradition and, in the case of women, the whole scriptural tradition has had a clearly detrimental and dangerous effect. There is no question that the way New Testament material speaks about Judaism contains within itself the seeds of much anti-Judaism;

and that the male community has found aid and comfort in its chauvinism in the name of the Bible is relatively easy to document in western culture. Thus I found myself increasingly drawn toward moving my teaching situation to what you might call the Public Health Department of biblical studies. What can be said? What can be done? What are the resources? What are the theological issues for an interpretation of the Scriptures that does not produce a harmful fallout, to use the metaphor from atomic power? That is not the most common role for exegetes or for preachers. We are usually sales people, and we often rightly speak about the good wares we have. Sheldon Blank has given us a sterling and stirring example of the way one can lift up the very best of a tradition. Even so, I have come to believe that the problem calls for frontal attention to what I have called the public health aspect of interpretation. How does the church live with its Bible without undesirable effects? I would guess that the last racists in this country, if there ever be an end to such, will be the ones with Bible in hand. There never has been an evil cause in the world that has not become more evil if it has been possible to argue it on biblical grounds. I think it is pretty clear that slavery in the western world would have been overcome considerably more quickly, had not slavery been part of the landscape in the Holy Book.

It is this aspect of application that I would like to focus upon in this presentation. To many of us, the first approach to this question seems to be, "Of course, the Bible is kosher (or that word's Christian equivalent); of course, if something goes wrong, it is because of insufficient depth, understanding, faith, and obedience of Christians." I do not find that argument convincing. It sounds to me a little like G. K. Chesterton's famous observation, "The Christian ideal has not been tried and found wanting. It has been found difficult and left untried."[2] That is clever rhetoric, but deeply unconvincing after two thousand years. There are questions here that cannot be handled without taking a harder look at the Scriptures themselves. For exemplification, I shall center my remarks on the question of women and the Bible.

The first and perhaps most popular way to handle such

issues is to make the best of what we have and stress whatever strikes us as positive. Sheldon Blank represents this approach to the Hebrew Scriptures in a most beautiful and moving manner. The same is constantly done in the New Testament field. We are told that Jesus recognizes women; that the Gospels mention a lot of women; and that Jesus liberated women from thinking they belong only in the kitchen, the point of the story about Martha and Mary (Luke 10:38-42). And there is the surprising statement Paul makes about total mutuality in relations between man and woman in marriage: "For the wife does not rule over her own body, but the husband does; likewise the husband does not rule over his own body, but the wife does" (1 Cor 7:4). There is no distinction, but total mutuality. Whether the idea of ruling over each other is the best theological understanding is another matter, but the mutuality is stunning in the setting of the times. Furthermore, there is in recent scholarship the happy rediscovery of a female apostle, Junia, in Romans 16:7.[3] Actually, the early Church Fathers knew of her. John Chrysostom—who is not a paragon of virtue in the fight against sexism—marvels when he considers the fact that even a woman could become an apostle.[4] Later tradition made her a male by referring to "Junias," which sounds like a male name—although there is no evidence that any such name existed.

I do rejoice in these and other points that can be made, but I think still it adds up to too little. If it be half and half, then it is the kind with one elephant and one canary. The basic impression of woman's subordination in practically all respects is part of the biblical tradition in its main thrust. The exceptions only prove the rule.

Another approach to interpretation is allegory. It is not very fashionable to give allegorical interpretations, but I always have liked Philo's note that anyone knows, of course, that a human being cannot be made out of a rib and that consequently the story in Genesis 2 must have a deeper meaning.[5] When something is contrary to what one perceives as scientific knowledge at that time, and instead of getting into a Scopes trial, one says "It has a deeper meaning," one is allegorizing. But the amount of humor it takes to allegorize became lost in Christian tradition, where biblicism coupled with pedantic rationalism drove out imaginative theology.

Of equally ancient origin is accommodation—the idea that God accommodated himself to the world-views, conceptions, structures, and so on, of the time into which the Bible came. The funny thing about accommodation is that once we acquire a more historical way of looking at these things, accommodation just does not work; accommodation, then, is not God accommodating himself—it is the biblical writers being influenced by their surrounding culture. And how can that add up to the pure Word of God? Once one started to look at matters historically, the high and precious doctrine of God's accommodation became a very difficult thing to handle.

Another approach is that of distinguishing, for example, between Paul and Deutero-Pauline writings. It so happens that one of the most derogatory "woman texts" we have in the New Testament is First Timothy 2:9-15, in the Pastoral Epistles. According to a broad scholarly consensus, they certainly were not written by Paul. Or, it can be shown rather convincingly that similar words in First Corinthians 14:33*b*-36 may well be a later interpolation in the manuscripts—and hence again, not the words of Paul.[6] That is interesting for the understanding of Paul; but from the point of view of the way the church lives with the Scriptures, does such an approach solve as many problems as it is intended to solve? I am not saying that these are irrelevant observations. I am only saying that as the church lives with the Bible, what kind of view of Bible does it suggest if one has such a gradation as this: Jesus knows best, Paul knows well, and the secondary Pauline tradition is not of truly revelatory quality? I would think, being the kind of Christian I am, that it is really the Bible that is the guide for the life of the church. And hence in a certain sense, it is interesting to know who within the rich variety of biblical writers said something, but it does not quite solve the problem—especially not in those circles where the maximum damage of "bibliolotry" is patent.

Much interesting work can be done in this department. There is, for example, a recent article by Karlfried Froehlich in a volume on the authority and the infallibility of the church, published jointly by Catholics and Lutherans.[7] Here we have a trench in the history of the interpretation of Galatians 2:11-14, the passage in which Paul tells how he stood up to Peter and challenged him severely. But once one recognizes the Bible and once one realizes that Peter has the authority he does in the church—with even infallibility added in the nineteenth century—then it becomes very difficult to come upon such controversies right in the Word of God. The problem engenders marvelous reflections through the ages. I especially like one reflection: Peter did not insist on his interpretation, but was willing to bow to reason; and since reason seemed to be on the other side, Peter did not insist on his authority.

Let me suggest a few more ways to interpret the Bible. One is to say that there are insights in the Scriptures that the apostles or the church did not manage to live up to. This is my own interpretation of the material on women. I happen to think Paul was a better theologian than implementer. When he, in a kind of theological rapture, says that in Christ there is neither slave nor free, neither Jew nor Greek, nor is there "male and female" (Gal 3:28), he spoke the truth. It is worth noting that he said "nor is there 'male and female'" in a context where there is no discussion about women; the context is that of "Jew and Greek," and the reference to male/female comes as the climax of an explanation that in Christ all dichotomies are overcome, even the basic one in creation—male and female.[8]

In specific situations, Paul found it a little hard to keep the vision. We are not quite clear about his thoughts on slavery, when it came down to the line. We have his letter to Philemon concerning Onesimus, but there Paul pleads for generosity; he does not lay down a clear Word of God as to the liberation of a slave. The ambiguity of the text in First Corinthians 7:21 is irritating.[9] As to Jew and Gentile, he had rather clear ideas, and I shall come back to those. But as to male and female, he had trouble; therefore, when he quotes this trilogy in Corinth (1 Cor 12:13), he chops off the third part—there is no speaking about male-and-female. When he discusses the relation between male and female in First Corinthians 7, he again discusses the first part and the second part—slave and free,

Jew and Gentile—but the woman issue is handled in another manner, although there is the mutuality clause to which we referred earlier (7:4). It seems that he saw a vision, but he did not know quite how to implement it fully.

If that be so, it would suggest the following question: If it is true that Paul saw a vision but that he was not ready to implement it, should we tie the church to the level of implementation Paul accomplished? Should we deepfreeze the church in Bible-land? Or is it right to say: "Here is a principle, an insight, a vision that will work itself out as the slavery issue worked itself out—only much too slowly, because the public health department of theology is not very well equipped?" That model appeals to me. Looking at it that way, one could sharpen up that view even further and make the following somewhat strange observation.

In First Timothy 2:9-15, which states that women should have no authority and do no teaching, that view is backed up by the story of the creation: We should remember that "Adam was not deceived but the woman was deceived and became a transgressor" (v. 14). Here we have a rather common view: that women are more susceptible to the snares of Satan; therefore they have only one way toward salvation and that is to have children—it says in that text—and they should not move into anything else. When I read that, I hear an echo of another text—the text of the Fall, in Genesis 3. You will remember that when God asks Adam why he is wearing those funny clothes, Adam, the courageous male, says, "Oh no, it wasn't I—it was she." He displays a typical pass-the-buck attitude. That is part of the Fall. It is that very fallenness of Adam that echoes so strongly in First Timothy 2. It is exactly the same creepy little Adam, blaming Eve, just as in the original story—the ultimate sign of the fallenness of Adam. But why should the church be so anxious to remain fallen? That is an interesting question, and one could ask whether much of the timidity of the church in these and other matters comes from some strange kind of devotion to those passages and signs in the Scriptures that belong to human fallenness.

There are many people who believe that such a way of thinking is wrong. I have the feeling that Sheldon Blank might think so, and also Richard McBrien. This kind of pendantry with texts may strike them as too halakhic; instead, we should find an overarching set of ideas or a theological system into which, to be sure, the Scripture feeds, and then we should resolve our questions within, or out of that system where all the different components of Scripture have been mixed together—perhaps partly canceling one another out—in the Catholic case, always hitting the perfect equilibrium. Or, one could do as various theologies have done—state a principle that becomes the guide and criterion for interpretation so that the texts really do speak in their own direct and crazy way with all their diversity. Then one usually has decided what it is about—and for Christians, it is usually about *love.* That seems to be a safe and popular theme.[10] Or *law and gospel.* Or one can read the whole of the Bible, as Luther sometimes did, in terms of *that which drives toward Christ.* Or one can attempt to recreate *the biblical view of man,* as it usually is called (the expression dates the approach). To me, that is another way to get things into the blender, get it all together; but then one is interpreting the totality—not the specifics, not the texts. And that is very attractive. In the Lutheran tradition, especially in its modern German forms, there is no question that it is Paul who understands the heart of Christianity, and one interprets the rest of the New Testament from that Pauline perspective. Pauline theology supplies the criterion for true Christianity.[11]

At the other end of the spectrum are those who would say, "It is written. There is the Word, and I take it as it stands." This can be done with various degrees of sophistication, but the unconscious adaptation remains hidden, and the intentionality of the original is covered up. Behind my own way of thinking about these things, there lies always the stress on the intentionality. I, for one, do not find any way to start on the interpretation other than to ask what the author intended. That intentionality then becomes the starting point from which one can move, cutting through all the layers of interpretation. What does it profit an exegete to understand the words and miss the intention?

If we try to examine the reason things sometimes tend to go wrong in Christendom, I think we will find that it is very hard to discover in Christian theology, and in the Christian church, a pure and simple devotion to justice. On the women's issue, it is very striking that if one says that this is a simple question of justice, Christians in general will feel that that solution is not Christian enough; it is not christological enough. One of the reasons the church has been so insensitive to justice is that justice is just not christological enough; it is something for which we do not need the more complicated equipment in our theological outfit, and that is humiliating. I think it really is that simple. Therefore we phase out the matter of simple justice.

Furthermore, it is very hard, and just as humiliating, for a Christian to live with a Bible that does not answer every question. We all have heard about the person who preached about gnashing our teeth in hell. And one parishioner said, "But what about those who have no teeth?" And the preacher answered, "Teeth will be provided." How did he know? Of course he did not, but he would feel terrible if he let the Bible down. When Paul was asked certain questions (actually they had to do with special cases in relation to marriage and divorce), he said, "On this one I do not have a commandment from the Lord" (1 Cor 7:25). I think he was the last preacher in Christendom to admit that. He just said, Sorry, Jesus had not thought about this. So what do we do? We pray about it, we think about it, we discuss it. "And what I tell you," said Paul, "is only my advice; it is not the Word of the Lord" (v. 12, cf. v. 6). "Just my advice." I have always wondered what a biblicist does when the Bible itself says that it is not the Word of the Lord.

"This is just my advice." That suggests to me that this is rather practical, that we should not be so anxious to close a lot of issues; that the church, as I speak about it and think about it, should allow a space in which some questions can remain open while we digest new information; for there are new data. A lot of religious people, especially if they are very well-read in history or the Bible, never can permit anything to be new. I mean, if one has studied history, it must pay off, so whatever happens is just a new twist on an old thing. And so also with Scripture—of course the answer has to be there. "What is not in the book cannot be in the world." There is a Rabbinic saying somewhat to that effect.

I think there are new data, especially in the whole realm of sexuality and homosexuality, that we need to listen to and digest. We need to beg for time, and we need to find a space and mutual trust that is sufficient to handle such a search. But often one looks at the church and the Bible as agents for closing issues, rather than for opening them. It is a bad habit.

I personally find it very striking when gay people say, "I have really not exchanged anything for anything"; Paul described the status of the homosexual who has exchanged the natural for the unnatural (Rom 1:26). This whole matter of homosexuality is historically very interesting. Of course, there is legislation in Leviticus against homosexuality.[12] The Koran is rather gruesome on this: It says that when women practice homosexuality, we should put them in a house and close the door with bricks and let them die; but if men practice homosexuality, then we should remember that Allah is compassionate *(Sura* 4:19-20). Do you hear the echo from the Fall? And if you feel superior to Islam, I think I could dig up things from Christian history that are not so far removed from such a double morality. Think of witches—they tend to be female. When Israel came into contact with Greek culture, one of the badges, one of the identity points, was in terms of homosexual acts: They do, we don't. Thus there was an upsurge in the attention toward homosexuality during that period; and Paul's writings are very much a part of that. It was the standard slogan when they thought about Greeks—they were homosexuals. We do need space for such questions to be reconsidered.

One distinct style of interpretation has developed into what we call liberation theology, a kind of theology that factors the power dimension into our reading of Scripture. Christians do not think much about power, and thus we disregard the power we actually have. Liberation theology takes hold of the fact that much of the biblical tradition is a tradition for and out of the oppressed. But something drastic happens when the language of the oppressed becomes the language of the oppressors. We "do not live by bread alone," said Jesus, quoting Deuteronomy 8:3, but he never said that to a hungry person. He did not mean to say "Let us be a little more spiritual." We have not often seen that clearly, for in our exegesis, we have not factored in the question of the haves and the have-nots, the power question.

I would like to ask the Jewish scholars whether it could be argued that in the Hebrew Scriptures, Israel is called "chosen" when she is in trouble; but whenever Israel wants to fall back on the fact that she is chosen when she has a full stomach (that was the situation in Deuteronomy 8:3) and is powerful, then Amos and the other prophets would appear and say, You think the day, the *yom adonay,* is light; but I will tell you that it is darkness; it is *hoshekh* (Amos 5:18). *Election* is God's marvelous way of throwing his vote into the balance when there is nothing else on our side. It is a way of giving dignity to those whose dignity is about to be extinguished. That could be the function of *election.* If that be true, one of the important insights for my public health department is this: You never can accomplish exegesis and you never can accomplish application without measuring the power question and weighing to whom the words were said and who speaks to whom.

This is, of course, also true where it comes to the relation between Christianity and Judaism. To be sure, the teaching of Jesus in his time was not one bit more scathing when it poked fun at the foibles of religious folk than was the teaching of the Pharisees, not to mention that of the Qumranites or the prophets of old. There was nothing un-Jewish in Jesus' critique of Judaism. It was just some of the good old prophetic stuff. What happened later was that his critique from within fell into alien hands and was thrown with glee by the Christians against the Jews in the synagogue across the street. And as that critique was then combined with power—when the Christians became the more powerful and the Jews were the minority—things went from worse to worse to worse. The apostle Paul, in the 50s of the Common Era, became aware of the fact that a certain snobbishness toward the Jews had developed among Gentile Christians in the Roman Empire. Therefore he told those Gentiles not to think that it was their calling to convert the Jews. The Jews were in God's hands, he said, and in due time God would save his own people. That is what Paul teaches in Romans 9–11. He said to the Gentile Christians, "I want you to be aware of the secret that God will save Israel lest you be conceited" (11:25). He does not say, "They will accept Christ"; he says, "They will be saved." He had perceived, in his great theological sensitivity, that for all practical purposes, the Jesus movement was to become a Gentile movement. That is quite some clear vision for the 50s.

Finally, one of the many things I have learned from Wilfred Cantwell Smith is that a religious tradition is a living thing. "All religions are new religions, every morning" (perhaps an unconscious allusion to Lam 3:23). The western habit of treating religion as a static given which must adjust to modern culture, technology, and so on, is just that: a habit of thought. For the believer, God is the creator of the whole universe, "all of the world, from the economics to art."[13] To put it another way, I do not believe in Christianity, but in God, Creator, Redeemer, and Sustainer. Neither a system (like Christianity) nor a book (like the Bible) is an object of faith. Rather, the church is my people, my fellow pilgrims, and the Bible is a rich and wise and saving guide on that pilgrimage, as we marvel and struggle and study and learn and reflect and sing together. Thereby the ancient Scripture is rejuvenated in the modern world. As to some of the history that lies between the "then" and the "now," we say unabashedly, "Beware, lest you repeat the mistakes that caused such calamities." Thereby we honor God and serve our sisters and brothers.

NOTES

Part One. Introduction

1. In Gal 1:12, Paul appeals directly to revelation in support of his message; other relevant passages are listed in W. G. Kümmel, *Introduction to the New Testament*, rev. ed., trans. Howard Clark Kee (Nashville: Abingdon Press, 1975), pp. 334-36.
2. Examples of this procedure can be found in Hag 2:10-13 and Zech 7:2-3; see also Mal 2:7.
3. *M. Qidd.* 4:14. One rabbinic text even claims that Abraham observed those traditions that came to be codified in the Talmud itself (*b. Yoma* 28b).
4. 2 Kgs 22–23. Most scholars regard this book as some form of the material in Deuteronomy, although the exact date of its authorship and its history prior to this discovery are the subjects of substantial discussion and disagreement. See A. D. H. Mayes, *Deuteronomy* (London: Oliphant, 1979), 80-108.
5. *T. Sota* 13:2; see also 1 Macc 9:27 and Josephus' *Contra Apionem* 1:8. The expectation for the return of prophecy can perhaps be traced to Joel 3:1 (2:28) and Mal 3:23 (4:5) and is reflected in such texts as 1QS 9:11 from Qumran; 1 Macc 4:46, 14:41; Matt 21:26; and John 1:21, 6:14, 7:40.
6. It was apparently on this basis that Ecclesiasticus, which refers to events long after the fifth-century end of prophecy, was excluded from the normative Jewish canon (*t. Yad. 2:13*), although there is ample evidence to show that it was regarded as authoritative in various Jewish circles; it is even quoted as Scripture once in the Talmud (*b. B. Qam.* 92b; see also *b. Hag.* 13a and *b. Yebam.* 63b). Other noncanonical books are treated similarly by the New Testament. The book of Enoch is cited in Jude 14, while references in John 7:38 and James 4:5 do not correspond to any known biblical passages.
7. A collection of essays dealing with this and related problems can be found in Sid Z. Leiman, *The Canon and Masorah of the Hebrew Bible* (New York: KTAV Publishing House, 1974).

8. The evidence for a separate process of canonization within the early church is described by A. C. Sundberg, Jr., *The Old Testment of the Early Church*, HTS 20 (Cambridge: Harvard University Press, 1964).

9. Kümmel, *Introduction to New Testament*, pp. 479-94.

10. Jer 23:16 and Ezek 13:3 describe prophets who invent messages, while 1 Kgs 22 raises the possibility that God used prophets to mislead the people; see also Isa 6:10.

11. E.g., ḇ *Sanh.* 86b-87a.

12. See Augustine's "Reply to Faustus the Manichaean," *A Select Library of the Nicene and Post-Nicene Fathers of the Christian Church*, ed. P. Schaff (Buffalo: Christian Literature Company, 1887) vol. 4, p. 310.

13. Christians include the New Testament, while Jews do not; Catholics include certain books rejected by both Protestants and Jews.

14. One rabbinic authority even implied that in the messianic future, only the Torah would be binding (*y. Meg.* 70d), while the eleventh-century exegete Rabbi Solomon ben Isaac (Rashi) clearly reflects the view that the narratives of Genesis and Exodus are little more than introduction to the legal material which makes up the essence of the Pentateuch (see his comment to Gen 1:1).

15. Prov 8:22-31, which describes wisdom as the first of God's creations and as an assistant in the subsequent process of creation, was understood by later Jewish tradition as referring to the Torah (e.g., *b. Pesaḥ.* 54a; *b. Ned.* 39b).

16. A similar kind of selectivity accounts for the fact that in the course of the debates on slavery that preceded the Civil War, both sides appealed to Scripture to support their positions, cf. T. Stringfellow, "A Scriptural View of Slavery," in *Slavery Defended: The View of the Old South*, ed. E. L. McKitrick (Englewood Cliffs, N.J.: Prentice-Hall, 1963), pp. 86-98; A. Barnes, *An Inquiry into the Scriptural Views of Slavery* (Philadelphia: Parry & McMillan, 1855).

Chapter 1. Avery Dulles, S.J.

1. Many of these documents are given in the original languages in H. Denzinger and A. Schönmetzer, eds. (hereafter cited as DS), *Enchiridion Symbolorum, Definitionum, et Declarationum de Rebus Fidei et Morum*, 32nd ed. (Freiburg: Herder, 1963). The most useful anthology in English is James J. Megivern, ed., *Bible Interpretation*, Official Catholic Teachings Series (Wilmington, N.C.: Consortium Books, 1978). The documents of Vatican II are available in English translation in W. M. Abbott and J. Gallagher, eds., *The Documents of Vatican II* (New York: America Press, 1966), and in A. Flannery, ed., *Vatican Council II: The Conciliar and Post-Conciliar Documents* (Northport, N.Y.: Costello, 1975). Except where otherwise noted, I shall follow the Abbott-Gallagher translation. The documents of Vatican II will be abbreviated according to their Latin titles:
   DV—*Dei Verbum (Dogmatic Constitution on Divine Revelation)*
   SC—*Sacrosanctum Concilium (Constitution on the Sacred Liturgy)*
   UR—*Unitatis Redintegratio (Decree on Ecumenism)*
   OT—*Optatam Totius (Decree on Priestly Formation)*

2. The historical limitations of doctrinal statements are indicated in the 1973 Declaration of the Congregation for the Doctrine of the Faith, *Mysterium Ecclesiae*, pt. 5; in Megivern, *Bible Interpretation*, pp. 431-32.

3. On this subject, see J. C. Turro and R. E. Brown, "Canonicity," in *The Jerome Biblical Comentary*, ed. R. E. Brown, J. A. Fitzmyer, and R. E. Murphy (Englewood Cliffs, N.J.: Prentice-Hall, 1968) no. 67.

4. See J.-M.-A. Vacant, *Etudes théologiques sur les Constitutions du Concile du Vatican: La Constitution "Dei Filius"* (Paris: Delhomme & Briguet, 1893), vol. 1, pp. 405-23.

5. The Response of the Biblical Commission of June 26, 1912, affirming the canonicity and authenticity of the last twelve verses of Mark (Megivern, *Bible Interpretation*, no. 443) no longer can be considered authoritative. For reasons, see R. E. Brown, *Biblical Reflections on Crises Facing the Church* (New York: Paulist Press, 1975), pp. 110-11.

6. P. Benoit, "La Septante est-elle inspirée?" in *Vom Wort des Lebens*, ed. N. Adler, Festschrift für Max Meinertz (Münster: Aschendorff, 1951), pp. 41–49; P. Auvray, "Comment se pose le problème de l'inspiration des Septante," *Revue Biblique* 59 (1952): 321-36.

7. See A. Bea, "Deus auctor sacrae Scriptura: Herkunft und Bedeutung der Formel," *Angelicum* 20 (1943): 16-43; also K. Rahner, *Inspiration in the Bible*, rev. trans. (New York: Herder & Herder, 1964), pp. 13-18.

8. G. Bardy, "L'inspiration des Pères de l'Eglise," *Recherches des sciences religieuses* 40 (1951–52):7-26, Mélanges J. Lebreton II; E. R. Kalin, "The Inspired Community: A Glance at Canon History," *Concordia Theological Monthly* 42 (1971):541-49.

9. See *Divino afflante Spiritu*, nos. 23-27; in Megivern, *Bible Interpretation*, nos. 739-44.

10. See Norbert Lohfink, *The Christian Meaning of the Old Testament* (Milwaukee, Wis.: Bruce Publishing Co., 1968), pp. 24-51.

11. *Divino afflante Spiritu*, nos. 28-30; in Megivern, *Bible Interpretations*, nos. 745-47.

12. *Divino afflante Spiritu*, no. 47.

13. *Luther's Works*, vol. 32, ed. George W. Forell (Philadelphia: Muhlenberg Press, 1958), pp. 112-13.

14. *Schemata Constitutionum et Decretorum*, series prima (Vatican City: Typis Polyglottis, 1962), no. 4, p. 10.

15. See P. C. Rodger and L. Vischer, eds., *The Fourth World Conference on Faith and Order* (New York: Association Press, 1964), rpt. of sec. 2, "Scripture, Tradition, and Traditions," pp. 50-61.

16. Council of Trent, 5th session, 2nd decree (A.D. 1547), in Megivern, *Bible Interpretation*, p. 181, no. 170.

17. To indicate the development in Catholic thought represented here, one need only refer to the 80th proposition of Paschasius Quesnel, condemned by Clement XI in 1713: "The reading of Holy Scripture is for all" (DS 2480).

18. J. Ratzinger, "Commentary on *Dei Verbum*, chapter 2," in *Commentary on the Documents of Vatican II*, vol. 3, ed. H. Vorgrimler (New York: Herder & Herder, 1969), p. 272.

Chapter 2. John H. Gerstner

1. *Form of Government* 18, 7(2), *et passim* (see Philip Schaff, *The Creeds of Christendom* [New York: Harper & Brothers, 1884], vol. 3, p. 606).

2. Sect. 1 (see Schaff, *Creeds*, vol. 3, pp. 93-94).

3. Sect. 5 (see Schaff, *Creeds*, vol. 3, p. 363).

4. Art. 6 (see Schaff, *Creeds,* vol. 3, p. 489).
5. Cf. Scots' Confession 1, 19 (see Schaff, *Creeds,* vol. 3, p. 464); First Helvetic, sec. 1-4 (see Schaff, *Creeds,* vol. 3., pp. 211-12; for English trans., see A. C. Cochrane, *Reformed Confessions of the 16th Century* [Philadelphia: Westminster Press, 1966], pp. 100-101); Belgic Confession, art. 7 (see Schaff, *Creeds,* vol. 3, pp. 387-89).
6. From the Reformation hymn, *Ein Feste Burg* ("A Mighty Fortress Is Our God").
7. Cf. H. Heppe, *Reformed Dogmatics,* trans. G. T. Thomson (London: George Allen & Unwin Ltd., 1950), pp. 12-46; R. Preuss, *The Inspiration of Scripture of the Theologians of Seventeenth-Century Lutheran Dogmaticians* (Edinburgh: Oliver & Boyd, 1955).
8. D. M. Beegle, *The Inspiration of Scripture* (Philadelphia: Westminster Press, 1963) is a notable early conservative example. More recently, Jack Rogers of Fuller Theological Seminary has edited a volume titled *Biblical Authority* (Waco, Tex.: Word Books, 1977). This is not truth in advertising, since the book does not attribute authority to all of the Bible. It therefore should be titled *Partial Biblical Authority,* with the subtitle *Unfortunately, We Do Not Know Which Part.* For a more adequate critique, see J. M. Boice, ed., *The Foundations of Biblical Authority* (Grand Rapids: Zondervan Corp., 1978).
9. Boice, *Biblical Authority,* pp. 35-36.
10. *Review of Metaphysics* 30 (December 1976): 306; cf. John Gerstner, "Jonathan Edwards and the Bible," *Tenth* (September 1979).
11. Kirsop Lake, *The Religion of Yesterday and Tomorrow* (Boston/New York: Houghton Mifflin Co., 1926), p. 61.
12. A meager list of current works representing this deviant modern view would include: Alan Richardson and W. Schweitzer, *Biblical Authority for Today* (Philadelphia: Westminster Press, 1951); J.K.S. Reid, *The Authority of Scripture* (New York: Harper & Brothers, n.d.); W. J. Koiman, *Luther and the Bible,* trans. John Schmidt (Philadelphia: Muhlenberg Press, 1961); E. R. Sandeen, *The Roots of Fundamentalism* (Philadelphia: Westminster Press, 1978); and esp. G. C. Berkouwer, *Holy Scripture,* trans. Jack Rogers (Grand Rapids: Wm. B. Eerdmans Publishing Co., 1975).
13. John W. Wenham, "Christ's View of Scripture," in *Inerrancy,* ed. N. L. Geisler (Grand Rapids: Zondervan Corp., 1979), pp. 3 ff.
14. Wenham, "Does the Lordship Demand an Inerrant Bible?" in *Authority of Scripture* (Dallas, Tex.: International Council on Biblical Inerrancy, n.d.).
15. K. Runia, *Karl Barth's Doctrine of Holy Scripture* (Grand Rapids: Wm. B. Eerdmans Publishing Co., 1962) finds it interesting that Barth charges orthodoxy with Docetism because of its doctrine of inerrancy, meaning that it does not take the humanity of the biblical writers seriously. Runia answers that charge by noting that Barth did not apply his own principle to Christ the God-man and attribute error to him.
16. Augustine, "The City of God," 22: 30, vol. 7, pp. 276-79, Loed Classical Library.
17. Council of Chalcedon (A.D. 451): "Our Lord Jesus Christ, at once complete in Godhead and complete in manhood, truly God and truly man," in Bettenson, *Documents of the Christian Church* (New York/London: Oxford University Press, 1947), p. 72.

18. I debated with K. Stendahl a few years ago on the authority of the Bible. One question from the floor concerned the Bible and the role of women. Dean Stendahl gave an even more conservative answer than I would have given, but then he intimated that he did not feel bound by Scripture, but by what he felt was later leading of the Spirit. I commented that that statement revealed our difference: The traditionalist is bound by Scripture; the modern Protestant theologian is not.

19. Bettenson, *Documents of Christian Church*, p. 285.

20. W. M. Abbott and J. Gallagher, eds., *The Documents of Vatican II* (London/Dublin: Geoffrey Chapman, 1966), pp. 117-18: "The task of authentically interpreting the word of God, whether written or handed on, has been entrusted exclusively to the living teaching office of the Church, whose authority is exercised in the name of Jesus Christ."

Chapter 3. Jacob Neusner

1. Yigael Yadin, *The Temple Scroll* (Hebrew), 3 vols. and suppl. (Jerusalem: Israel Exploration Society, 1977).

2. Isaac Hirsch Weiss, ed., *The Sifra*, reprint (New York: n.p., 1947) is a running commentary on the book of Leviticus, based on early Rabbinic (tannaitic) legal traditions.

3. See Jacob Neusner, *History of the Mishnaic Law of Purities* (Leiden: E. J. Brill, 1974-77), vols. 1-22.

4. These deal with regulations regarding the proper observance of the sabbath and of festivals.

5. Morton Smith, *Palestinian Parties and Politics That Shaped the Old Testament* (New York: Columbia University Press, 1971), pp. 57-81, 138.

6. *Ibid.*, pp. 138-139.

7. This description of the mishnaic system derives from Neusner, *History of Law of Purities*, vols. 1-22; *History of the Mishnaic Law of Women* (Leiden: E. J. Brill, 1979-80), vols. 1-5; *History of the Mishnaic Law of Appointed Times* (Leiden: E. J. Brill, 1981), vols. 1-5; and *History of the Mishnaic Law of Damages* (Leiden: E. J. Brill, 1982), vols. 1-5. It is further worked out in Jacob Neusner, *Method and Meaning in Ancient Judaism* (Missoula, Mont.: Scholars Press, 1979), *Method and Meaning in Ancient Judaism, Second Series* (Missoula, Mont.: Scholars Press, 1980), and *Judaism: The Evidence of the Mishnah* (Chicago: University of Chicago Press, 1981).

8. See Baruch A. Levine, *In the Presence of the Lord* (Leiden: E. J. Brill, 1975).

Part Two. Introduction

1. *B. Menah.* 29b.

2. The aggadic traditions of Judaism do reflect a value-orientation, but are not accorded the same authority as the *halakha* ("law") within Jewish tradition; see *Encyclopedia Judaica*, s.v. "Aggadah" (Jerusalem: Keter Publishing, 1972), vol. 2, pp. 354-56. A collection of aggadot reflecting the diversity of such material can be found in C. G. Montefiore and H. Loewe, *A Rabbinic Anthology* (Philadelphia: Jewish Publication Society,

1963), which contains an index of the biblical verses cited in the rabbinic quotations it contains.

3. The relatively recent development of this orientation is traced in considerable detail by J. B. Rogers and D. McKim, *The Authority and Interpretation of the Bible, An Historical Approach* (San Francisco: Harper & Row, 1979).

4. One interpretive technique, for example, was limited to those cases in which it already had been applied (*y. Pesah.* 6:1, 33a). A discussion of the possible Greek influence on the development of these hermeneutical methods can be found in S. Lieberman, *Hellenism in Jewish Palestine* (New York: Jewish Theological Seminary of America, 1950), pp. 47-82.

5. See Neh 8. The sectarian commentary on Habakkuk found among the Dead Sea Scrolls claims that "God told Habakkuk to write down that which would happen to the final generation, but He did not make known to him when time would come to an end"; whereas to their own Teacher of Righteousness, "God made known all the mysteries of the words of His servants the prophets."

6. This has led one scholar to speak of that period as characterized by the coexistence of several distinct "Judaisms"; see S. Sandmel, *The First Christian Century in Judaism and Christianity* (New York: Oxford University Press, 1969), p. 58.

7. This is explicitly stated within both Jewish and Christian traditions, e.g., Augustine, "The Usefulness of Belief," 3:5, *The Library of Christian Classics* (Philadelphia: Westminster Press, 1953), vol. 6, p. 294; Num Rab 13:15.

Chapter 4. Michael Fishbane

1. M. Fishbane, "Revelation and Tradition: Aspects of Inner-Biblical Exegesis," *Journal of Biblical Literature* 99 (1980): 343-61.

2. In regard to the development of laws, note, for example, the way the slave laws of Exod 21:2-6 have been transformed in Deut 15:12-18 by exhorting manumission gifts; by desacralizing the procedure for permanent servitude; and by incorporating and reinterpreting the old laws of concubinage (Exod 21:7-11), thereby giving new status to female slaves.

3.. Cf. Fishbane, "Revelation and Tradition."

4. The changing meanings of the verb *darash* from biblical to Rabbinic literature has been charted by Y. Heinemann, "Regarding the Development of the Technical Terms of Bible Exegesis," *Leshonenu* 14 (1945-46): 182-89 (Hebrew); he has dealt with other terms in *Leshonenu* 15 (1946-47): 108-115; 16 (1947-48): 20-28. Another valuable contribution is B. Gertner's "Terms of Scriptural Interpretation: A Study in Hebrew Semantics," *BSOAS* 25 (1962): 1-27.

5. Cf. Pss 1, 119; Ezra 9; Neh 8, 13:1-3.

6. CD 15:10-13.

7. 1QS 5:7-12; 8:15-16; 9:13-14, 18-20; CD 3:12-16.

8. See J. Neusner, *Fellowship in Judaism* (London: Vallentine, Mitchell, 1963); C. Rabin, *Qumran Studies* (New York: Schocken Books, 1975), ch. 1.

9. *ARN,* A 12, end, Schecter ed. reprint (New York: Feldheim, 1967), p. 56.

10. *Ibid.,* A 5, p. 25.
11. See the discussion of texts and literature cited in E. E. Urbach, *The Sages, Their Concepts and Beliefs* (Jerusalem: Magnes, 1969), ch. 12 (Hebrew).
12. See Josephus, *Ant.* 18.10.6, and next n.
13. See J. Lauterbach, *Rabbinic Essays,* reprint (New York: KTAV Publishing Hse., 1973), pp. 23-48.
14. Of the many discussions, see the most recent, J. Fraenkel, "Hermeneutical Problems in the Study of the Aggadic Narrative," *Tarbiz* 47/2-4 (1978): 149-57, Hebrew.
15. Characteristic of Ishmael's method is *Sif Num* 112; regarding Akiva's method, see *b. Baba Qama* 41b; *Sif Deut* 133, 269.
16. For the hermeneutical principles, see *Sifra* 3a (Weiss ed.); *Baraita of R. Ishmael,* end; *Tos. Sanh.* 7:11. For discussion, cf. H. Strack, *Introduction to the Talmud and Midrash* (New York: Meridian Press/Philadelphia: Jewish Publication Society, 1963), ch. 11; M. Elon, *HaMishpat Ha-Ivri* (Jerusalem: Magnes, 1973), vol. 2, pp. 270, 302; *Encyclopedia Judaica,* s.v. "Hermeneutics."
17. See D. Daube, "Rabbinic Methods of Interpretation and Hellenistic Rhetoric," *Hebrew Union College Annual* 22 (1949): 239-64; cf. S. Lieberman, *Hellenism in Jewish Palestine* (New York: Jewish Theological Seminary, 1962), pp. 56-68.
18. See J. Heinemann, *Darkei Ha-Aggadah* (Jerusalem: Magnes, 1956), still the most valuable survey of midrashic modes and features.
19. For the contents of this literature, see *Encyclopedia Judaica,* s.v. "Mishnah," s.v. "Talmud, Babylonian."
20. On the *Dorshei Reshumot,* see L. Ginzberg, *On Jewish Law and Lore* (New York: Meridian Press/Philadelphia: Jewish Publication Society, 1962), p. 133; *Encyclopedia Judaica,* s.v. "Allegory."
21. For a full discussion, see H. Wolfson, *Philo, Foundations of Religious Philosophy in Judaism, Christianity, and Islam,* 2 vols. (Cambridge: Harvard University Press, 1947).
22. *Abot* 3:11. The italicized clause is not found in ms. Kaufmann, ms. Cambridge, or ARN A 26. Urbach, *Sages,* p. 263, understands the clause as a reference to allegories. For other views, see his n. 31.
23. See S. Lieberman's critical edition of the text in G. Scholem, *Jewish Gnosticism, Merkabah Mysticism, and Talmudic Tradition* (New York: Jewish Theological Seminary, 1960), pp. 118-26, appendix D.
24. See G. Scholem, *On the Kabbala and Its Symbolism* (New York: Schocken Books, 1965), pp. 56-62; W. Bacher, "L'Exegese Biblique dans le Zohar," *Revue d'Etudes Juives* 22 (1891): 33-46, 219-29.
25. See M. Zucker, *Rav Saadya Gaon's Translation of the Torah; exegesis, halakha and polemics in R. Saadya's Translation of the Pentateuch* (New York: Feldheim, 1959), Hebrew with English summary.
26. For a convenient catalogue of examples of Ibn Janah's method, see N. Sarna, "Hebrew and Bible Studies in Medieval Spain," in *The Sephardi Heritage,* ed. R. Barnett (London: Vallentine, Mitchell, 1971), pp. 346-49.
27. On Moses Chiquitilla and Ibn Balaam, see Sarna, "Hebrew and Bible Studies," pp. 350-52. Sarna has also collected some remarkable passages from medieval Jewish exegesis which reflect awareness of post-Mosaic elements in the Pentateuch: See his "Some Unusual Aspects of Medieval

Biblical Exegesis," to appear in a forthcoming tribute volume in memory of S. Rawidowicz, edited by A. Ivry and B. Ravid.

28. Cf. the comment of *Da'at Zekenim Mi-Ba'alei Ha-Tosafot* on Deut 6:4; the remarks of R. Joseph Kimhi in *The Book of the Covenant* (Toronto: Pontifical Institute of Medieval Studies, 1972), pp. 32-35, 43-53.

29. From intro. to ch. 1. On Maimonides' Bible exegesis, see W. Bacher, *Die Bibelexegese Moses Maimumi's* (Budapest: Alkalay, 1896); more generally, see J. Guttmann, *Philosophies of Judaism* (New York: Holt, Rinehart, & Winston, 1964), pp. 152-82.

30. Of more than passing interest is Nahmanides' comment on Maimonides' discussion of the Talmudic principle *'ayn Miqra yotzei midei peshuto* ("Scripture never loses its plain/contextual sense" [*b. Shab.* 63a]). Nahmanides remarks: "They have not said 'Scripture is only according to its *peshat*,' for we have the midrashic-exegesis [of Scripture] together with its *peshat*-meaning, and it [Scripture] never loses [the sense] of either one. For [truly] the text is able to sustain it all, and they are both truth; i.e., the *derash* [level of meaning] does not cancel out the *peshat*: both remain meaningful." See *Hasagot HaRamban*, 2nd root, 27.

31. See the introduction to Nahmanides' Bible commentary. This has been translated by R. C. Chavel, *Ramban, Commentary on the Torah: Genesis* (New York: Shilo Publishing House, 1971), esp. pp. 14-15.

32. *Zohar II*, 99a-b; trans. in Scholem, *Kabbala and Symbolism*, pp. 55-56.

33. *Zohar II*, 63b; in G. Scholem, *Zohar, The Book of Splendor* (New York: Schocken Books, 1963), pp. 81-82.

34. According to the tradition of R. Moses Hayyim Ephraim of Sudilkov, *Degel Ephraim*, Parshath Eqev, beginning.

35. See J. Weiss, "Via passiva in early Hasidism," *Journal of Jewish Studies* 2 (1960): 149-54.

36. See *Franz Rosenzweig, His Life and Thought*, ed. N. Glatzer (New York: Schocken Books, 1953), pp. 257-58.

Chapter 5. Bruce Vawter, C.M.

1. I have summarized the patristic notion of the Bible in Vawter, *Biblical Inspiration*, Theological Resources (Philadelphia: Westminster Press, 1972), pp. 20-42.

2. Augustine, *De Genesi ad litteram* 2.9, Migne, *PL* vol. 34, p. 270.

3. Aquinas, *Summa Theologiae* (hereafter cited as *ST*), Ia, q. 70, art. 1 ad 3.

4. J. D. Mansi, *Sacrorum Conciliorum nova et amplissima collectio*, reprinted and cont. by L. Petit and J. B. Martin (Paris: n.p., 1889-1927), vol. 9, p. 223.

5. Cf. Bruce Vawter, "The Fuller Sense: Some Considerations," *CBQ* 26 (1964): 85-96.

6. Cf. Erik Persson, *Sacra Doctrina; Reason and Revelation in Aquinas*, trans. Ross Mackenzie (Philadelphia: Fortress Press, 1970), pp. 83-90. See also Aquinas, *ST*, Ia, q. 1, art. 2 ad 2; q. 1, art. 3.

7. Aquinas, *ST*, Ia, q. 29, art. 3 ad 1.

8. Yves Congar, *A History of Theology*, trans. Hunter Guthrie, S.J. (New York: Doubleday & Co., 1968), pp. 113-14.

9. Second ed. (Oxford: Basil Blackwell, 1952).

10. Vawter, *The Bible in the Church* (New York: Sheed & Ward, 1959).

11. Barbara W. Tuchman, *A Distant Mirror: The Calamitous 14th Century* (New York: Alfred A. Knopf, 1978).
12. Henricus Denzinger and Adolfus Schönmetzer, S.J., *Enchiridion Symbolorum* (hereafter cited as DS), 34th ed. (Barcelona: Herder & Herder, 1967), §§ 1501-503.
13. Cf. Jack N. Lightstone, "The Formation of the Biblical Canon in Judaism of Late Antiquity: Prolegomenon to a General Reassessment," *SR* 8 (1979): 135-42.
14. DS § 1501. On the propriety of translating "under the inspiration," see n. 17 below.
15. Cited in Eduard Stakemeier, *Die Konzilskonstitution über die göttliche Offenbarung* (Paderborn: Bonifacius-Druckerei, 1966), pp. 27-28.
16. George H. Tavard, *Holy Writ or Holy Church, The Crisis of the Protestant Reformation* (New York: Harper & Brothers, 1959) pp. 208-209. Tavard's summation of the situation at the Council of Trent is excellently excised from the minutes of the sessions, see pp. 195-209.
17. DS § 3006.
18. W. M. Abbott and J. Gallagher, eds., *The Documents of Vatican II* (New York: Guild Press, 1966), pp. 119-21.
19. DS § 3006.
20. DS §§ 3288-90.
21. Cf. *DBS* 4, 144-46.
22. DS § 3653.
23. See Vawter, *Biblical Inspiration,* pp. 122, 177.
24. DS §§ 3898-99.
25. Vawter, *Biblical Inspiration,* p. 123 n.
26. Athanasius Miller, O.S.B., "Das neue biblische Handbuch," *Benediktinische Monatschrift* 31 (1955): 49-50; A. Kleinhans, "De nova Enchiridii Biblici editione," *Antonianum* 30 (1955): 63-65. Kleinhans later incorporated this interpretation in "Bibelkommission," *LTK* 2: 359-60. See also *CBQ* 17 (1955): 50-53, 450-51; E. F. Siegman, C.Pp.S., "The decrees of the Biblical Commission," *CBQ* 18 (1956): 23-29; J. Dupont, O.S.B., "A propos du nouvel Enchiridion Biblicum," *RB* 62 (1955): 415-19.
27. *AAS* 56 (1964): 712-18.
28. Cf. Joseph A. Fitzmyer, S.J., "The Biblical Commission's Instruction on the Historical Truth of the Gospels," *TS* 25 (1964): 386-408.
29. Abbott and Gallagher, *Documents of Vatican II,* p. 124.
30. "Women and Priestly Ministry: The New Testament Evidence," *CBQ* 41 (1979): 608-13.
31. James Barr, *Fundamentalism* (Philadelphia: Westminster Press, 1978), pp. 40-41.
32. Karl Rahner, *Studies in Modern Theology* (Freiburg: Herder, 1965), p. 31.
33. Cf. Oswald Loretz, *Galilei und der Irrtum der Inquisition* (Kevelaer: Butzon & Bercker, 1966), pp. 182-209.
34. There are exceptions, of course, but the rule is exemplified in such citations as those which appear in n. 2, 3 above.
35. Vawter, "Biblical Interpretation and the Positive Sciences," *Homiletic and Pastoral Review* 71 (1961) 1127-38.
36. Loretz, *Galilei,* pp. 72-100.

37. Santillana, *Crime of Galileo* (Chicago: University of Chicago Press, 1955), p. 307.
38. Otto Semmelroth and Maximilian Zerwick, *Vaticanum II über das Wort Gottes,* SBS 16 (Stuttgart: Katholisches Bibelwerk, 1966), pp. 28-34.
39. Cf. Abbott and Gallagher, *Documents of Vatican II,* p. 119, esp. n. 31.
40. Franz Hesse, *Hiob,* Zürcher Bibelkommentare AT 14 (Zürich: Theologisches Verlag, 1978).
41. *AAS* 29 (1937): 151.

Chapter 6. David H. Kelsey

1. Werner Georg Kümmel, *The New Testament: The History of the Investigation of Its Problems,* trans. S. MacLean Gilmour and Howard C. Kee (Nashville: Abingdon Press, 1972), p. 27; cf. p. 412, n. 20, 21; for rules, pp. 28-30.
2. Cf. Geoffrey W. Bromiley, "The Church Doctrine of Inspiration," in *Revelation and the Bible,* ed. Carl F.H. Henry (Grand Rapids: Baker Book House, 1958), pp. 205-217.
3. Gerhard Ebeling, *The Word of God and Tradition,* trans. S. H. Hooke (Philadelphia: Fortress Press, 1968), pp. 102-148.
4. Kümmel, *History of Investigation,* p. 26.
5. Reinhold Seeberg, *Text-book of the History of Doctrines,* trans. L. E. Hay, 2 vols. (Grand Rapids: Baker Book House, 1966), vol. 2, p. 300.
6. John Calvin, "Commentary on Romans 10:6," "Commentary on *A Harmony of the Evangelists," Calvin's New Testament Commentaries,* ed. David W. Torrance and Thomas F. Torrance, 12 vols. (William B. Eerdmans Publishing Co.), vol. 3, p. 177; vol. 8, p. 224.
7. John Calvin, *Commentary on Genesis* (1:14-15), Christian Classics, vol. 23.
8. Cited in Jack B. Rogers and Donald K. McKim, *The Authority and Interpretation of the Bible* (New York: Harper & Row, 1979), pp. 83, 727.
9. *Ibid.,* p. 85, n. 97.
10. In regard to the New Testament, cf. Kümmel, *History of Investigation,* pp. 31-50.
11. *Ibid.,* p. 76.
12. *Ibid.,* ch. 2.
13. *Ibid.,* p. 95, referring to work by Karl Hase.
14. Charles W. Wood, "Finding the Life of a Text: Notes on the Explication of Scripture," *SJT* 31 (1978): 102-103; for Wolff's influence on subsequent theology, cf. Hans W. Frei, *The Eclipse of Biblical Narrative: A Study in Eighteenth and Nineteenth Century Hermeneutics* (New Haven: Yale University Press, 1974), pp. 96-104.
15. For this entire section, cf. Frei, *Eclipse,* ch. 15.
16. Cf. Rogers and McKim, *Authority and Interpretation,* ch. 3.
17. Cf. Albert Schweitzer, *The Quest of the Historical Jesus* (New York: Macmillan Co., 1950), ch. 14; H. Richard Niebuhr, *Radical Monotheism* (New York: Harper & Brothers, 1960), ch. 3; James M. Robinson, *A New Quest of the Historical Jesus* (London: SCM Press, 1959); Wolfhart Pannenberg, "Did Jesus Really Rise from the Dead?" *Dialog* 4 (1965): 128-35.
18. Immanuel Kant, *Religion Within the Limits of Reason Alone,* trans.

Greene and Hudson (New York: Harper Torchbooks, Harper & Brothers, 1960), bk. 3.

19. Frei, *Eclipse,* chs. 12-14.

20. Rudolf Bultmann, *Jesus Christ and Mythology* (New York: Charles Schribner's Sons, 1958) and "The Problem of Hermeneutics," in *Essays,* trans. James C. G. Greig (New York: Macmillan Co., 1955), pp. 234-62; cf. David H. Kelsey, *The Uses of Scripture in Recent Theology* (Philadelphia: Fortress Press, 1975), pp. 74-83. Despite enormous differences between Paul Tillich and Rudolf Bultmann, Tillich may be placed with this group, too, insofar as he holds that biblical writings are the symbolic expressions of the transformation of people's subjectivity as they come to the "revelation," or existential insight that they have been accepted by God, or the "power of being itself," and consequently find their lives reshaped by the "power of new being."

21. Van A. Harvey, *The Historian and the Believer* (New York: Macmillan Co., 1966), ch. 8.

22. Cf. Kelsey, *Uses of Scripture,* pp. 39-50. Hans W. Frei has a similar proposal in *The Identity of Jesus Christ* (Philadelphia: Fortress Press, 1975). In his proposals concerning the theologically most fruitful way to go about biblical exegesis, Brevard Childs seems to hold a similar view about what constitutes the meaning of a biblical text and how its literal and religious meanings may be held together—see his *Introduction to the Old Testament as Scripure* (Philadelphia: Fortress Press, 1979), pt. 1. Although the content of his theology differs from Barth's in important ways, Jurgen Möltmann's uses of Scripture, especially in *Theology of Hope,* trans. James W. Leitch (New York: Harper & Row, 1967), seem to rely on a similar view of the "location" of its meaning.

23. Cf. Gerhard Ebeling, *Word and Faith,* trans. James W. Leitch (Philadelphia: Fortress Press, 1960), pp. 30-60; Langdon Gilkey, "Cosmology, Ontology, and the Travail of Biblical Language," *Journal of Religion* 41 (1961): 194-205.

Part Three. Introduction

1. Thus Cicero urges that "our oratory should be accommodated to the ear of the multitude" (*De Oratore,* ed. A. S. Wilkens [Hildesheim: Georg Olms Verlagsbuchhandlung, 1965], Bk. 2, ch. 38, p. 306). The development of this doctrine within Christian theology is traced by F. L. Battles, "God Was Accommodating Himself to Human Capacity," *Int.* 31 (1977): 19-38.

2. *B. Yebam.* 71a; and often in the Talmud.

3. Examples of such interpretations are cited by James Barr, *Fundamentalism* (London: SCM Press, 1977), pp. 40-55.

4. The New Testament doctrine of "turn the other cheek" (Matt 5:38), and the rabbinic teaching that injuries inflicted require monetary compensation (*b. B. Qam.* 83b-84a) demonstrate within both Judaism and Christianity a tendency away from physical retribution.

5. See P. Trible, *God and the Rhetoric of Sexuality* (Philadelphia: Fortress Press, 1978), pp. 105-15.

6. M. Greenberg, "Some Postulates of Biblical Criminal Law," in *The Jewish Expression,* ed. J. Goldin (New York: Bantam Books, 1970), pp. 18-37.

7. Precisely this question regarding Hanukkah is discussed in *b. Shabb.* 23a, where Deut 17:11 is cited as mandating the authority to make such innovations. The doctrine of Mary's Immaculate Conception did not become the official position of the Roman Catholic Church until the bull *Ineffabilis Deus* of Pope Pius IX was issued in 1854, although its roots go back many centuries.

Chapter 7. Sheldon H. Blank

1. The text and the perhaps unfamiliar translation of this rule may call for some comment and a defense of the views that *rea'*, neighbor, means more than "fellow Israelite" and that "(he is) like you" is a proper translation of *kamokha*, usually rendered "as yourself": You shall love your neighbor as yourself.

    Neighbor is an adequate rendering of the Hebrew *rea'*, but it need not mean a fellow Israelite, one of the tribe. Long before the emergence of the Hebrews, the builders of Babel were reduced to a condition in which one could not understand another's speech, *'ish sefat re'ehu*, the language of his neighbor, his *rea'*. And just a few paragraphs before, we notice a passage in the same "holiness chapter" (Lev 19:34) in which the *ger*, the stranger from another land or culture, is to be loved even as the *rea'* in the Golden Rule: You shall love him, (the *ger*, the stranger who resides with you), *kamokha*, (he is) like you, (remembering that) you were strangers in the land of Egypt.

    The translation of *kamokha* as "(he is) like you" is an insight I owe to the late revered Rabbi Leo Baeck and to the German philosopher Franz Rosenzweig (see *The Star of Redemption* [New York: Holt, Rinehart & Winston, 1970], p. 240; trans. in UAHC, *The Torah: Leviticus*, comm. of B. J. Bamberger, pp. 217, 335). It is syntactically justified by the three occurrences in historical narrative of the idiom *kamoni khamokha*, as in 1 Kgs 22:4. There Ahab, the king of Israel, urges Jehoshaphat of Judah to join in an attack upon Aram. Jehoshaphat consents, saying *kamoni khamokha, ke'ami khe'amekha*, "I am as you are, my people as your people, my horses as your horses" (cf. 2 Kgs 3:7; 2 Chron 18:3). In the idiom here, *kamokha* equals "like you, as you are." Similarly: You shall love your neighbor—slave—stranger—fellow man; (he is) like you, as you are, your counterpart. NEB translates: "You shall love your neighbor as a man like yourself." Raphael Jospe has kindly drawn my attention to the earlier comment of the German philosopher Moses Mendelssohn. In his German translation and Hebrew commentary *(bi'ur)* to the Pentateuch, *Netivot Hashalom*, completed in 1783, Mendelssohn understands Lev 19:18 as: "You shall love your neighbor, he is like you, your equal and your counterpart *(shehu' kamokha, shaveh lekha vedomeh lekha)*."

Chapter 8. Richard P. McBrien

1. *Dei Filius,* Vatican Council I.
2. See Gabriel Moran, *Scripture and Tradition: A Survey of the Controversy* (New York: Herder & Herder, 1963).

3. See Herbert Vorgrimler, ed., *Commentary on the Documents of Vatican II* (New York: Herder & Herder, 1969), vol. 5, p. 81 *et passim*.
4. For an understanding of sacramentality, cf. Richard P. McBrien, *Catholicism*, 2 vols. (Minneapolis: Winston Press, 1980).
5. Vatican Council II, *Pastoral Constitution on the Church in the Modern World*, 39.
6. See, e.g., Edward Schillebeeckx, *Jesus: An Experiment in Christology* (New York: Seabury Press, 1979), esp. pp. 105-271.
7. See *Dogmatic Constitution on the Church*, 5.
8. Paul VI, apostolic letter, *Octagesima Adveniens*, *AAS* 63 (1971): 401-441; English trans., *Catholic Mind* 69 (November 1971): 37-58.
9. John Paul II, encyclical letter, *Redemptor Hominis, AAS* 71 (1979): 257-324.
10. *Iustitia in Mundo, AAS* 63 (1971): 923-42; English trans., *Catholic Mind* 70 (March 1972): 52-64.
11. *Pastoral Constitution*, 4.
12. I have tried to summarize that history in McBrien, *Catholicism*, vol. 2, pp. 928-37.
13. See *ibid.*, pp. 1027-33 for my summary of the discussion.
14. Gilleman, *The Primacy of Charity in Moral Theology* (Westminster, Md.: Newman Press, 1959); Häring, *The Law of Christ*, 3 vols. (Westminster, Md.: Newman Press, 1961-66).
15. *Dogmatic Constitution*, ch. 5, and 40, 41, 42.
16. *Pastoral Constitution*, 24.

Chapter 9. Krister Stendahl

1. For development of the tradition about the seventy translators, see S. Jellicoe, *The Septuagint and Modern Study* (Oxford: Clarendon Press, Oxford University Press, 1968); reprint (Ann Arbor: Eisenbrauns, 1978), pp. 38-47.
2. Chesterton, *What's Wrong with the World* (New York: Sheed & Ward, 1956), p. 29.
3. For a balanced discussion of the evidence, see C.E.B. Cranfield, *The Epistle to the Romans,* ICC 1975; 1979, pp. 788-90. The main issue here is not one of different readings in the manuscripts, but the accents added by later editors (*Iouniān* is masc.; *Iounían* is fem.). On the wider ramifications, see Bernadette Brooten, "Inscriptional Evidence for Women as Leaders in the Ancient Synagogues" (Ph.D. diss., Harvard University, 1982).
4. See John Chrysostom, "Homilies on Romans," no. 31 to Rom. 16, in *Nicene and Post-Nicene Fathers,* ed. P. Schaff, ser. 1, vol. 11, p. 555; cf. Migne, *PG* vol. 60, cols. 669-70.
5. Philo Judaeus, *Leg. Alleg.* II. 19; LCL vol. 1, pp. 237-38.
6. See the commentaries, e.g., H. Conzelmann, *1 Corinthians,* Hermeneia Series (Philadelphia: Fortress Press, 1975), p. 246; cf. W. O. Walker, Jr., "I Corinthians 11:2-16 and Paul's Views Regarding Women," *JBL* 94 (1975): 85, n. 6.
7. Froehlich, "Fallibility Instead of Infallibility? A Brief History of the Interpretation of Gal. 2:11-14," in *Teaching Authority and Infallibility in*

the Church, ed. Paul C. Empie et al. (Minneapolis: Augsburg Publishing House, 1978), pp. 259-69.

8. It is also worth noting that Paul does not say "neither male nor female," as in most translations, but "nor is there 'male-and-female,'" a direct quote from Gen 1:27.

9. RSV gives the alternative: *"Or make use of your present condition instead."* The ambiguity lies in the Greek expression and is not due to uncertainty about the manuscripts. See now S. Scott Bartchy, *Mallon Chresai: First-Century Slavery and the Interpretation of 1 Corinthians 7:21,* JBL diss. series, no. 11 (Missoula, Mont.: Scholars Press, 1973).

10. In my courses in preaching, I have worked out some commandments. One reads: "Thou shalt not use the word *love* unless it is in the text." That sobers up a lot of preachy rhetoric, for when preachers do not know quite what to say, they tend to speak about love.

11. See, e.g., the preface in E. Käsemann, *Commentary on Romans* (Grand Rapids: William B. Eerdmans Publishing Co., 1980).

12. Lev 18:22, 20:13 (always only male homosexuality). Whether the story about Sodom was about hospitality or homosexuality is a totally open question. In the Koran the story is about homosexuality *(Sura 7:78).*

13. See Smith, "Traditional Religions and Modern Culture," in *Religious Diversity,* ed. W. G. Oxtoby (New York: Harper & Row, 1976), pp. 68, 72.

INDEX

Abhandlung von freir Unters-chung des Canons, 144
Abortion, 202
Accommodation theory, 57, 208
Aggadic midrash, 98-99
Akiva, Rabbi, 71, 87, 98
Alexandrian Judaism, 22
Allegorical interpretation, 100, 206;
  and Immanuel Kant, 156;
  in understanding Scripture, 89
Allegorical theories as exegesis, 164
Altar as center of life, 84
Anathema, 16, 18
Anti-Judaism in New Testament, 204
Antiochenes, 114
Apostolic tradition, 203
Aquila, 118
Aquinas, Thomas, 28, 113-16
Augustine, 21, 54, 113, 118;
  and classical rhetoric, 163;
  on saving truth in Bible, 124;
  and Septuagint, 22

Baal Shem Tov, 108

Babylonian captivity, 180
Barr, James, 128
Barth, Karl, 45, 114, 158
Bauer, Walter, 122
ben Azariah, Elazar, 96
Benedict XV, 15, 124;
  on uses of Bible, 37
ben Meir, Samuel, 104
ben Zakkai, Yochanan, 96, 98
Biblical Commission. *See* Pontifical Biblical Commission
Book of Splendor. See Zohar
Buber, Martin, 109
Bultmann, Rudolf, 114, 156;
  and historical Jesus, 157

Calvin, John, 136, 138, 140
Canaanite practices, 176;
  idolatry, 163
Canon, 27;
  and Catholic Church, 18;
  as content of Old Testament, 11;
  and inspiration, 23;
  and papal conciliar documents, 15-16
Canonical powers, 36

Canonization
   history of, 10;
   and sacred books, 18
Canon of Florence, 18
Canons of Trent, binding force
   of, 32
Chesterton, G. K., 46, 205
Christian Moral Teaching as Re-
   alization of the Kingdom of
   God, 197
Chrysostom, John
   and concept of *synkatabasis*,
   113;
   and Junia, 206
Church Dogmatics, 158-59
Classicist moral theology, 199
Clement of Alexandria, 19;
   and Septuagint, 22
Congar, Yves, 116
Congregation for the Doctrine
   of the Faith, 125
Congregation of the Council,
   125
Congregation of the Holy Office,
   125-26
Congregation of the Inquisition,
   125-27
Consensus fidelium, 122
Consensus theologorum, 122
Constitution of the Sacred Lit-
   urgy, 37
Council of Florence, 15;
   and authorship of Scriptures,
   24;
   and decree of union, 18
Council of Lyons, 114
Council of Trent, 15-16, 18,
   20-21, 120, 125, 131, 136;
   and authorship of Scriptures,
   24;
   and interpretation of Scriptures, 30;

and multiple uses of Scripture,
   37;
   and response to Martin Luther,
   33;
   on sacramental worship, 36;
   and Septuagint, 118;
   on *sola Scriptura*, 119;
   and traditions, 35
Covenant, 158
Covenant code
   and framers of Mishnah, 76;
   and Sinaitic Law, 93
Curran, Charles, 198

Dalman, Gustav, 114
Darwin, Charles, 146
Darwinism, 202
Dead Sea Scrolls, 95
Decree of Union, 18
Decree on Ecumenism, 39
Decree on Priestly Formation,
   199
Dei Verbum, 15, 130-31. *See also*
   Dogmatic Constitution on
   Divine Revelation
Deuterocanonical, 20, 22
Deuteronomic laws and framers
   of Mishnah, 76
Dignitatis Humanae (On Human
   Freedom), 193
Divine authority, 93, 171
Divine authorship, 24-25
Divino afflante Spiritu, 15, 17,
   22, 27-28;
   as liberating encyclical, 125
Doctrina sacra
   and Thomas Aquinas, 115
Dogmatic Constitution on Divine
   Revelation, 15, 21, 26, 34,
   38. *See also Dei Verbum*

Eastern churches, 21

Ecclesiastical authority, classical Protestant pattern of, 60
Ecclesiastical magisterium. *See* Magisterium
Ecclesiastical ministry and apostolic revelation, 36
Ecumenism. *See Decree on Ecumenism*
Edwards, Jonathan, 46
Eichhorn, J. C., 143, 145
Election, 213
Enchiridion Biblicum, 127
Encyclical letter, 125-26; definition of, 124; of John Paul II, 192; of Pius XII, 17
Esdras, 19
Esoteric Torah, 102
Essay on the Development of Christian Doctrine, 122
Essenes, 67. *See also* Qumran
Ethical judgments, 189
Evangelicals, 55; and inerrancy, 53
Evangelical zeal in Protestant tradition, 204
Evangelists and apocalyptic prophecy, 66
Exoteric Torah, 95, 101

Faith and Order Commission, World Council of Churches, 33, 112
Family and the Bible, 59
First Vatican Council. *See* Vatican I
Flacius, Matthaeus Illyricus, 136-37, 139, 149
Franciscans and Thomas Aquinas, 115
French Confession of Faith, 43
Froehlich, Karlfried, 207

Fuchs, Joseph, 198
Fundamentalism, 202

Galileo, ecclesiastical condemnation of, 129. *See also* Congregation of the Inquisition
Gaudium et Spes, 185-86, 191. *See also Pastoral Constitution on the Church in the Modern World*
Genesis Rabba, 99
Gilleman, Gerard, 198
Gimzo, Nahum, 98
Graf, Karl H., 145
Guide for the Perplexed, 105
Gunkel, Hermann, 145

Halakha, 101
Hanukkah, 165
Häring, Bernard, 198
Hasidism as heir of Kabbala, 108
Hellenization, age of, 78-79
Herder, J. G., 144
Hermeneutics, 202
Hesse, Franz, 130-31
Hillel, 96, 98; and Avtalyon, 97; and the Mishnah, 69
Hirsch, Samson Raphael, and enlightened orthodoxy, 109
Hirscher, Johann Baptist von, 197-198
Historical Jesus, 145-46, 157; quest of, 155
Historical sense of Scripture, 141, 143, 147-48, 151, 159-60
The Historical Truth of the Gospels, 27
Holy Office, 15
Homosexuality, 176, 197, 212
Humani Generis, 125
Hummelauer, Franz von, 124-26

ibn Ezra, Abraham, 103-104, 106
ibn Janah, Jonah, 103
Immaculate Conception, 166
Industrial Revolution, 191
Interrancy of Scripture, 26-27, 44, 48-50, 56-57, 128, 130, 152
Infallibility
  of church, 207;
  of pontiff, 123
Infallible pronouncements, 16
Inspiration, doctrine of, 23
Inspired literature, 24-25
Integrationist orientation, 186, 200
Interpretation of Scriptures, 30
Irenaeus and Septuagint, 22
Ishmael, Rabbi, 97-98
Isidore and Septuagint, 22
Iustitia in Mundo (*Justice in the World*), 191, 193

Jacobites, 18
Jehoshaphat, 10
Jerome, 20, 22, 118
Johannine comma, 126
John XXIII and Vatican II, 39
John Paul II, 131, 191, 193;
  encyclical of, 192;
  and Galileo, 126
Josephus, 97, 99
Josiah, 10
Joy and Hope. See Gaudium et Spes
Judah the Patriarch as scribe, 72
Jülicher, Adolf, 49
Junia, 206
Justice, 173-74

Kabbalists, 108;
  and *raza dimehemanutha*, 107

Kant, Immanuel, 109, 156
Karaites, 90, 103
Kenosis, doctrine of, 48-52
Key to the Scriptures, 135-36
King James Version, 204
Koran
  as inspired literature, 25;
  on homosexuality, 212
Küng, Hans, 131

Lagrange, Marie-Joseph, 126
Lake, Kirsop, 46
Lamentabil, decree of Holy Office, 126
Law of Christ, 198
Lazzatto, S. D., 109
Legalism and Catholic moral theology, 197
Leo XIII, 15, 25, 124, 126, 190-91;
  on uses of Bible, 37
Lessing, G. E., 144
Leviticus Rabba, 99
Lex talonis, 170
Liberation theology, 202, 212
Luther, Martin, 62, 116, 136, 139-40, 210;
  and ecclesiastical pattern, 61;
  and Illyricus, 135;
  and inerrancy, 44;
  and Scriptures, 33
Lutheran Formula of Concord, 43
Lutheran theologians, 20

Maccabees, 19
Magisterium, 17, 21, 32, 122-25, 127-28;
  authority of, 88
  and interpretation of Scriptures, 31;
  and meaning of Scriptures, 30;

Magisterium *(continued)*
  versus individual interpreta-
    tion, 62
Maimonides, 105-106
Male chauvinism and the Bible,
  204
Marcionism, 130
Masoretic tradition, 22
Mausbach, Joseph, 198
Mekhilta of R. Ishmael, 97
Mendelssohn, Moses, 108
Miqra, 94, 97-98
Mishnah, 68-85, 97, 99;
  and Priestly Code, 66-67
Mit brennender Sorge, 131
Moral judgments, 200
Moral theology in 19th century,
  197
Moses
  God's revelation to, 71;
  and Mishnah, 68
Muratorian canon, 131

Nahmanides, 106
Nehemiah as *tyrannos*, 78
Nehuniyah bar haQaneh, 98
Neo-Protestants and inerrancy,
  45
Newman, John Henry, 122
Nomistic perspective, 12

Octagesima Adveniens, 192
Oracular revelation, 113. *See
  also* Revelation
*Orthodoxy and Heresy in Ear-
  liest Christianity*, 122

Pacem in Terris, 191
Papal concilar documents, 15
PaRDeS, 102, 107
Pascendi encyclical, 126
Passover, 177-78

*Pastoral Constitution on the
  Church in the Modern World*,
  192-95. *See also Gaudium et
  Spes*
Patriarchal society, 171
Paul VI, 131
Pauline theology, 210
Peckham, John (Archbishop of
  Canterbury), 115
Pentateuch
  authority attributed to, 12;
  influence on Priestly Writers,
    79
Pesher literature, 95
Pharisees, 213;
  and divine authority of Scrip-
    tures, 97;
  and Law, 96;
  and Priestly Code, 66
Philo of Alexandria, 28, 100,
  114, 206;
  exegesis of, 101;
  and mantic prophecy, 113
Philosophical exegesis, development of, 104
Pietism, 154
Pius X, 124, 126
Pius XI, 190-91;
  and *Mit brennender Sorge*, 131
Pius XII, 15, 17, 22, 28, 126, 131,
    190;
  and authority of magisterium,
    31;
  and *Humani Generis*, 125;
  and uses of Bible, 37
Pontifical Biblical Commission,
    15;
  of Leo XIII, 126;
  and letter to Cardinal Suhard,
    125;
  under Pius X, 124
Postexilic period, 181

Priestly Code
  as basis of Mishnah, 85;
  and framers of Mishnah, 76-82;
  laws of, 66
Priestly Writers
  and cultic cleanness, 74;
  influence of hellenization on,
    79
*Primacy of Charity in Moral
  Theology*, 198
Prophetic religion and historic
  Judaism, 182
The Prophets, 178
Protocanonical books of Bible,
  22
Providentissimus Deus, 15, 25-
  26, 124

Quadragesimo Anno, 191
Qumran
  discoveries at, 22;
  and Essene cultic activity, 82;
  and language of Scriptures, 67
Qumranites, 213

Rabbinic Judaism
  and difference between prac-
    tice and Scriptures, 87;
  and Priestly Code, 66
Rabbinic midrash and Torah,
  104
Rabbinic sages, 170
Rabbis, role of, 12
Rahner, Karl, 128
Rashi, 106
Redaction criticism, 144
Redemptive presence of God,
  187
Redemptor Hominis, 192
Reform Jews, 169, 182;
  and binding nature of Scrip-
    ture, 171;

oral tradition of, 90
Reformation, locus of, 62
Reformers, 135, 140, 142, 151,
  153, 161;
  and authority of Scripture,
    137;
  and Council of Trent, 18;
  and freedom to criticize, 138;
  and grammatical method, 136;
  and Protestants, 141;
  and reliance on Scripture, 12;
  and Resurrection, 149
  and stress on Christ, 139;
  and understanding of faith,
    150
Rerum Novarum, 190-91
Revelation
  direct, 11;
  oracular, 113;
  sources of, 33
Rhetorical criticism, 142
Rosenzweig, Franz, 109

Saadia, Gaon, R., 103
Sacramentality and integration-
  ist approach, 186
Sacraments and apostolic revela-
  tion, 36
Sacred history, Bible as, 152-53,
  158
Sadducees
  and divine authority of Scrip-
    ture, 97;
  and Law, 96
Santillana, Giorgio di, 129
Schilling, Otto, 198
Schleiermacher, Friedrich, 149-
  51, 157
Scholasticism, 154
Scholastic theology in 16th cen-
  tury, 153
Scopes trial, 202, 206

Scriptural truth, different dimensions of, 12
Scripture, religious sense of, 141, 148, 151, 157, 160
Second Council of Constantinople, 114
Second Vatican Council. *See* Vatican II
Seeberg, Reinhold, 139
Semler, Johan, 144
Septuagint, 204;
  authority of, 22
Sexual behavior, 176
Sexuality, 212
Shammai, 96;
  and Mishnah, 69
Shekina as personification of *sod*, 107
Sifra
  and exegesis of Leviticus, 70;
  and Mishnah, 71
Simon, Richard, 144
Sin, 185
Sinaitic revelation and the Sadducees, 97
Skydsgaard, Krister Eynar, 120
Slavery, 205
Smalley, Beryl, 117
Smith, John, 46
Smith, Morton, 79
Smith, Wilfred Cantwell, 214
Social doctrine of Roman Catholic Church, 190
sod, 107
Sola fide, 138
Sola gratia, 137
Sola Scriptura, 138
Source criticism and Synoptic Gospels, 144
Sources of revelation, 33. *See also* Revelation
Sovereign will of God, 189

Spain and Jews in Middle Ages, 103
Spinoza, Baruch, 108, 144
Spiritus paraclitus, 15, 124
Steinbuechel, Theodore, 198
Study of the Bible in the Middle Ages, 117
Suborthodox Christology, 52
Sufficiency of Scripture, 35
Suhard, Cardinal, and Pontifical Biblical Commission, 125
Symmachus, 118
Synoptic Gospels, 143-45

Tablets of Sinai, 10
Talmud, 99, 170;
  and Mishnah, 70
Tavard, George H., 120
Tempier, Stephen (Archbishop of Paris), 115
Ten Commandments, 177
Theism and inerrancy, 44
Theodore of Mopsuestia, 113
Theodotion, 118
Theopneustos, in 2 Tim. 3:16, 113
Third International Synod of Bishops, 191
Tillmann, Fritz, 198
Torah, 175;
  centrality of, 94;
  and divine wisdom, 100;
  esoteric, 95;
  exoteric, 96;
  and the Law, 171, 176;
  as literature, 66, 80;
  and metaphysics, 12;
  and Mishnah, 69;
  mystical exegesis of, 101;
  as origin of Word, 9;
  and sephirotic structure of cosmos, 107;

Torah *(continued)*
  and use of human language,
    163
Tractates
  On Appointed Times, 73;
  On Purities, 73;
  and reliance on Scripture,
    74-75;
  and structure of Scriptures, 68
Tradition and the Traditions, 112
Transvestism, 176
Typology, 89
Tzvi, Shabbetai, 108

Uncleanness, the tractates and,
  73
United Presbyterian Church, 43

Vatican I, 15-16, 18, 21, 121,
  123;
  on authorship of Scriptures,
    24;
  on inerrancy, 130;
  on inspiration, 23;
  on interpretation of Scrip-
    tures, 30
Vatican II, 15-17, 21, 26-27, 121,
  127-28, 131-32, 186, 191-93,
  198;
  on authorship of Scriptures,
    24;
  on biblical revival, 39;
  on easy access to Scripture,
    38;
  on inerrancy, 130;

on inspiration, 23;
and integrationist approach,
  185;
on interpretation of Scripture,
  30;
on liturgy and revelation, 40;
and magisterium, 31;
on meaning of Scriptures, 29;
and rejection of Sources of
  Revelation schema, 34;
and revealed truth, 33;
on sacramental worship, 36;
on tradition and patrimony of
  faith, 35;
on uses of Bible, 37
Vincent of Lerins, 122
Virtue, 185;
  and Catholic theology, 184
Vosté, J. M., 126
Vulgate, 21;
  authority of, 15

Wellhausen, Julius, 145
Westminster Confession of Faith,
  43
Westminster Shorter Catechism,
  58
Wolff, Christian, 147
Women
  and the church, 206, 208-209;
  and justice, 211
World Council of Churches, 185
The Writings, 178

Zohar, 107